JERUSALEM

A BIBLICAL AND HISTORICAL CASE
FOR THE JEWISH CAPITAL

JAY SEKULOW

TRILOGY
CHRISTIAN
PUBLISHING

TRILOGY
CHRISTIAN
PUBLISHING

Trilogy Christian Publishers
A Wholly Owned Subsidary of Trinity Broadcasting Network
2442 Michelle Drive
Tustin, CA 92780

First Trilogy Christian Publishing hardcover edition May 2018

Trilogy Christian Publishing/ TBN and colophon are trademarks of Trinity
Broadcasting Network.

For information about special discounts for bulk purchases, please contact
Trilogy Christian Publishing.

Cover design, Diane Whisner

Manufactured in the United States of America

10   9   8   7   6   5   4   3   2   1

Library of Congress Cataloging-in-Publication Data is available.

ISBN 978-1-6408-8077-1
ISBN 978-1-6408-8078-8 (ebook)

DEDICATED

To my Grandchildren

ACKNOWLEDGEMENTS

The completion of this comprehensive work on this important and complex topic is nothing short of extraordinary. This endeavor would not have been possible without the tireless efforts and expertise of my colleagues.

I want to thank Robert W. Ash, Senior Counsel for the ACLJ, who provided invaluable legal expertise throughout this process. Shaheryar Gill, Senior Litigation Counsel for the ACLJ, provided a valuable amount of religious and cultural insights over the last year that was helpful in my approach to the issues discussed. John Monaghan provided insightful historical and archeological background through his assistance in research.

Dr. Mark Goldfeder, Special Counsel for International Affairs at the ACLJ provided a uniquely important combination of legal, historical, and religious insights within this project.

I also want to thank Allen Harris, who served as our developmental editor on this project. He worked quickly and tirelessly with the invaluable assistance of Joseph Williams in editing this work. These efforts combined made this a better book. I would be remiss to not mention the efforts of our literary agent Curtis Wallace and our Chief of Staff Miles Terry who both worked to bring this project to completion.

CONTENTS

SECTION V: JERUSALEM, THE ETERNAL CAPITAL OF ISRAEL

SECTION VI: ISRAEL AND THE LAW: ANCIENT PRINCIPLES AND MODERN LAWFARE

SECTION VII: CONCLUSION

LEBANON
• Damascus

SYRIA

Acre •

Haifa •
(Sea of Galilee)

(Nazareth) •

Mediterranean Sea

Nablus •

WEST BANK

Tel Aviv •

Ramallah •
• Amman

ISRAEL
• Jericho

Jerusalem •
Bethlehem •
GUSH ETZION

Hebron •
(Dead Sea)

GAZA

(Ein Gedi) •

Be'er Sheva •

(Negev Desert)

JORDAN

EGYPT

0 miles   50

0 kilometers   50

Note: Ancient places in parentheses

Eilat •

Gulf of Aqaba

© 2018 Jeffrey L. Ward

INTRODUCTION

This book is about the history of Israel. I had no idea when I started writing it, though, that this would be one of the most important and historic years in Israel's long history. Soon after I completed the first draft of this book, something wonderful happened: President Donald J. Trump announced that the United States would move its embassy from Tel Aviv to Jerusalem and officially recognize Jerusalem as the capital of Israel. Of course, the Jerusalem Embassy Act of 1995, which easily passed the House and the Senate, called for both these things more than twenty years ago. However, Presidents Bill Clinton, George W. Bush, and Barack Obama all kicked the can down the road every time they had a chance to put the resolution into effect. Those delays came to an end in December 2017, when President Trump finally took action on this important piece of legislation.

I was personally and tremendously touched on many levels that day. I have the honor of serving as Counsel to the 45th President of the United States, and I was in Washington with the president on the very day he announced the historic recognition of Jerusalem as Israel's Capital. My entire family, including my grandchildren, were with me. We were able to spend time with the president, and I told him how proud we all were for what he had done. It was a day we will never forget. And now, as this book goes to print, the U.S. Embassy has been relocated to Jerusalem. We are truly living history.

The December 2017 decision should not have been a surprise. Just six months earlier, in June of that year, the U.S. Senate unanimously passed a resolution reaffirming the Act and calling on the President to abide by all its provisions. And yet, when President Trump did just that, the world erupted into a panic. World leaders, the United Nations, news media, and even U.S. senators who had reaffirmed the Act months earlier now criticized and attacked the president. These criticisms were devoid of any factual basis, and the unbelievable cognitive dissonance of some legislators became painfully apparent. They showed themselves to be friends with Israel and supporters of her rights in theory but certainly not in practice. This kind of disagreement and duplicity shows why a book like this is absolutely necessary—now more than ever.

"This will kill the two-state plan," they screamed from Europe. "This will result in violence," they yelled from around the Middle East. "Oslo accords are dead," proclaimed Mahmoud Abbas, leader of the Palestinian Authority.[1] And yet, for all this blustering, what actually happened? Thanks to God's good grace, absolutely nothing. President Trump was right. Standing up for Israel's rights—not to mention the United States' right to have our embassy where we want it—did not lead to massive riots. As significant as the recognition of Israel has been for the Israeli people, it has effectively changed nothing for the rest of the world. Saudi Arabia, Turkey, and Jordan have all continued to develop and even expand inroads made unilaterally with Israel in terms of diplomatic and economic projects. Even now, the development of NEOM, a technologically advanced city on the coast of Saudi Arabia, may serve as one of the strongest bonds between countries in the area. On the other side of the Suez, Egypt and Israel have continued to work together on shared security concerns, such as those posed by Hamas in the Gaza Strip and ISIS in the Sinai. On the Friday following the announcement, Jews were able to pray at the Western Wall, Muslims continued to pray at the Al-Aqsa Mosque, and life continued as normal.

This begs the question: *If nothing really changed, why was this such a momentous occasion?* First, there is the history. All throughout Israel, archaeological digs have turned up artifacts showing connections between the land and the Jewish people. Just a few weeks before I sat down to write this preface, Israel discovered the seal of the prophet Isaiah in Jerusalem, right near the Temple Mount. It was Isaiah, of course, who prophesied that the Jewish people would one day regain sovereignty over that very mountain and that the nations of the world would bear witness. To say the Temple Mount and its Western Wall have no historical significance to the Jews (a claim that has been repeated endlessly by Israel's detractors) is simply absurd—and it's way past time the world stopped trading in these absurdities.

Second, there is the practicality of the matter. For modern Israelis, there's no question that Jerusalem is the capital of Israel. It's a fact of life for them. But, if others need further convincing, just look at the objective facts:

- Legally, Jerusalem is home to the Supreme Court of Israel, its parliament (the Knesset), and the Office of the Prime Minister.

- Culturally, Israel's National Museum and Yad Vashem, the World Holocaust Remembrance Center, are in Jerusalem.

- From a census perspective, the bulk of Israel's population resides in Jerusalem. The *combined* populations of the next two largest cities—Tel Aviv and Haifa—amount to only *half* of Jerusalem's 1.2 million residents.

- Economically, Jerusalem is the economic capital of Israel. The population of Jerusalem swells every workday, as people travel from their homes in Tel Aviv to their jobs in Jerusalem. The government has invested $2 billion USD into a high-speed rail system just to reduce traffic and decrease the travel time for these commuters.

- As a destination city, Jerusalem represents a huge source of tourism from around the world. In 2013 alone, 75% of Israel's tourists visited Jerusalem.[2]

- As far as industry, an entire industrial park devoted to international technology companies now sits in Har Hotzvim, providing further industrial power to an ever-growing Israeli technology sector. Jerusalem is currently transitioning into an even larger metropolis, with plans to build skyscrapers throughout the city while still protecting its historical roots. Educationally, Jerusalem is home to domestic universities and to extension campuses of other overseas universities.

All this development took decades of hard work and careful planning—all centered in Israel's unwavering commitment to Jerusalem as its eternal heart, soul, and capital.

Third, the United States' acknowledgment of Jerusalem as Israel's capital, though fundamentally right and good in and of itself, may do the exact opposite of what many detractors claim and ultimately move peace negotiations forward. The peace process has stalled and stagnated for decades. Without any shakeup in the process, there has been no incentive to reach a lasting resolution. To this end, the Palestinians have completely turned their backs on the peace process and have tried to force Israel into capitulating due to pressure from the international community. For whatever reason—and there are several—the Palestinian Authority has done everything they can do to avoid the negotiation table. Now, they are aware that procrastination has consequences. They know Israel's rights will not be held hostage forever and that, if they don't come to the table, the world will move forward without them.

The next round of negotiations will recognize what everyone already knows is true: Jerusalem is and will always be the eternal capital of the Jewish state and the Jewish people. In his announcement, President Trump made it abundantly clear. "This is nothing more, or less, than a recognition of reality. It is also the right thing to do. It's something that has to be done....This decision is not intended, in any way, to reflect a departure from our strong commitment to facilitate a lasting peace agreement. We want an agreement that is a great deal for the Israelis and a great deal for the Palestinians." [3]

It is a simple matter for the United States to recognize Jerusalem as Israel's capital. But, as you'll see in this book, Israel didn't need the U.S.'s recognition. Jerusalem is and always has been the capital of Israel. No sovereign nation needs another nation's permission to establish its capital anywhere within its legal borders; Israel has the historical, biblical, and legal authority to place its capital wherever it wants. As we dive into the research and case law, it's my hope that you will understand once and for all why the headlines you see everyday matter in the world—and perhaps understand how and why much of the world is lying to you about what Israel is and what it wants in the Middle East.

With a lifetime of experience and advocacy behind me, and with my heart and mind firmly planted with the Jewish people, I humbly offer this examination into the rich history and legal underpinnings of Israel.

SECTION I

OPENING ARGUMENTS

1

OPENING STATEMENT

"If I speak in heat, I speak in zeal. You ask what I wish: my answer is, a national existence, which we have not. You ask me what I wish: my answer is, the Land of Promise. You ask me what I wish: my answer is, Jerusalem. You ask me what I wish: my answer is, the Temple—all we have forfeited, all we have yearned after, all for which we have fought—our beauteous country, our holy creed, our simple manners, and our ancient customs." [1]
—BENJAMIN DISRAELI

Where's Jordan? Where is my son?
That was the singular, overwhelming thought racing through my mind as the echoes of the explosions and sirens rang in my ears. I was relatively safe in a command bunker in Ashkelon on the border of Gaza, where I had been meeting with key Israeli leaders. As chief counsel of the American Center for Law and Justice (ACLJ), I was in Israel discussing a response to the ridiculous claims that the Israeli self-defense measures against Hamas constituted "war crimes." To get a good picture of what life looked like under the threat of Hamas, I had asked to visit the border of Gaza myself. I wanted to see what the people of Israel faced every day. I just didn't expect to see it *quite* so up close and personal.

My son Jordan, an attorney who works with me at the ACLJ, was outside the command bunker when the warning sirens went off. The sirens back in 2008 only gave us a fourteen-second warning. Fourteen seconds to get to shelter. Fourteen seconds of terror, of not knowing what was about to happen, and, worst of all, of wondering if my son was safe. The missile bombardment went on so long and the bombs were so massive that they could not let us leave the bunker for thirty minutes. As a lawyer championing the rights of Israel, I was outraged. As a parent fearing the safety of my child, I was terrified. I was there because I wanted to know what the Israeli people felt day in and day out, and now I knew. And I can never forget.

A Hamas rocket landed just seventy-five yards from my son. The trajectory of the rocket and the shape of its payload drove the blast away from his position. By the grace of God, Jordan was safe, but he watched the whole thing happen. He saw the earth explode less than a football field away from where he was standing. He felt the earth shake beneath a huge cloud of dust, dirt, and shrapnel.

Jordan and I were obviously shaken, but I'll never forget the demeanor of the Israeli officials and soldiers who were with us. This was—and continues to be—simply a part of their daily lives. They live in a constant state of war, facing an enemy who wants nothing less than their absolute and total destruction. Whereas you and I may get up and worry about a busy day or a demanding project at work, this entire population worries about making it through the day with their lives—and national sovereignty—intact. And, I'm ashamed to say, most of the world doesn't seem to care.

They live in a constant state of war, facing an enemy who wants nothing less than their absolute and total destruction.

THE NEW WAR ZONE

We at the ACLJ can't do much about the rockets flying over Israeli airspace, but we can wage war on the latest battleground in the fight for Israel. After decades of endless war, Israel's enemies are taking the battle to a new war zone, one that is potentially more dangerous than any other: the world's courtrooms.

Litigating Israel's Right to Exist

The outcome of every trial I've been a part of in my thirty-seven years of law practice has come down to one thing: evidence. From local trial courts to the Supreme Court of the United States, it is all about the evidence. That's *real* law, though. The case against Israel is something else entirely.

On March 7, 2016, a two-hundred-page federal lawsuit hit my desk with a thud. After almost four decades as both a government lawyer and as the chief counsel of the ACLJ, I've seen a lot of lawsuits. I can usually judge their merits rather quickly by examining the evidence and the legitimacy of the plaintiffs. That's what made this particular complaint so troubling. There was a list of plaintiffs without real identification. The allegations in the complaint were certainly lengthy and dense, but they weren't "legal" in any true sense of the word. The more I read, the more confused I became about what was really going on here.

Then it dawned on me. This lawsuit wasn't about the law at all. I don't think it was even meant to be at its heart. What I was reading, what I was about to engage in, was a political exercise in the guise of a lawsuit. It was an at-

> **It was an attempt to litigate the very existence and legitimacy of the Jewish State of Israel.**

tempt to litigate the very existence and legitimacy of the Jewish State of Israel.

Representing Warriors

We represent the Gush Etzion Foundation, and I couldn't be prouder to be associated with an organization with such a fine heritage. Built on land acquired by the Jewish community in the 1920s and 1930s, Gush Etzion is a collection of Jewish settlements that has a famed history. This region, located in the Judean Hills less than ten miles from Jerusalem, played a pivotal role in the defense of Jerusalem during the 1948–1949 Israeli War of Independence, which we will discuss at length in this book.

On May 12, 1948, enemy Arab forces reached Gush Etzion on their destructive march to capture Jerusalem. The Arab armies knew that, if they could plow through Gush Etzion quickly, they could sack a relatively undefended Jerusalem with ease. But they could not have expected the resistance they'd face in the valiant defense at Gush Etzion. Soldiers and civilians alike did all they could to hold the line until the next day, when it became clear that they could fight no longer. But that daylong battle gave Israeli reinforcements just the time they needed to mount a final defense in Jerusalem.

Sadly, every Israeli soldier and remaining civilian resident who was not evacuated from Gush Etzion was massacred by the Arab forces that day. However, their sacrifice was not in vain. By holding off the Arab forces for that one critical day, the people of Gush Etzion helped save Jerusalem. Jewish reinforcements arrived and were prepared to turn back the enemy by the time the Arab forces were able to get through the line at Gush Etzion.

The day after Gush Etzion fell, Israel declared its independence. David Ben-Gurion, Israel's first prime minister, eulogized the defenders of Gush Etzion with the following words: "I can think of no battle in the annals of the Israel Defense Forces which was more magnificent, more tragic, or more heroic than the struggle for Gush Etzion. . . . If there exists a Jewish Jerusalem, our foremost thanks go to the defenders of Gush Etzion."[2]

A lot has changed in the seventy years since that battle, but one thing remains true today: The people of Gush Etzion, as represented by the Gush Etzion Foundation, are still prepared to go to war to defend the Jewish people of Israel. And this time, I was going with them.

MAKING THE CASE

As you will see throughout this book, Israel has many enemies and faces all manner of attacks every day. Those attacks come in the form of missiles flying overhead, boycotts, attempted sanctions, and an endless stream of legal battles. Even though Israel is a sovereign nation fully recognized by the United Nations (UN), its opponents want nothing less than Israel's complete destruction.

I have had some unique experiences during my legal career. Over the last three decades, I have appeared before the Supreme Court of the United States, as well as before numerous courts of appeal, before the International Criminal Court (ICC) in The Hague, and in numerous congressional hearings. But this particular issue—defending the legitimacy of the Jewish State of Israel—led me into one of the most incredible experiences of my career: appearing before the General Assembly of the United Nations on May 31, 2016. I had talked to representatives from other nations before, but here, on this momentous day, I was talking to *all* of them. The pressure was on.

As we begin this discussion about Israel's very right to exist, I want to take you into the UN so you can understand where my passion for Israel comes from. It's literally in my blood and in the blood of my family. And that blood boils when I hear of pro-Israel students and professors being silenced or punished on college campuses across the United States. There is a wave of anti-Israel hysteria sweeping across college campuses right now, fueled by the Boycott, Divestment, and Sanctions (BDS) movement, whose goal is nothing short of the complete delegitimization of Israel's right to exist. That's what my speech to the UN was all about. In reading parts of that speech, you'll start to see why this issue is so important to me, and why it should become important to you as well.

I'll admit, walking into the General Assembly room at the United Nations building in New York City was intimidating. Presidents, kings, dictators, and tyrants have stood at that massive marble podium. The room looks enormous from that perspective, with what seems like an endless sea of seats filled with world leaders. But the audience for this session wasn't just those who were seated before me. The audience this day, in that setting, was the whole world.

After my formal introduction, I was escorted to the podium as a video was presented to the General Assembly. The video showcased the rampant discrimination that pro-Israel students and professors were facing on college campuses across the country. At the end of the video, I began my first presentation to the United Nations. Below is a partial transcript of that speech:

> Mr. Ambassador, Your Excellency, Justice Rubinstein, Justice Amin, Ambassador Lauder, friends: what you saw in that video, taking place on America's college campuses, is unacceptable.
>
> It is unacceptable in a country governed by a constitution. It is unacceptable as a matter of law.
>
> I'm before you today, and it's a humbling experience for me. My grandfather, Schmulik Sekulow, traveled from Russia in 1914 aboard a boat that took him past the Statue of Liberty. He came through Ellis Island and was a fruit peddler in Brooklyn, New York.
>
> His grandson—me—I get to argue cases at the Supreme Court of the United States, at international tribunals, and now appear before you. It is humbling.
>
> But the task that we have before us is great, and we have no time for delay. In one of my very first Supreme Court arguments, one of the legal journals said I was rude, aggressive, and obnoxious.
>
> We won that case unanimously. After we won the case, that periodical said I remained undeterred during intense questioning. In 2009, we opened our permanent office in Jerusalem. One year later, I found myself before the International Criminal Court in The Hague—the ICC. The Palestinian Authority, much like the BDS movement of today, sought to utilize an international tribunal for one purpose and one purpose only—to delegitimize the Jewish State of Israel.
>
> I argued the law, and the law was clear: the Palestinian Authority was not a state, and it had no business being before the ICC. And the case must be dismissed.
>
> Two years later that law was established, and the court did dismiss that action. That's a victory, but the fact of the matter

is BDS is the flip side of that same coin. We call it *lawfare*—utilizing the legal system to delegitimize a people or a group. Now, this is an ongoing battle at the ACLJ.

[Part of our strategy is to] expose the true nature of the BDS movement for what it is, and make no mistake about it—it is not a civil rights movement. It is a movement with one aim and one aim only. It is a long-term project created by anti-Israel and anti-Jewish activists that is designed with one purpose: to delegitimize and destroy the State of Israel. To delegitimize the Jewish people. To delegitimize those non-Jewish people that stand with Israel.

This is the agenda. They cloak it in the garb of the civil rights movement. This is no civil rights movement; this is an unconstitutional and illegal advocacy taking place in the United State of America. Make no mistake, the goal is unambiguous. The intent is clear. It is to create an environment so hostile that those students of you that are here today would be afraid to say the words, "I am a Zionist. I am a Jew."

Never, never, on the memory of our families, should we allow that to take place in the least in the United States of America.

In the past year, ACLJ lawyers have briefed 30 state legislators on passing laws specifically to protect students, businesses, and others from this Boycott, Divestment, and Sanctions scheme. We believe that this year we will see that legislation passed in a number of states.

I want to talk about the legal issues. You know, I make my living practicing law. I have represented a variety of groups around the globe. We have offices in Strasbourg, France, Jerusalem, two in Africa, in Moscow. But in the United States of America, we are seeing right now a marked upswing on college campuses and universities concerning this BDS targeting.

And it comes in multiple forms. It is sometimes aimed at a student, who merely speaks out—exercises his or her free speech right. One of those students, from Loyola University, is with us today. She's brave. She's a hero. She stood up for her people and she did it in her college, and she was the one brought up on charges.

Now hear me: she exercised free speech rights, was non-disruptive, was being harassed by the BDS proponents of Loyola University in Chicago. She spoke out for her rights, and [as a result] she was being prosecuted by the college. That student, Talia Neiman, is here today. I'd like her to stand up please for a moment.

We had the privilege and honor to work with her, to put the College—the University—on notice that you better read your own rules. You better read your own regulations. You better read your own accrediting agencies' principles because it does not allow targeted discrimination because someone is Jewish or pro-Israel. And that fact, by the way, got Loyola to back down. That's some good news.

But let me take it a step further: it is not just students. There are professors. We are handling a number of those right now. Some of those professors are Israeli, most of them are Americans. Most of them—but not all of them—are Jewish. They have stood up for their rights as well. . . .

Friends, there's a website that our coalition partners put together. EndBDS.com. For the students that are here: as you can tell, you're not alone. Between us and our partners, there are hundreds, I will say thousands, of lawyers here in the United States and around the globe willing to defend—*desiring* to defend—[who are] winning these cases if we fight back.

I said we win these cases when we fight back. The truth is, we *must* win—we have no other option. This is our time and this is our moment.

I remember smiling when I read the part about being called "rude, aggressive, and obnoxious" and "undeterred" in defense of my clients. Depending on your perspective, I imagine all of those are true of me at some time or another. As it pertains to this debate, if you fall on the side of the anti-Israel Boycott, Divestment, and Sanctions camp, you're definitely going to find me rude, aggressive, obnoxious, and undeterred. That's because I believe that whole movement is built on a stack of lies, and I'm going to call them out one by one.

> I believe that whole movement is built on a stack of lies, and I'm going to call them out one by one.

My team at the ACLJ and I are not ashamed to stand with Israel and its right to exist. We are fighting for Israel, and we're fighting with everything we've got. We won't back down. As I told you at the start of this book, Hamas even dropped a bomb on my son, but it didn't stop us. You know what we did when the dust settled

> Hamas even dropped a bomb on my son, but it didn't stop us.

that day in Gaza? Jordan and I walked to the blast zone and picked up pieces of the rocket that almost killed him. I had those pieces set into a pair of cuff links, and I wore those cuff links the day I presented my case to the United Nations. I wear them as a reminder of the terror Israeli citizens live with every day and of the persecution Jewish and pro-Israel Americans face here in the United States.

A BATTLE WE MUST WIN

Litigating the legality of Israel in a federal court in Washington, DC, is not really litigation. It is lawfare, an attempt to use judicial systems as a weapon. It is warfare with briefs instead of bullets, with arguments instead of armaments. The aim—the destruction of the Jewish State—is the same, but the enemies' tactics have changed. They've brought

> They've brought the battle into the court of law, but make no mistake: Israel is under attack today in courtrooms around the world.

the battle into the court of law, but make no mistake: Israel is under attack today in courtrooms around the world.

In the federal lawsuit I'm working on with the Gush Etzion Foundation, the allegations in the complaint harkened back to the history of the Israeli-Palestinian conflict. In a court of law, I am limited in the length of the brief by a word and page count; not so in this book. Here, I want to answer the complaint more fully and present the law and evidence in support of the legitimacy of the Jewish State.

I don't hesitate to say the *Jewish* State of Israel. That is precisely what it is—uniquely Jewish and Democratic. Then-outgoing Secretary of State John Kerry said of Israel in December 2016, "Israel can be either Jewish or Democratic. It cannot be both."[3] I respectfully—and vehemently—disagree. But don't just take my word for it. Trust the evidence.

> Secretary of State John Kerry said of Israel in December 2016, "Israel can be either Jewish or Democratic. It cannot be both." I respectfully—and vehemently—disagree.

This book will concisely, accurately, and beyond the shadow of a doubt establish the legal and historical right for Israel to exist as a Jewish State. I will use biblical history, extra-biblical history, archaeology, and international law to make my case. You'll see clearly why the Jewish people lay claim to the land, that there has been an enduring Jewish presence in Palestine (Israel) for almost four millennia, why Jerusalem should be considered their eternal capital, and how modern Israeli law is built upon the bedrock principle of human rights. And as we go, I will also give you a clear picture of the enemy we're fighting and what's at stake for the Jewish people—and the world—if we fail. We—*you and I*—cannot allow that to happen.

Let me be clear up front as we begin this tour through history and international law together. It is my intention to make this an *exhaustive* resource, to settle the matter of Israel's right to exist as a Jewish state once and for all using every critical piece of history, every piece of archaeological evidence, every biblical record, and every legal principle available. As you read, you'll see that I really haven't left any stones unturned. That means you may come across some pages that you'll need to read and then read again as you process the vast amount of information presented here. That's okay. Do it. Fight through it. This is a critical issue on the world stage, and every fact I'm entering into evidence here further establishes the firm foundation on which the Jewish State of Israel stands today.

In this book, inasmuch as I am able, I will argue the evidence and facts of the case with the same "aggressive" attitude that I take with me into the Supreme Court. I have no choice. As I told the UN General Assembly, this is a war we *must* win.

We have no other option.

This is our time. This is our moment.

Let's get started.

2

THE NEW TOOLS OF WARFARE

Warfare: military operations between enemies; also, an activity undertaken by a political unit (as a nation) to weaken or destroy another.[1]

Israel has been engaged in seemingly endless military conflict since its creation. The Jewish people have been on the receiving end of spears, clubs, swords, arrows, guns, tanks, bombs, missiles, and even extermination camps throughout Israel's almost four-thousand-year history. Each generation, it seems, had to learn how to defend itself against a new breed of warfare. The methods were ever-changing but the goal was always the same: the destruction of the Jewish nation and the Jewish people. After four millennia of conflict, the most significant battle has moved off the field of war and has been focused on another increasingly relevant arena: modern lawfare.

> **After four millennia of conflict, the most significant battle has moved off the field of war and has been focused on another increasingly relevant arena: modern lawfare.**

The bulk of this book will delve into the rich, often contentious history of Israel as a nation, how it came to be, and how its neighbors have reacted to it. As we dig into the details throughout these chapters, you'll see that Israel's enemies have accused it of racism, intolerance, colonialism, apartheid, illegal occupation, crimes against humanity, and more. Even more common than these baseless accusations against Israel are the great lengths to which its enemies will go to slander and defame the most progressive and accepting country in the Middle East. We will explore all of this in further detail in later chapters, but for now, let's put a modern face on the conflict. Before we dive into four thousand years of Jewish history, I want you to see the enemy we're facing *today*. Doing so, however, means that you may not yet understand the full context of the accusations against Israel that I'll mention below. I promise, though, that you will understand it all as you delve deeper into this book. For the time being, I think it is enough to say that we will prove that Israel has a legal right to the land within its borders; however, many of its neighbors and much of the international community disagree. This dispute over the land and Israel's right to exist as a Jewish state are at the heart of the ongoing conflict that we'll discuss here.

WAGING WAR IN THE COURTROOM

As we'll see throughout this book, Israel is under attack—not just from bombs, but from something even more insidious: legal efforts to boycott and delegitimize its people and its place in the world. "Lawfare" is a term that has entered the academic, political, and legal lexicon only over the last several decades. First described in a 2001 essay by Colonel (now Major General) Charles J. Dunlap of the USAF, lawfare has been increasingly used to describe how many conflicts today, both domestic and abroad, are being waged in the courtroom, as opposed to or in addition to those being waged on the battlefield.[2]

In some ways, the evolution into lawfare can be viewed as a good thing. Prior to a more formalized rule of law concerning warfare, soldiers and states were left to the mercy of their enemies. The rampant destruction and violence that soldiers experienced during the First World War marked a change in how wars were to be fought moving forward. Aside from the horrors of trench warfare, World War I was one of the first times that the world experienced true *industrialized* war, which pitted human beings against the likes of tanks, land mines, mustard gas, automatic weapons, aerial combat, air strikes: what we've come to know as modern warfare.

By the end of World War I, the nations of the world faced the harsh reality that warfare as they knew it had changed forever. Left unchecked, the advancements in the destructive forces unleashed in times of war could ultimately destroy the world. The result was the beginning of an international legal framework that outlined new rules of war and engagement that many nations rely on today. While it wasn't enough to stop the crisis that led to World War II, it was the start of a new sense of order to give some boundaries to the world's ongoing international conflicts, especially as applied to those between nation-states. In a strange way, the law helped make warfare safer.

As often happens, however, the law also made things more complicated and, in a way, more dangerous to the long-term effects of war. Governments and advocacy groups have long used the law and legal strategies, like treaties and negotiations, to avoid the armed physical violence of the past. However, this new idea of lawfare—waging war in a legal sense—has empowered and emboldened groups and organizations to use the law as an *offensive* tool of conflict. As the "newest feature of twenty-first century combat," lawfare defines the way the law is being used as an active force for change, often

> **This new idea of lawfare—waging war in a legal sense—has empowered and emboldened groups and organizations to use the law as an *offensive* tool of conflict.**

with groups using or exploiting the law to achieve specific political, social, or cultural ends.[3] Nowhere is this legal exploitation more obvious or egregious than it is in the hands of Israel's enemies.

THE ARAB LEAGUE BOYCOTT

One of Israel's first battles in modern lawfare came in the mid-1940s, before Israel even declared its independence as a Jewish state. In the years leading up to Israel's formal establishment in 1948, the entire Arab political structure inside Palestine and beyond deemed Israel—and the Jewish people as a whole—to be an unwanted presence in the region without a single shred of nuance or balance.

Throughout the early-to-mid 1940s, Jewish immigrants from all over the world were arriving in Israel, both to escape oppression and discrimination in their home countries during World War II and to establish a significant enough Jewish population to eventually form a viable Jewish autonomous state that, as we'll discuss later, the Jewish people had been working toward since the end of the First World War.[4] Many of these new immigrants contributed to the incredible economic growth and industrialization experienced in the region during that time. Recognizing this growth, surrounding Arab governments were disturbed at the idea of a permanent Jewish sovereign state in the region, and they immediately sought to destroy this fledgling nation before it could attain statehood.

Even before a formal boycott was ever issued, informal anti-Jewish boycotts in Palestine began to appear. Arab Palestinians were often physically attacked for conducting business with their Jewish neighbors.[5] Then, on December 2, 1945, the Arab League—at the time comprising Egypt, Iraq, Lebanon, Transjordan (now Jordan), and North Yemen (the historical predecessor to modern-day Yemen)—issued a declaration that stated: "Products of Palestinian Jews are to be considered undesirable in Arab countries. They should be prohibited and refused as long as their production in Palestine might lead to the realization of Zionist political aims."[6]

This declaration effectively instituted a geopolitical treaty that forbade Arab governments—and to a large extent, private Arab business enterprises—from engaging in economic relationships with Jewish industries in the region. It is noteworthy that this boycott was not directed at *Israeli* businesses—which would have been impossible, since Israel as a state did not yet exist—but at the Jewish people themselves. This shows that the Arab League boycott of Israel—largely a model and philosophy that the modern-day BDS movement is built upon today—was originally based on inherently anti-Semitic philosophies that sought to cleanse the region of any Jewish religious or ethnic presence in what was then Palestine.

In addition to the innate animosity toward the Jewish people, the boycott declaration also specifically spoke out against the creation of a Zionist state. The intent of the Arab League boycott, then, was clear. Not only did the Arabs have no intention of working with Israel, they wanted to prevent others from doing so as well. This is an example of the kind of existential harm the Arab League boycott posed by not merely choosing to cease its own dealings with Israel, but also pressuring others to stop.

The Arab League boycott had an undeniable effect on the political power and legitimacy of Israel in the Middle East and beyond for years after. However, the boycott did little to inhibit Israel's incredible economic growth in the ensuing decades—an economic boom that brought new energy and vitality to the region. It is ironic that the Arab people were unable to benefit from this time of growth and prosperity because of their governments' obstinate refusal to accept and cooperate with the Jewish State.[7]

Unfounded Accusations of Racism

The Arab League boycott gradually weakened over the next few decades following Israel's establishment as a state in 1948. This was due to the inherent impracticality of enforcing the boycott, as well as the peace made between Israel and several Arab governments in the 1970s and 1990s.[8] However, the notion of boycotting Israel in its modern form was reinvigorated in the early 2000s, this time with the disappointing facilitation and support of the United Nations.

> **The notion of boycotting Israel in its modern form was reinvigorated in the early 2000s, this time with the disappointing facilitation and support of the United Nations.**

In 2001, the United Nations hosted the World Conference Against Racism (WCAR) in Durban, South Africa. The conference had been authorized by General Assembly Resolution 52/111 in December 1997, which focused on eliminating racism, racial discrimination, xenophobia, and related intolerance. The plan for the conference was to make some real headway in human rights issues, but it sadly turned into a venue to attack Israel. To the exclusion of some Western nations, many nations wanted to push for the broader discussion of regional, national, and international issues surrounding compensation for colonialism and slavery.[9] The result is that this broader discussion dominated the conference preparation, with perceived Palestinian oppression and discrimination by the Israeli government being a prominent topic time and time again.

Many of these discussions focused on politically motivated and biased accusations against Israel for allegedly violating international humanitarian laws in their treatment of the Palestinians. Furthermore, much of the discussion condemning Israel focused not only on Israeli security and ethnic policy but on the entire Zionist philosophical ideology. Partly inspired by the now-defunct UN General Assembly Resolution 3379 of 1975 (which also equated Zionism with racism), the resolution sought to confirm that Zionism—the political philosophy that Jews as a historically oppressed minority are entitled to security in a Jewish majority state—is racist and therefore antithetical to international human rights and international humanitarian law.[10] And so, in resolutions prepared before the conference even started, Zionism was equated with racism.

This represented an evolution in the international anti-Israel movement's chief strategy. The past was clearly filled with direct assaults on the state, as seen in both the Arab League boycott and the various armed conflicts waged against Israel by its Arab neighbors in the years since its independence. The future, it seemed, would focus on exploiting international legal principles and legal forums with the purpose of delegitimizing, demonizing, and ultimately dismantling the Jewish State.

Ultimately, the United States and Israel condemned the language equating Zionism with racism, and both parties withdrew from the conference when it became clear that the deadlock over the language could not be addressed.[11] Once both delegations were gone, the conference and its outcomes were subject to greater suspicion and scrutiny by the international community, and in the end both the anti-Zionism language and the proposed reengineered language were left out.[12] However, the damage was already done. Not only had the conference on racism failed to have any lasting positive change, but its violently biased criticism of Israel and Zionist ideology, coupled with a complete failure to condemn the human rights abuses and racial bias of Israel's Arab neighbors, actually led to more baseless and misinformed criticism of Israel and heightened hatred for the Jewish people.

BDS: The Latest Face of Anti-Semitism

In hindsight, the Durban Conference was the formal rollout for a rebranding of the Arab League boycott that led to the Boycott, Divestment, and Sanctions movement as it is known today.[13] The BDS movement is a global network of organizations and individuals with the express goal to "end international support for Israel's oppression of Palestinians and pressure Israel to comply with international law."[14] BDS as a political and economic movement formally began in 2005 with this public announcement accredited to "Palestinian Civil Society":[15]

> We, representatives of Palestinian civil society, call upon international civil society organizations and people of conscience all over the world to impose broad boycotts and implement divestment initiatives against Israel similar to those applied to South Africa in the apartheid era. We appeal to you to pressure your respective states to impose embargoes and sanctions against Israel. We also invite conscientious Israelis to support this Call, for the sake of justice and genuine peace.[16]

However, this call for BDS did not originate in grassroots Palestinian civil society. In fact, it did not come from within the Palestinian territories at all. Instead, the call for BDS can be attributed to a group of intellectuals living and working in Israel and the West who were sympathetic to the Palestinian cause but without any roots or connections in Palestinian political society.[17] Only later did Palestinians living inside the territories fall in line with the movement and its goals.[18] Thus, BDS is a product of a familiar trope in Palestinian society: outside manipulation exploiting the ongoing lack of Palestinian leadership to continually obstruct peace, to the detriment of both the Israelis and the Palestinian people themselves.

> **BDS is a product of a familiar trope in Palestinian society: outside manipulation exploiting the ongoing lack of Palestinian leadership to continually obstruct peace, to the detriment of both the Israelis and the Palestinian people themselves.**

According to the Palestinian Campaign for the Academic and Cultural Boycott of Israel (PACBI) and the Palestinian BDS National Committee, the main objectives of the BDS movement are threefold:

1. End Israel's occupation and colonization of all Arab lands and dismantle the security barrier that stretches across Gaza's land border.

2. Recognize the fundamental rights of the Arab-Palestinian citizens of Israel to full equality.

3. Respect, protect, and promote the rights of Palestinian refugees to return to their homes and properties as stipulated in UN Resolution 194.[19]

You may not yet understand the nuances of these objectives, but you certainly will by the end of this book. Regardless, it is clear, based on these objectives, that the BDS movement is not focused on thoughtful and balanced peacemaking with the Israeli government or the Israeli people. Further, these objectives do not recognize the Palestinian leadership's culpability in continuing to destabilize the peace process and the region.

Instead, the BDS movement is focused on creating a demographic shift that would fundamentally change Israel. If the BDS movement succeeded in its goals, the entire region, from the Jordan River to the Mediterranean, would be given to the Palestinian people, thereby destroying the Jewish State and displacing the more than nine million Jews who currently call Israel their homeland.

In the sixteen years since Durban and the twelve years since the call from Palestinian "civil society," the number of states, nongovernmental organizations (NGOs), and other institutions that have embraced the BDS movement as official policy has exploded. The movement has become a loosely connected yet highly organized network with supporters and representatives in nearly every country around the world.

Even church and student groups have engaged with and openly supported the BDS movement's hateful ideology. Many faith-based Christian organizations around the world have used millions of dollars of government funding to contribute to anti-Israel and pro-BDS organizations. Inspired by the message of the Durban Conference (in which many Christian denominations participated) and a sense of global Christian solidarity, Christian groups from across the denominational spectrum have used taxpayer money to support certain Palestinian NGOs' goal of the destruction of the Jewish State.[20]

College campuses in particular have become battlefields in this renewed brand of lawfare, with many students aligning themselves with the BDS movement in the name of international human rights and anti-colonialism, a charge often aimed at Israel for reasons we will discuss at length in this book. At campuses across the country, Israeli academic works and even Israeli academics themselves have been demonized and excluded from campus academic and cultural life. Furthermore, active BDS groups on campus, like the Students for Justice in Palestine, regularly organize threatening and aggressive programs, protests, and demonstrations on college campuses. These events leave not only Jewish students but the entire student bodies of these schools feeling intimidated about sharing their personal perspectives on campus. We will examine how the ACLJ is fighting back against this on-campus discrimination in Chapter 15 of this book.

Perhaps most disturbingly, many Western anti-Israel organizations actually have links to fundamentalist terrorist organizations currently attacking the Jewish State in Palestinian territories and across the Middle East. For example, individuals associated with American Muslims for Palestine have previously been involved with organizations held civilly liable for providing funding to Hamas, the internationally recognized terrorist organization that currently controls the Gaza Strip and regularly fires rockets into Israel, targeting civilian areas.[21] At a minimum, a group that claims to want peace and acceptance welcomes individuals who support a known terrorist organization. That is the kind of misdirection and duplicity that we have seen in so many of Israel's enemies.

THE THREE STRATEGIES OF THE BDS MOVEMENT

While much of their actions and initiatives are wrapped in a false blanket of openness, inclusion, and peace, the BDS movement is completely up front with their end goals in the campaign against Israel. Their goal is the complete dissolution of the Jewish State, and they have put the three parts

> **Their goal is the complete dissolution of the Jewish State.**

of their plan in the very name of the campaign: Boycott, Divestment, and Sanctions. To understand the opposition, we must understand their tactics. Let's examine each part.

BOYCOTT

The use of boycotts to protest Israel's rights goes back to the Arab League boycotts of the 1940s and beyond. Today, BDS advocates have begun actively boycotting a wide range of corporations and individuals, including entertainers, artists, and athletes. Even more troubling, as we've mentioned, they have taken this boycott into the educational arena, cutting off entire educational institutions solely because of where in the world—namely Israel—they are based.

When it comes to Israeli-made products, however, the BDS efforts have become even more disturbing. One of their most effective campaigns to date has been their push to have all goods made or produced in Israeli-controlled regions throughout disputed parts of Palestine, such as Judea and Samaria, labeled as such. This, coupled with their strong marketing and education efforts, make it easier for anti-Israel advocates around the world to avoid any Israeli-made products, thereby extending the reach and ease of the boycotts.

This labeling effort has gained traction around the world over the past several years. For example:

• In December of 2009, the British government issued official recommendations to business owners, asking that all Israeli products that were produced in these contested areas be labeled so that those who want to boycott can do so more easily. Essentially, the British government is trying to avoid saying they are in agreement with the boycott, but they do want to make it easier for their citizens to engage in it.

• Denmark took it a step further in 2012 by formally adopting this special label system. When asked about it, Danish foreign minister Villy Søvndal said, "This is a step that clearly shows consumers that the products are produced under conditions that not only the Danish government, but also European governments, do not approve of." [22]

• In 2012, the Swiss supermarket chain Migros declared that all products previously labeled as "Made in Israel" that were made in Judea and Samaria would now be labeled as coming from the West Bank, essentially creating two different kinds of products from Israel. Like the British approach, the argument was to make boycotting easier for the boycotter.

• In November 2015, the European Union adopted the labeling policy over the overwhelming condemnation of the Israeli government, but much to the delight of the Palestinian Authority and their president, Mahmoud Abbas.

These tactics do not demonstrate intelligent, healthy debate about difficult topics. Instead, they show the BDS preference for bullying nations and businesses to bend to the demands of the BDS movement. One very public example of this practice occurred when BDS País Valencià, a BDS group based in Spain, pressured the Rototom Sunsplash reggae festival to force Matisyahu, a Jewish reggae artist, to make a

These tactics do not demonstrate intelligent, healthy debate about difficult topics. Instead, they show the BDS preference for bullying nations and businesses to bend to the demands of the BDS movement.

statement of support for BDS. The ultimate goal was to have him not only endorse the BDS movement but to specifically call for Palestinian statehood.[23]

The anti-Semitic tendencies of the BDS movement were magnified in this specific incidence, because there was rampant racism throughout the whole affair. Aside from the public racism of speaking out against the Jewish State, there was a more subtle racism at play here when you realize that Matisyahu was the only Jewish performer at the event, is not Israeli, and was the only one pressured to issue a public statement of support for the BDS efforts. There is no doubt that he was targeted simply because he was Jewish. Matisyahu refused to issue the endorsement, withdrew his support for the festival, and only performed in the end after the festival staff apologized for the entire affair.

In other circumstances, Sabra hummus, Israel-grown Medjool dates, and Hewlett-Packard computer equipment have been singled out by some advocates as goods to avoid because their producers either do business with Israel generally or in the areas of Judea and Samaria specifically. Of those businesses targeted by the BDS boycott campaign, the case of SodaStream is perhaps the most interesting, given that many Palestinians living in the area depended on SodaStream as a source of work.

The company, which produces machines that allow consumers to make their own carbonated drinks using plain water and SodaStream flavored syrups, was formerly located in the West Bank, which Pal-

estinians claim is illegally occupied by Israel. In 201
left the West Bank factory and moved its operation
cility two hours away within Israel's undisputed bor
cofounder asserts the move was the result of BDS bo
but the company understandably denies it. Whether S
located due to BDS pressure or not, the bottom line
tory moved, the move cost four hundred Palestinian
good-paying jobs, and the BDS movement somehow
move a victory.[24] How this sad affair counts as a win fc
a mystery. Perhaps it is because the proponents of the I
don't actually have the best interests of everyday Arab ʁ ᴀⅼᴇᵴᵗⅰⁿⁱᵃⁿˢ ⁱⁿ
mind after all.

DIVESTMENT

"Divestment" is a financial term that refers to the practice of reducing one's assets, often for political or ethical reasons. Think of it as the opposite of an investment. When you *invest*, you put money into something; when you *divest*, you pull money out of something. That's what the BDS movement wants individuals and businesses to do: pull their money out of all investments or assets that currently provide a benefit to any Israeli or Jewish companies.

> That's what the BDS movement wants individuals and businesses to do: pull their money out of all investments or assets that currently provide a benefit to any Israeli or Jewish companies.

As a result, banks, pension funds, corporations, and other entities are pressured not to invest their funds in any company that they think serves Israeli or Jewish interests. By this mandate, then, financial advisers are prevented from serving the best interests of their clients because they are intentionally steered away from a wide variety of otherwise sound investment opportunities. These are not financial decisions; they are the result of coercion based on religious and ethnic lines.

Many believe that their rights to free speech extend to putting their money where they want to put it. That's not what the BDS wants. They don't want you to put your money where you want it;

they want you to put it where *they* want it. Even though every individual has the freedom of choice in where to invest their money, that choice should not be dictated by such divisive and bigoted reasons as religion and ethnicity.

SANCTIONS

Perhaps the most punitive of all the methods, the BDS movement attempts to pressure the nations of the world to legislate and create economic sanctions that are meant to punish Israel, its citizens, and Jewish people in general. These broad restrictions come in the form of trade penalties, bans, arms embargoes, the severing of diplomatic ties, and expensive tariffs that hurt both the people within that country and the people in Israel. Engaging in political trade wars like these leads to weaker economies and products, but the insidiousness of this is that it is still all based on a backward mentality that is racist against Jews and discriminatory against the Jewish people.

In the sixteen years since Durban's failed World Conference Against Racism, the number of states, nongovernmental organizations, and other institutions that have embraced the BDS movement as official policy has exploded. The response to combating these methods has been swift, with groups like the ACLJ stepping in and protecting those who need protection. And as the BDS movement has grown increasingly popular in the United States, state governments—deciding to take a decidedly pro-Israel stance—have passed legislation to protect the economic and business relationships between Israel and the states by refusing to issue contract work to organizations and corporations who have a public pro-BDS stance.[25] Pro-BDS groups have responded to such legislation by crying that these laws run afoul of their constitutional First Amendment rights, such as freedom of speech, and have engaged in lawfare to advance these allegations.[26]

However, constitutional analysis and case law both affirm that such state legislation is perfectly legal and the BDS movement's boycotts of Israel and Israeli goods are not constitutionally protected activity or speech. Furthermore, the BDS movement's claims that their constitutional rights have been violated are further discredited by the fact that many pro-BDS organizations are not only participating in economic boycotts of Israel but are unfairly targeting the American Jewish community for that community's overwhelming support of Israel.[27]

Through these tactics, many in the BDS movement are engaging in unprotected activity as well as in racist and anti-Semitic discrimination that is in itself unconstitutional. While some easily see and understand the seedy underbelly of many in the BDS movement, more and more are drawn to the BDS movement's shaky, false, but nevertheless appealing-to-elites message of protecting international human rights and domestic civil liberties. The BDS movement puts forth a veneer of peace and inclusion, but it is really a tired form of hate and racism in disguise. This is not the first time many anti-Israel advocates have tried clever bait-and-switch approach.

It is clear that the BDS movement has completely transformed the idea of the international boycott. What had once been seen by much of the world as an effectively dead policy based on racism, bigotry, and anti-Semitism is now renewed and repackaged with deceptive buzzwords and slogans. To their credit, the Arab League boycott has effectively done what most CEOs and moguls wish they could do: take something bad and rebrand it among some communities as good.

THE NEW AND OLD FIGHT AGAINST RACISM

I want to be abundantly clear: Racism in all its forms is disgusting, and racism hiding behind the banner of peace and inclusion, as we see with the BDS movement, is especially grotesque. As you probably know, and as we'll see in detail in later chapters, the Jewish people have been the victims of racism and discrimination for literally thousands of years. However, the ACLJ, other like-minded nongovernmental organizations, and

I want to be abundantly clear: Racism in all its forms is disgusting, and racism hiding behind the banner of peace and inclusion, as we see with the BDS movement, is especially grotesque.

the Israeli government have made it abundantly clear that the injustice waged against Israel and the Jewish people for decades will not be allowed to rear its ugly head once again.

Open Hatred

Many BDS organizations do little to hide their hatred for Israel and anyone who supports Israel, openly calling for Jewish and other pro-Israel students to be expelled from campus or even to be subjected to violence.[28] The rise in organizations supporting BDS on college campuses and beyond has led to increased anti-Israel sentiment around the world, with Israel often becoming the litmus test for how the general community views their Jewish neighbors. This has led to an increase in anti-Semitic speech and violence committed against innocent Jews based on BDS supporters' perception that even Jews living outside of Israel are directly responsible for any suffering of the Palestinian people.

Many of the most violently hateful BDS supporters, especially in the United States, feel justified or even protected in expressing these views because of First Amendment rights to freedom of speech. However, just as the BDS movement has used constitutional law to continue to express anti-Semitic vitriol, the pro-Israel movement can use our legal system and foundational principles to expose the fact that the types of activities engaged in by the BDS movement are, at best, not protected under the Constitution and, at worst, exactly the type of biased racism and discrimination they claim to be victims of themselves.

Anti-BDS Legislation Is Not Unconstitutional

As multiple state legislatures across the country have passed anti-BDS legislation, which effectively denies any company engaging in BDS activities from contracting with the government, many in the BDS movement have attacked these pieces of legislation as unconstitutional and a violation of their First Amendment rights. This assertion is simply not true. Anti-BDS legislation is not unconstitutional, and I can prove it. For anti-BDS legislation to be unconstitutional, the bills would have to meet two conditions:

First, the anti-BDS legislation would have to be a restriction on *private* speech. These bills are not restrictions on private speech. Any private individual can choose to boycott any individual, organization, or even state by choosing, as a private citizen, not to purchase their goods or engage in business with them.

Instead, these pieces of state legislation affect only the freedom of the *government* by ensuring that the state will not engage in business with organizations and corporations that publicly endorse or align themselves with BDS ideology. The fact is that the government is seeking to distance itself from a political movement that openly discriminates against a group of people based on religion and national origin, which is itself a constitutional violation.

The second condition that must be met for anti-BDS legislation to be considered unconstitutional is that BDS activity must be the kind of speech protected under the First Amendment. And I can say with confidence that BDS is not a type of protected boycott activity as defined by the Constitution and American case law. The reason for this has to do with the very nature of the boycotts themselves.

Primary boycotts, in which private individuals decide for themselves whether or not to do business with a company, are protected by the Constitution. Any individual can make that decision for himself. However, the BDS movement is not engaging in a *primary* boycott. Instead, they practice what is called a *secondary* boycott. A secondary boycott occurs when an individual or group (like BDS) pressures another individual or group (you and/or your state government) to stop doing business with a third group (Israeli and Jewish businesses). Basically, it is a case of a third party injecting themselves into your private buying decisions. I have personally argued a secondary boycott case at the U.S. Court of Appeals for the Second Circuit and won unanimously. I know the law well here: We helped establish it.

Past case law demonstrates that secondary boycotts are not only detrimental to the economy, they are also not the kinds of boycotts and expressions of free speech that merit constitutional First Amendment protections.[29] Furthermore, in the case of BDS boycotts, the

BDS movement is not focusing on the specific organization that they feel is responsible for their grievances. If they were, they would direct all of their efforts specifically at the Israeli government. Instead, the BDS movement is engaging in economic warfare against businesses and organizations that have no direct link to the Israeli government at all. These individuals and organizations are being targeted simply because they are Israeli and/or Jewish.

Secondary boycotts hurt business, communities, individuals, and nations. In the case of the BDS movement, however, the boycott hurts not only Israel and ally countries economically, but also further harms the entire Israeli population, and by proxy, the entire community of Jews around the world.

NOW WHAT?

We began this chapter by discussing lawfare and how Israel's enemies have moved the most intense anti-Israel campaigns off the battlefield and into the courtroom. I hope it's already become clear that you can add a new member to Israel's list of public enemies: Iran, Hamas, Hezbollah, and now the Boycott, Divestment, and Sanctions movement. Each of these have the same goal: the elimination of the Jewish State of Israel.[30] I also hope it's equally clear that what's happening within the BDS movement isn't just legal maneuvering and manipulating the court of public opinion; it is a full-scale assault against the existence of the Jewish State.

> I also hope it's equally clear that what's happening within the BDS movement isn't just legal maneuvering and manipulating the court of public opinion; it is a full-scale assault against the existence of the Jewish State.

It is my job as the chief counsel for the ACLJ to present the definitive defense for Israel as a Jewish state, and that is my intent in this book. Now that we know the game we're playing, who the enemy is, and what's at stake, it's time to dive into the evidence of the case, the biblical, historical, and legal proof that Israel deserves its right to exist as a Jewish state and to hold the land it currently claims. We'll start in the next section of this book by exploring the rich biblical history of the Jewish people and the Land of Promise in order to get an idea of who these people are and why they feel entitled to this land in the first place.

KEY TAKEAWAYS

1. "Lawfare" is a term that describes exploiting the legal system to use it as a weapon against one's opponents in an effort to damage or delegitimize them.

2. The Boycott, Divestment, and Sanctions (BDS) movement is a discriminatory campaign against Israel and the latest iteration of the continuing effort to eliminate the Jewish State. BDS hides behind the progressive language of peaceful protest; but in reality, it is clearly anti-Semitic and undermines real efforts for peace by hurting both Israelis and Palestinians on the ground.

SECTION II

THE BIBLICAL EVIDENCE

This is what the Sovereign LORD says: "I will take the Israelites out of the nations where they have gone. I will gather them from all around and bring them back into their own land. I will make them one nation in the land, on the mountains of Israel."

—EZEKIEL 37:21–22 (NEW INTERNATIONAL VERSION)

3

THE LAND OF PROMISE

Covenant
1: a usually formal, solemn, and binding agreement: COMPACT
2: . . . a written agreement or promise usually under seal between two or more parties especially for the performance of some action . . . [1]

've been to Israel many times. These days, I like to take friends with me and show them around the key holy and historical sites, as well as the military sites. Seeing the Holy Land from their perspective is always refreshing. I can see the awe and wonder in their faces. I can see the deep spiritual connection they make almost immediately with the land that is so fundamentally tied to their faith and traditions. Most Jews and Christians have this reaction in some form or another when they first step onto the land they've read about in their holy books. I, however, wasn't so fortunate.

When looking back to my first trip to Israel in 1987, I call it "the Tour by Night." I wasn't there on a pilgrimage or spiritual odyssey; I was there on business. I was litigating one of my first cases involving organizations operating in Israel, and we arrived late in the evening, well after dark. My friend Baruck, who showed us around, jokingly said something like, "If you could see in the dark, that would be Mount Hebron over there. If you could see over there, that would be the Western

Wall of the Temple." Sure, I saw some sites during that trip, but what I mainly saw were conference rooms. As a lawyer litigating an important case in Israel, I didn't have the luxury of having an emotional experience. My clients didn't need me to be emotional; they needed me to be on my game, to stay focused on the matter at hand, to stay clearheaded and objective. And, for good or bad, that's been my perspective every time I've been in the Holy Land. For me, it's business. It has to be.

Israel—the Holy Land—is of great significance to the world's three great monotheistic religions: Judaism, Christianity, and Islam. All three faiths believe the Holy Land has been chosen by God to be a location of special significance. It is, therefore, the most coveted piece of real estate in the world, as evidenced by the strife that has taken place between Jews, Muslims, and even Christians vying for control of the region. Jews (the descendants of Isaac) and Arabs (the descendants of Ishmael) call the land holy and lay a claim to it. While the Holy Land has a special significance to Christians as the location where Jesus was born, crucified, and rose from the dead, today Christians do not claim the land in the way Jews and Muslims do.

Since the modern State of Israel came into being in 1948, it has been continuously attacked by Muslim Palestinians, its Arab neighbors, and groups like Hamas and Hezbollah attempting to gain control of Jerusalem. Terrorist groups and individuals have carried out numerous indiscriminate attacks on innocent Israeli civilians with a declared aim to destroy the nation of Israel. To put it simply, different religions throughout history have laid claim to this land, and they have killed and died for it. We need to understand why.

> **To put it simply, different religions throughout history have laid claim to this land, and they have killed and died for it. We need to understand why.**

WHY LOOK TO THE BIBLE?

Judaism and Christianity both esteem the Scriptures as holy. The Jewish people, of course, hold to what the Christian world calls the

Old Testament, which focuses on the biblical record before the time of Jesus. This includes the Torah (the Law), the history of the Jewish people, the wisdom and poetic writings, and the records of the prophets. Christians embrace both the Old and New Testaments, extending the biblical record into the life and ministry of Jesus and well into the establishment and spread of the Christian church. Muslims, as we'll discuss in more detail, also revere many aspects of what we know as Old Testament history, as much of it is included in the Quran. Muslims also view Jesus as a powerful, influential Muslim prophet.

Whether you are a person of faith or not, it is hard to dismiss the Bible's historical importance. It is the most complete record of the Jewish people's beginnings, enslavement, wandering, kingdoms, and interactions with other nations. I understand that you may come to the Bible with a preexisting bias for or against its teachings. In later chapters, we'll see how extra-biblical history and archaeology support the biblical history. For now, though, I am going to present the information in the Bible as a key piece of evidence for two main reasons:

1.   to demonstrate why the Jewish people feel such a connection to and ownership of this land in the first place; and

2.   to show that there has been an enduring presence of Jews in Israel for four thousand years.

Throughout this section, I'm going to use phrases like "God said," "God's covenant," and "God promised." I don't do this because of my own faith commitment; I'm doing this because this is what the Jewish people earnestly believe—and have believed for four thousand years. If you want to understand why the Jewish people feel so bound to the land of Israel, you have to read the history from their perspective, which is one of faith. So let's do that.

> If you want to understand why the Jewish people feel so bound to the land of Israel, you have to read the history from their perspective, which is one of faith.

THE BIBLICAL COVENANT: GOD'S PROMISE TO ABRAHAM

It's surprising to many that Judaism, Christianity, and Islam all agree that God (or, in Islam's case, Allah) promised to give the land of Canaan to the children of Israel. The Bible and the Quran both call the Holy Land the "Promised Land" because God promised to give it to the children of Israel. God made a covenant with Abraham, Isaac, Jacob (later named Israel), and the children of Israel that He would give the land of Canaan to them and their descendants. To understand the scope of that promise, we must start all the way back at the beginning. From there, we'll do a quick sprint through hundreds of years of biblical history, dropping in on key moments of Israel's existence and explaining why these milestone people, places, and events still matter today.

CREATION AND THE FLOOD

Genesis 1:1, the very first verse in the Bible, proclaims that God created the heavens and the earth.[2] Everything belongs to God—the world and everything in it—but God gave *dominion* of the earth to mankind (Psalm 24:1; Gen. 1:28). Genesis 1:26 explains that God made man in His own image to "rule over the fish in the sea and the birds in the sky, over the livestock and all the wild animals, and over all the creatures that move along the ground."

Many generations later, as the sixth chapter of Genesis explains, God regretted making mankind due to the horrendous evil in the world. He determined to send a great flood to wipe out the human race because "[t]he LORD saw how great the wickedness of the human race had become" and how man's every intention "was only evil all the time" (Gen. 6:5). However, one man in all the world found favor with God, and God chose to spare Noah and his family from the Flood, thereby reiterating His command of dominion to Noah and his offspring (Gen. 9:1–3).

Genesis chapters 9 to 11 record the genealogy of Noah, starting with his three sons, Shem, Ham, and Japheth, from whom all the nations of the earth are descended. We're going to run through a long list of names for just a minute, but I promise it's relevant because every nation on earth can literally be traced to these three sons of Noah. Ham's sons were Cush, Egypt, Put, and Canaan. The Canaanites descended from Ham's son Canaan, and the Philistines descended from Ham's son Egypt. The Canaanite clans included the Hittites, the Jebusites, and the Amorites, among others. These clans came to occupy a large territory of land stretching from modern-day Lebanon in the north all the way to Gaza in the south, which was known as the land of Canaan. Noah's son Japheth also had many sons, including Gomer, Magog, and Madai, from whom the coastland clans descended. Finally, Noah's son Shem had five sons, Elam, Ashur, Arphaxad, Lud, and Aram. If you've started tuning out because of this long list of ancient names, here's why all of this matters to our discussion: It is from Shem's line that both the Jews and the Arabs descended.

One of Shem's direct descendants was Terah, who lived in a land Genesis 11:28 calls "Ur of the Chaldeans," located in modern-day Iraq.[3] Ur occupied the southern portion of ancient Mesopotamia, near the Persian Gulf.[4] It was there that Terah's son was born—a man named Abram (Gen. 11:27). I cannot overstate the importance of Abram in the history of the Jewish people or the land of Israel. Abram, who would later be known as Abraham, would become the patriarch of every Jew, Christian, and Muslim.[5] He is *the* central figure in Jewish and Israeli history.

> **Abram, who would later be known as Abraham, would become the patriarch of every Jew, Christian, and Muslim. He is *the* central figure in Jewish and Israeli history.**

GOD'S PROMISE TO ABRAM

Abram was born into a world that had once again departed from the knowledge and worship of God, a world that was steeped in polytheism, the worship of many gods.[6] Joshua 24:2 even indicates that Abram's father Terah was himself an idol worshipper. Abram, however, was unique in his time, breaking tradition with his own family and culture in his devotion to the one true God.[7] Eventually, Abram set out from Ur with his father, his wife Sarai (later renamed Sarah), and his nephew Lot to go to Canaan. However, once they reached Harran, a region north of Canaan, they stopped and settled there (Gen. 11:31).

A dutiful son, Abram stayed with his father in Harran until Terah's death (Gen. 11:32). However, it was not God's plan for Abram to stay in Harran. The Lord declared to Abram:

> "Go from your country, your people and your father's household to the land I will show you.
>
> "I will make you into a great nation,
> and I will bless you;
> I will make your name great,
> and you will be a blessing.
> I will bless those who bless you,
> and whoever curses you I will curse;
> and all peoples on earth will be blessed through you."
>   (Gen. 12:1–3)

This remarkable promise, as we'll explore in more detail, marks the beginning of God's close, intimate relationship with the "nation" referred to here. From this command to leave his home, Abram would go on to be the father of a great nation that has outlasted practically every other ancient civilization. And it all started with this divine promise.

> From this command to leave his home, Abram would go on to be the father of a great nation that has outlasted practically every other ancient civilization.

God's command required two responses from Abram: faith and obedience. And, as we read in the Bible, Abram was up to the challenge. He demonstrated remarkable faith in God when he chose, at the age of seventy-five, to leave Harran and all he knew to set out on a journey at God's command, not even knowing where the journey would take him—let alone what it would ultimately mean for the world (Gen. 12:4–5). So great was his faith that Abram was noted among the most faithful men in history in the New Testament book of Hebrews: "By faith Abraham, when called to go to a place he would later receive as his inheritance, obeyed and went, even though he did not know where he was going" (Hebrews 11:8).

When Abram arrived in Canaan, the Lord appeared to him near Shechem, just west of the Jordan River, and said, "To your offspring I will give this land" (Gen. 12:7). Remarkably, almost four thousand years later, this land is the modern-day State of Israel. After hearing God's voice, Abram built an altar to the Lord.

Later, Abram and Lot separated because the land could not provide for both of their families. When Lot departed, God again said to Abram in much clearer terms:

"Look around from where you are, to the north and south, to the east and west. All the land that you see I will give to you and your offspring forever. I will make your offspring like the dust of the earth, so that if anyone could count the dust, then your offspring could be counted. Go, walk through the length and breadth of the land, for I am giving it to you." (Gen. 13:14–17)

Abram was more than seventy-five years old at this time and did not yet have any children, so he was surely puzzled by God's promise to grant the land to his "offspring," but he again built an altar to the Lord in the plain of Mamre at Hebron (Gen. 13:18).

There are two key promises that I want to point out in God's word to Abram in Genesis 13:14–17. First, God made Abram look all around in all directions and said, "All the land that you see I will give to you and your offspring forever" (Gen. 13:15). This is clearly a promise of the land. Here, God is promising Abram and his descendants the land of Israel. It is upon this promise and the coming covenant that the Jewish people have based their ownership of the land for thousands of years. Second, God promised Abram's descendants would be as innumerable as the dust of the earth. This refers to not only the Jewish people but also the Christians who claim Abraham as their spiritual father. In this promise, we see the beginning of not only the Jewish people's claim to Israel but also of two of the three great monotheistic religions of the world that have endured for millennia.

Sometime later, God again appeared to Abram, and Abram said, "Sovereign Lord, what can you give me since I remain childless and the one who will inherit my estate is Eliezer of Damascus? . . . You have given me no children; so a servant in my household will be my heir" (Gen. 15:2–3). This shows that Abram's faith was beginning to waver. Still childless and growing ever older, Abram began to see Eliezer, the steward of his home, as his heir.

The Lord said to him, "This man will not be your heir, but a son who is your own flesh and blood will be your heir. . . . Look up at the sky and count the stars—if indeed you can count them. . . . So shall your offspring be" (Gen. 15:4–5). God further said to Abram, "I . . . brought you out of Ur of the Chaldeans to give you this land to take possession of it" (Gen. 15:7). There it is again: the twin promises of the land and of descendants to inherit it. Genesis 15:6 says that Abram believed in this promise from the Lord, and God counted Abram righteous because of this demonstration of faith.

Abram, seeking clarity, asked God in Genesis 15:8 how he would know for certain that he would inherit the land. With this, God began one of the most powerful, most important acts in history: His covenant with Abraham. As described in Genesis 15:9–21, God commanded Abram to gather a heifer, a goat, a ram, a dove, and a pigeon—giving specific instructions for each. Pursuant to the legal covenant practices of the day, Abram divided each animal

> God began one of the most powerful, most important acts in history: His covenant with Abraham.

(except the birds) in half, laying the halves beside each other. Later that night, according to Scripture, God Himself walked between the pieces, making an unbreakable covenant with Abram and saying, "To your descendants I give this land, from the Wadi of Egypt to the great river, the Euphrates" (Gen. 15:18). I cannot overstate how critical this covenant act was between God and Abram, and we will explore its rich meaning and impact in a later chapter. For now, let's get back to the history lesson.

DESCENDANTS OF THE COVENANT

The story of how God fulfilled His covenant promise is a long, some-times complicated, sometimes joyful, sometimes mournful tale of obedience followed by rebellion followed by repentance. As we'll see in this and later chapters, this cycle has repeated over and over for thousands of years, but it started with Abram himself, despite his renowned faithfulness.

TAKING MATTERS INTO HIS OWN HANDS

Ten years after God had promised to make Abram the father of many, Abram still had no offspring by his wife, the now-elderly Sarai (Gen. 16:1). So, despite his initial show of faith, Abram did not wait for God to fulfill His promise. Instead, he and Sarai took matters into their own hands and thought of a way to fulfill God's covenant prom-ise through other means. What happened at this point sounds like a modern-day soap opera, but Abram's and Sarai's desire for a child was so great that they made a decision that would haunt them—and the Jewish people—from then to this very day.

Genesis chapter 16 recounts the sordid affair: Sarai convinced Abram to take her maidservant Hagar as another wife, hoping she could bear Abram a son as the means to fulfill God's promise. As soon as Hagar conceived for Abram, she despised Sarai, and Sarai regretted suggesting the arrangement in the first place. There was severe contention between the two women, and Sarai's harsh treat-ment of Hagar eventually caused the pregnant servant to flee into the wilderness. There she was met by an angel of the Lord, who told her to return and submit to Sarai. The angel promised her that her son would be blessed and that he would be the father of a great nation. The angel also told Hagar that her child would be a wild and unruly man who would be a trouble to his brother. Hagar returned to her mistress and soon bore a son to Abram, whom they called Ishmael. Ishmael would later become the father of the Arab people.

THE PROMISE FULFILLED

Years later, nearing one hundred years old—a full twenty-five years after God's initial call to leave the land of Ur—Abram heard from the Lord once again. Genesis chapter 17 recounts God's renewal of His covenant promise with His faithful servant, saying, "This is my covenant with you: You will be the father of many nations" (Gen. 17:4). It is here that God changes Abram's name to Abraham and reminds the future patriarch once again of His promises of the land and of endless heirs, proclaiming:

> "No longer will you be called Abram; your name will be Abraham, for I have made you a father of many nations. I will make you very fruitful; I will make nations of you, and kings will come from you. I will establish my covenant as an ever-lasting covenant between me and you and your descendants after you for the generations to come, to be your God and the God of your descendants after you. The whole land of Canaan, where you now reside as a foreigner, I will give as an everlasting possession to you and your descendants after you; and I will be their God." (Gen. 17:5–8)

The name change is significant when you see the meanings behind each name. Abram means "exalted father," while Abraham means "father of many."[8] In changing Abraham's name, God was putting His promise front and center. Abraham would have many heirs, and those heirs would inherit the land. Furthermore, as Genesis 17:15–16 makes clear, God would fulfill His promise through Sarai, whom He at that point renamed Sarah.

> **In changing Abraham's name, God was putting His promise front and center. Abraham would have many heirs, and those heirs would inherit the land.**

Believing he and Sarah were simply too old to conceive, Abraham asked God to fulfill His promise through Ishmael instead. At this point, God specifically promised Abraham that "your wife Sarah will bear you a son, and you will call him Isaac. I will establish my covenant with him as an everlasting covenant for his descendants after him" (Gen. 17:18–19). Hearing Abraham's concern for his firstborn son Ishmael, God assures the old father in Genesis 17:20–21, "And as for Ishmael, I have heard you: I will surely bless him; I will make him fruitful and will greatly increase his numbers. He will be the father of twelve rulers, and I will make him into a great nation. *But my covenant I will establish with Isaac . . .*" (emphasis added). After Isaac's miraculous birth a little more than a year later, God reinforced Isaac's role in His promise: *"It is through Isaac that your offspring will be reckoned"* (Gen. 21:12, emphasis added).

TESTING ABRAHAM'S FAITH

Years later, when Isaac was a young boy, Abraham was called by God to make a heartbreaking decision. Genesis chapter 22 tells of God's call upon Abraham to take his son Isaac—who represented the fulfillment of God's covenant promises—to Mount Moriah as a sacrifice unto God. The faithful servant complied and led Isaac to the place God had directed him to. When they arrived, Abraham bound his son and prepared to sacrifice him. At the last moment, an angel appeared and called on Abraham to stop. Through the angel, God said, "Do not lay a hand on the boy. . . . Do not do anything to him. Now I know that you fear God, because you have not withheld from me your son, your only son" (Gen. 22:12). Then God provided a ram caught in a thicket as a sacrifice in Isaac's place. After this remarkable demonstration of faith and obedience on Mount Moriah, God again renewed His covenant promise:

> "I swear by myself, declares the LORD, that because you have done this and have not withheld your son, your only son, I will surely bless you and make your descendants as numerous as the stars in the sky and as the sand on the sea-

shore. Your descendants will take possession of the cities of their enemies, and through your offspring all nations on earth will be blessed, because you have obeyed me." (Gen. 22:16–18)

Here, we see that God's promise to Abraham isn't only for descendants beyond measure; it is for descendants who will bless all the nations of the earth.

ISAAC AND JACOB

Having fully established the importance of Abraham and God's covenant promise to him, we can speed up a bit in our run through biblical history by looking at some key moments over the next several generations in Abraham's line.

Abraham was told repeatedly before Isaac's birth that God would fulfill His covenant promise through Isaac. Many years later, after Abraham had died, God appeared to a now-grown Isaac and confirmed His covenant with him, as He had done with Isaac's father. This occurred during a period of famine, when Isaac was considering journeying to Egypt, but God said:

> "Do not go down to Egypt; live in the land where I tell you to live. Stay in this land for a while, and I will be with you and will bless you. For to you and your descendants I will give all these lands and will confirm the oath I swore to your father Abraham. I will make your descendants as numerous as the stars in the sky and will give them all these lands, and through your offspring all nations on earth will be blessed, because Abraham obeyed me and did everything I required of him, keeping my commands, my decrees and my instructions." (Gen. 26:2–5)

This was a significant moment, as it marked the first time God issued His covenant promise to anyone other than Abraham. Although He had proclaimed it from the start, now there was no doubt that Abraham's line through Isaac would carry the blessing and the promise.

God blessed Isaac and his wife, Rebekah, with twin sons, and He told Rebekah while she was still pregnant that her sons would become two nations (Gen. 25:21–25). Telling Rebekah "the older will serve the younger," God made it clear that, even before birth, He had chosen Isaac's younger son, Jacob, to inherit the covenant rather than the elder son, Esau (Gen. 25:23).

> God made it clear that, even before birth, He had chosen Isaac's younger son, Jacob, to inherit the covenant.

Here, Genesis chapter 27 describes another family drama that could be ripped from today's headlines. As the boys grew into young men, despite God clearly saying that Esau would serve Jacob, an aging Isaac still intended to give the blessing of the firstborn to his elder son, Esau. However, Jacob and Rebekah took matters into their own hands by deceiving Isaac and tricking him into giving the blessing of the firstborn to the younger son. Fearing Esau's retaliation, Jacob then fled his home. He would spend years on the run from his brother, afraid for his life if Esau ever caught him.

Genesis chapter 28 describes a miraculous encounter on Jacob's journey. On his way toward Harran, Jacob stopped and made camp to sleep. There he had a dream in which he saw "a stairway resting on the earth, with its top reaching to heaven, and the angels of God were ascending and descending on it" (Gen. 28:12). God spoke to Jacob in his dream: "I am the Lord, the God of your father Abraham and the God of Isaac. I will give you and your descendants the land on which you are lying. . . . I will bring you back to this land. I will not leave you until I have done what I have promised you" (Gen. 28:13–15). This was the first time God had spoken of His covenant to the third generation from Abraham. To make the passing of the covenant promise perfectly clear, God later reminded Jacob of His covenant: "The land I gave to Abraham and Isaac I also give to you, and I will give this land to your descendants after you" (Gen. 35:12). This took place on what is now known as the Temple Mount.

After spending twenty years away from his home and out of Esau's reach, Jacob, at God's command, returned home to the land of his fathers (Gen. 31:3, 38). On the journey home, immediately before confronting his brother Esau, an angel of the Lord appeared to Jacob and wrestled with him throughout the night (Gen. 32:24–29). As the sun began to rise, the angel asked Jacob to let him go, but Jacob replied, "I will not let you go unless you bless me" (Gen. 32:26).

The angel said, "Your name will no longer be Jacob, but Israel, because you have struggled with God and with humans and have overcome" (Gen. 32:28). Jacob renamed that place Peniel because, he said, "I saw God face to face, and yet my life was spared" (Gen. 32:30). From that point on, not only did Jacob have a new name; God's people had a new name as well. That name, Israel, has remained a fixture of the world for the thousands of years since.

> "Your name will no longer be Jacob, but Israel, because you have struggled with God and with humans and have overcome."

> From that point on, not only did Jacob have a new name; God's people had a new name as well. That name, Israel, has remained a fixture of the world for the thousands of years since.

JOSEPH AND EGYPTIAN CAPTIVITY

After settling in Canaan, Jacob had twelve sons who later became the twelve tribes of Israel: Reuben, Simeon, Levi, Judah, Issachar, Zebulun, Joseph, Benjamin, Dan, Naphtali, Gad, and Asher (Gen. 33:18; 35:23–26). Joseph, Jacob's favorite son and the firstborn of his favorite wife, inspired envy and hatred in his half brothers, and they conspired to kill him (Gen. 37:4, 18). Due to a last-minute impulse of mercy from one of the brothers, they decided to spare his life and sell him into slavery instead (Gen. 37:26-27). Years later, although Joseph had grown into a model servant to his masters, he was wrongly accused of a crime and ultimately ended up in an Egyptian prison (Gen 39:1-20). And yet, even in prison—having been separated from his loving father, sold into slavery, and imprisoned for a crime he didn't commit—the Bible continually states that "the LORD was with him . . ." (Gen. 39:21).

After spending several years in prison, where he quickly earned the respect and trust of his guards, Joseph's supernatural ability to interpret dreams gave him an opportunity to leave his cell and enter into the Pharaoh's service (Gen. 39:21–23; 40–41). His strong work ethic and blessing from God led Joseph not only out of prison but into the ultimate seat of authority as viceroy over all of Egypt, second only to Pharaoh himself (Gen. 41:40).

Soon after, a great famine spread across Egypt and Canaan, and Joseph was in charge of stockpiling and rationing all of the food. His father, Jacob, who had believed for years that Joseph was dead, sent his family from Canaan to Egypt in the hopes of finding food. Ultimately they reconnected with Joseph, who convinced them to settle in the land of Goshen (Gen. 45:19–20, 28; Gen. 46:6; Gen. 47:27). This was an emotional move for Jacob, whom God had named Israel, because it meant leaving the land God had promised to him and his descendants. So, on the way down to Egypt, God appeared in a dream and reassured him, "I am God, the God of your father . . . Do not be afraid to go down to Egypt, for I will make you into a great nation there. . . . [A]nd I will surely bring you back again [to Canaan]" (Gen. 46:1-4).

The people of Israel prospered in Egypt and their numbers increased dramatically (Ex. 1:7). After Joseph's death, however, there arose a new pharaoh of Egypt "which knew not Joseph" and who grew fearful of the vast multitude of Israelites in Egypt (Ex. 1:8-9, KJV). The new pharaoh enslaved the Israelites, making "their lives bitter with harsh labor in brick and mortar and with all kinds of work in the fields" (Ex. 1:14). Yet, the more the Egyptians enslaved and persecuted the Israelites, the more the Israelites multiplied and grew (Ex. 1:12).

After more than four hundred years of captivity in Egypt

(Ex. 12:40), God raised up Moses as a leader of the Israelites (Ex. 3:9–10). God commanded Moses to go to Pharaoh and demand that he let the Israelites go. Moses demanded ten times before Pharaoh acquiesced (Ex. 12:31). Each of Pharaoh's denials was followed by a plague from the hand of God. Only after the tenth plague did Pharaoh relent and let the Israelites go. Yet, as the Israelites were finally leaving Egypt, Pharaoh changed his mind about releasing them and pursued them with his army (Ex. 14:5–9). God miraculously created a dry path through the Red Sea for the Israelites to escape, and once they had all crossed the sea safely, the waters returned to their place and drowned the pursuing Egyptian army (Ex. 14:28). At that point, for the first time in hundreds of years, the Israelites were heading back to the Promised Land of Canaan.

This exodus from Egypt is celebrated in the Jewish community with the holiday of Passover. It is one of my family's favorite Jewish holidays. It speaks of liberation, freedom, and hope. The message of the Passover is timeless. It speaks to each generation, imparting the desire for the God-given right of freedom.

A few months after their miraculous escape from Egypt, before arriving in the Land of Promise, the Israelites followed God's call to Mount Sinai for an absolutely critical step (Ex. 19:1–2). For the first time ever, at Mount Sinai, God brought the *entire* nation of Israel into the covenant. Whereas before it had been a personal message to Abraham, Isaac, and Jacob, God was now presenting His promise to the entire nation. In return, the people agreed to obey and follow God's commands. At Mount Sinai, after God gave the law to Moses,

> **For the first time ever, at Mount Sinai, God brought the *entire* nation of Israel into the covenant.**

Moses went and told the people all the LORD's words and laws, [and] they responded with one voice, "*Everything the LORD has said we will do.*" Moses then wrote down everything the LORD had said. He got up early the next morning and built an altar at the foot of the mountain and set up twelve stone pillars representing the twelve tribes of Israel. . . . Then he took the *Book of the Covenant* and read it to the people. They responded, "*We will do everything the* LORD *has said; we will obey.*" (Ex. 24:3–4, 7, emphasis added)

Here, the *entire* Israelite nation agreed to obey God's law and keep His commands. By agreeing to obey the law, they entered into God's covenant and received the right to possess the Promised Land. As we'll see later, this condition of obeying God's commands would prove to be crucial in Israel's ongoing enjoyment of the land.

This has been a quick sprint through hundreds of years of early biblical history, and it should in no way be considered exhaustive. However, I've tried to hit the high points as it pertains to God's covenantal promise to the nation of Israel. We've traced it from before the time of the Great Flood, through the line of Abraham, and onto the entire nation of Israel under Moses. In the next chapter, we'll see how that covenant promise remained true during the highs and lows of Israel's reigns of kings. Each time we see God speaking to His people about His promise, we see two things: the enduring nation and the land God has promised to them. The people and the land. These are the promises that Jews have passed down from generation to generation for thousands of years, and this is a big reason why the Jews have always felt tied to the land of Israel.

> Each time we see God speaking to His people about His promise, we see two things: the enduring nation and the land God has promised to them. The people and the land.

THE LINE OF ISHMAEL AND THE ARAB WORLD

Remembering His promise to Abraham, God also made his son Ishmael's descendants into a great nation, beginning with his twelve sons (Gen. 25:12–16). But, as God had warned Hagar, Ishmael's descendants have always had a contentious relationship with the children of Israel.[9] In modern times, the Arabs—the descendants of Ishmael—claim that the Holy Land belongs to them because Jews— the descendants of Isaac—no longer have a right to it. Despite this modern conflict, many non-Muslims and perhaps some Muslims themselves may be surprised to learn that the Quran, the Muslim holy book, actually affirms the fact that Allah made a covenant with the children of Israel to make them a vehicle of his message to mankind. The Muslim holy book also records Allah's promise to give the Holy Land to the people of Israel.

> **The Quran, the Muslim holy book, actually affirms the fact that Allah made a covenant with the children of Israel to make them a vehicle of his message to mankind.**

As we turn our eyes to the Quran's teaching on these things, let me set one thing straight up front. I will not get into a debate about whether or not the God of the Quran is the same as the God in the Old Testament. However, because we are viewing the Quran's perspective here, I will refer to the God of Islam as Allah.

THE QURAN'S TEACHING ON THE LAND

Like the Bible, the Quran states that Allah "created the heavens and the earth in six days."[10] "To Allah belongeth the dominion of the heavens and the earth; and Allah hath power over all things."[11] The Quran extensively talks about the covenant Allah made with the children of Israel. It speaks of the Israelites being a people set apart for a special purpose (i.e., spreading Allah's message). Consider the following verses, for instance:

> O Children of Israel! call to mind the (special) favor which I bestowed upon you, and fulfil your covenant with Me as I fulfil My Covenant with you . . . (Quran 2:40)
> O Children of Israel, call to mind the special favor which I

bestowed upon you, and that I preferred you to all others (for My Message). (Quran 2:122; 2:47)

And remember We took your covenant and We raised above you (The towering height) of Mount (Sinai): (Saying): "Hold firmly to what We have given you . . ." (Quran 2:63)

And remember that Abraham was tried by his Lord with certain commands, which he fulfilled: He said: "I will make thee an Imam to the Nations." He pleaded: "And also (Imams) from my offspring!" . . . (Quran 2:124)

Allah did aforetime take a covenant from the Children of Israel, and we appointed twelve captains among them. And Allah said: "I am with you: if ye (but) establish regular prayers, practice regular charity, believe in my apostles, honour and assist them, and loan to Allah a beautiful loan, verily I will wipe out from you your evils, and admit you to gardens with rivers flowing beneath; . . ." (Quran 5:12)

Clearly, the children of Israel had a special place in Allah's plan from the early Muslim perspective.

Furthermore, the Quran specifically states that Allah gave the Holy Land to the children of Israel. We see in chapter 5:

Remember Moses said to his people: "O my people! Call in remembrance the favour of Allah unto you, when He produced prophets among you, made you kings, and gave you what He had not given to any other among the peoples. O my people! Enter the holy land which Allah hath assigned unto you, and turn not back ignominiously, for then will ye be overthrown, to your own ruin." (Quran 5:20–21)

While commenting on these verses, Abdullah Yusuf Ali, a revered translator of and commentator on the Quran, says, "Israel was chosen to be the vehicle of Allah's message, the highest honor which any nation can receive."[12]

Consider a few more Quranic passages discussing how Allah fulfilled his promise and led the Israelites out of Egypt to the Promised Land:

> And We made a people, considered weak (and of no account), inheritors of lands in both east and west, — lands whereon We sent down Our blessings. The fair promise of thy Lord was fulfilled for the Children of Israel, because they had patience and constancy, and We levelled to the ground the great works and fine buildings which Pharaoh and his people erected (with such pride). (Quran 7:137)
>
> We settled the Children of Israel in a beautiful dwelling-place, and provided them sustenance of the best . . . (Quran 10:93)
>
> And We [Allah] said thereafter to the Children of Israel, "Dwell securely in the land (of promise)" . . . (Quran 17:104)

Over and over again, the Quran demonstrates Allah's intention to give the land of Israel to the Jewish people.

Chapter 20 of the Quran talks specifically about the covenant made on Mount Sinai:

> O ye Children of Israel! We delivered you from your enemy, and We made a Covenant with you on the right side of Mount (Sinai), and We sent down to you Manna and quails: (Saying): "Eat of the good things We have provided for your sustenance, but commit no excess therein, lest My Wrath should justly descend on you: and those on whom descends My Wrath do perish indeed!" (Quran 20:80–81)

Verse 86 of that chapter goes on to say, "So Moses returned to his people in a state of indignation and sorrow. He said: 'O my people! did not your Lord make a handsome promise to you? Did then the promise seem to you long (in coming)? . . .'"

Further commenting on the Israelites' escape from Egyptian slavery, the Quran says:

Truly Pharaoh elated himself in the land and broke up its people into sections, depressing a small group among them: their sons he slew, but he kept alive their females: for he was indeed a maker of mischief. And We wished to be Gracious to those who were being depressed in the land, to make them leaders (in Faith) and make them heirs, To establish a firm place for them in the land . . . (Quran 28:4–6)

Commenting on these verses, Yusuf Ali says, "What Pharaoh wished was to crush [the Israelites]. But Allah's plan was to protect them as they were weak, and indeed to make them custodians and leaders in His Faith, and to give them in inheritance a land 'flowing with milk and honey.' "[13]

Amid the recent decades of conflict between Jews and Palestinians, some Palestinian leaders have claimed that Jerusalem was never a Jewish city or that the Jewish Temple never existed on the Temple Mount.[14] As we'll see later in this book, these leaders are not only denying historical and archaeological facts but their own holy text, the Quran. Interestingly, the land of Canaan is called the "Promised Land" in the Quran because of Allah's promise to the children of Israel. The Quran called it the "Holy Land" long before there was any Islamic influence over the land or any Islamic monument, such as the Al Aqsa Mosque, was envisioned or built. In other words, even according to the Quran, the land is holy because of its connection to the Jews, not Muslims. In 2014, Sheikh Ahmed Aladoan of Amman, a member of Jordan's well-known Adwan tribe, acknowledged that Allah is the protector of the children of Israel and Allah "gave the Holy Land to the sons of Israel *until the Day of Judgment.*"[15] Sheikh Aladoan further stated that Muslims who deny these facts "distort the words of the Koran."[16]

THE PEOPLE AND THE LAND

This chapter has documented passage after passage not only of the Bible but also of the Quran that attest to the existence and nature of God's covenant with His chosen people, Israel. Yes, I quoted a lot of passages here, but I hope you see the point in that barrage of Scripture: Whenever we see the covenant, we see it tied to a specific people and to a specific land. There is no covenant concerning the Jews and the Holy Land—whether in the Bible or the Quran—that doesn't include both aspects. This rich, deep history is crucial in understanding why the Jewish people feel so intimately connected with the land of Israel. It is theirs by God's promise, a fact that even their enemies' most holy text affirms over and over again. As we will see in subsequent chapters, this is an eternal promise that has remained in effect ever since—even during the Israelites' periods of disobedience, rebellion, and captivity.

KEY TAKEAWAYS

1. Regardless of any disagreement about what happened later in history, all three of the great monotheistic faiths believe that God promised the land of Israel to the Jewish people and gave it to them.

2. This happened long before the Christian and Muslim faiths had even come into being.

4

HOPE FOR THE NATION

"My people, I am going to open your graves and bring you up from them; I will bring you back to the land of Israel. Then you, my people, will know that I am the LORD *. . .* I will put my Spirit in you and you will live, and I will settle you in your own land."
—EZEKIEL 37:12–14 (EMPHASIS ADDED)

I n my legal career now going on forty years, I have had the privilege of working with presidents, prime ministers, foreign ministers, and members of multiple legislative bodies. I have spoken twice at the United Nations General Assembly. I don't say this to boast; I say this to let you know that I have seen government from the inside. If there's anything all those years and all that experience has taught me, it's that governing is fraught with setbacks. That is the nature of politics.

For example, I remember having lunch one afternoon years ago with an esteemed cabinet member of the Israeli government. As we enjoyed our meal, he got an important phone call that changed his life. During that short phone conversation, he found out that his party was no longer part of the coalition government and his portfolio as cabinet member was revoked. The whole mood of the lunch changed radically. Within the span of one phone call, this man's entire political career came to an abrupt end.

In my work around the globe, I have developed close working relationships with world leaders who, like my lunch companion, were leaders of their country one minute and out of office the next. I also have had to work with leaders who knew their time was short and were trying to get as much done as possible in the time they had left. This sense of endless political upheaval is especially true in Israel, where the political climate is always tense. This is nothing new. In fact, the daily drama of modern politics may not even hold a candle to what Israel went through during the biblical reign of the kings.

> **The daily drama of modern politics may not even hold a candle to what Israel went through during the biblical reign of the kings.**

FAITHFULNESS AND DISOBEDIENCE DURING THE REIGN OF THE KINGS

In the previous chapter, we traced the history of God's covenant relationship with His chosen people, Israel, from the time of the Great Flood through the time of Moses. Whereas God had revealed His covenant promise only to individuals in Abraham's line up to that point, He chose to bring the entire nation of Israel into the covenant at Mount Sinai following the Israelites' miraculous deliverance from Egypt. Now let's skip ahead about three hundred years into the reign of the kings to get a snapshot of Israel's life in the land God had given them—and in a new political system they had never known before. As we run through about one thousand years of biblical history, we'll see many highs and lows. However, no matter what was happening politically or militarily, the Israelites never lost their ownership of the land. As we've seen, God gave them the land, and no one else will ever gain title to it.

> **No matter what was happening politically or militarily, the Israelites never lost their ownership of the land. As we've seen, God gave them the land, and no one else will ever gain title to it.**

SOLOMON AND THE DIVIDED KINGDOM

King Solomon was not the first Israelite king, but he was certainly a central figure in Israel's early history as a kingdom in the land God had given to the Jews. Solomon was the son of David, a man whom the Bible describes as "a man after [God's] own heart" (1 Sam. 13:14). David had been a hero of Israel and a beloved king. Although he wasn't a perfect human being, God's anointing was on David— so much so, in fact, that God promised David an eternal kingdom through David's line: "Your house and your kingdom will endure forever before me; your throne will be established forever" (2 Sam. 7:16). Jews traditionally take this as a foreshadowing of the coming Messiah, while Christians see this Messianic promise as being fulfilled in Jesus (Matt. 1:1). Moreover, David's reign was so great that it was considered the highest praise for future kings to be compared or traced back to David.

As king, Solomon was greatly revered for his remarkable wisdom. The Bible makes it clear that this wisdom was a gift from God:

> Solomon answered . . . "Your servant is here among the people you have chosen, a great people, too numerous to count or number. So give your servant a discerning heart to govern your people and to distinguish between right and wrong. For who is able to govern this great people of yours?"
>
> The LORD was pleased that Solomon had asked for this. So God said to him . . . "I will do what you have asked. I will give you a wise and discerning heart, so that there will never have been anyone like you, nor will there ever be." (1 Kings 3:6–12)

Through Solomon's wise rule, God ushered in a time of great prosperity for the Israelites, crowned by the magnificent Temple for the Lord that was constructed in Jerusalem.

Despite this grand national success and the supernatural wisdom that God had given the king, Solomon continually fell to his primary weakness: women. He directly contradicted the Lord's commands by taking hundreds of wives from among the pagan nations:

> King Solomon . . . loved many foreign women. . . . They were from nations about which the LORD had told the Israelites, "You must not intermarry with them, because they will surely turn your hearts after their gods." Nevertheless, Solomon held fast to them in love. (1 Kings 11:1–2)

And, just as God had warned, these wives

> turned [Solomon's] heart after other gods, and his heart was not fully devoted to the LORD his God, as the heart of David his father had been. He followed Ashtoreth the goddess of the Sidonians, and Molek the detestable god of the Ammonites. So Solomon did evil in the eyes of the LORD; he did not follow the LORD completely, as David his father had done.
> On a hill east of Jerusalem, Solomon built a high place for Chemosh, the detestable god of Moab, and for Molek, the detestable god of the Ammonites. He did the same for all his foreign wives, who burned incense and offered sacrifices to their gods. (1 Kings 11:4–8)

Solomon's slip, due largely to the influence of so many pagan wives, led to nothing but trouble for the rest of his years and for the next several generations of Israel's history.

Because of God's love for Solomon's father, David, He did not take away the kingdom from Solomon directly. Instead, as 1 Kings chapters 11 and 12 recount, God promised to take the kingdom away from Solomon's son and give it to one of his son's servants. God also raised up three enemies to trouble Solomon for the remainder of his reign: Hadad the Edomite; Rezon, king of Syria; and finally Jeroboam, Solomon's own servant. As God had promised, soon after Solomon's death, the servant Jeroboam led a rebellion against Solomon's son Rehoboam. This resulted in the ten northern tribes of Israel completely rejecting Rehoboam as king, leaving only Judah and Benjamin for Solomon's son Rehoboam to rule. Israel, from that point forward, was split into the Northern Kingdom of Israel—ruled by kings in Samaria—and the Southern Kingdom of Judah, ruled by kings in Jerusalem.

Despite not only witnessing but actually playing an instrumental part in the punishment God sent for Solomon's idolatry, Jeroboam followed suit and instituted further idolatry in Israel:

> The king made two golden calves. He said to the people, "It is too much for you to go up to Jerusalem. Here are your gods, Israel, who brought you up out of Egypt." One he set up in Bethel, and the other in Dan. And this thing became a sin; the people came to worship the one at Bethel and went as far as Dan to worship the other.
>
> Jeroboam built shrines on high places and appointed priests from all sorts of people, even though they were not Levites. He instituted a festival on the fifteenth day of the eighth month, like the festival held in Judah, and offered sacrifices on the altar. This he did in Bethel, sacrificing to the calves he had made. And at Bethel he also installed priests at the high places he had made. On the fifteenth day of the eighth month, a month of his own choosing, he offered sacrifices on the altar he had built at Bethel. So he instituted the festival for the Israelites and went up to the altar to make offerings. (1 Kings 12:28–33)

So, within two generations of the great king David, the entire Israelite kingdom was divided and ten of the twelve tribes of Israel were bowing down to idols in the Northern Kingdom.

Things weren't any better in the Southern Kingdom. As 1 Kings 14:21–26 relates, Rehoboam ruled wickedly in Judah. He was the son of one of Solomon's Ammonite wives. As such, he himself was the product of Solomon's refusal to obey God's command against intermarrying with the enemies of the Lord. Scripture tells us that Judah, under the reign of Rehoboam, did even greater evil than the Israelites had in earlier generations by worshipping idols in the high places:

"They also set up for themselves high places, sacred stones and Asherah poles on every high hill and under every spreading tree" (1 Kings 14:23). As punishment for this wickedness, God sent Shishak, the king of Egypt, to raid Jerusalem and steal the treasures out of the Temple and the house of the king. God's message was clear: If the children of Israel would not obey His commands, He would remove the blessings He had bestowed on them. And, as we've seen several times now, when God removes His blessings from the people of Israel, the consequences show up in the peace and security of the land itself.

> When God removes His blessings from the people of Israel, the consequences show up in the peace and security of the land itself.

The Cycle of God's Blessings Given and Taken Away

The biblical history of the Israelites during the reign of the kings isn't all bad. There were, in fact, several bright spots over the centuries when a righteous ruler would rise up and return the nation to God's ways. And, not surprisingly, the Lord's blessings would return during those times. One such ruler was Asa, king of Judah, the grandson of Rehoboam. We see in 1 Kings 15:11–12 that "Asa did what was right in the eyes of the LORD, as his father David had done. He expelled the male shrine prostitutes from the land and got rid of all the idols his ancestors had made." Asa even went so far as to remove his own mother from being queen "because she had made a repulsive image for the worship of Asherah. Asa cut it down and burned it in the Kidron Valley" (1 Kings 15:13).

Asa presents an interesting contrast to Solomon. Whereas Solomon forsook the Lord in favor of his many wives, Asa's faithfulness to God was so deep that he forsook his own mother in order to follow the Lord. First Kings 15:14 records that "Asa's heart was fully committed to the LORD all his life." God blessed Asa with a long reign of forty-one years, and he lived to reach old age (1 Kings 15:10, 23). Still, the wickedness of idolatry was not completely curbed because "he did not remove the high places" (1 Kings 15:14). Due to this disobedience and failure to follow God's purpose as a holy nation, the Promised Land remained divided during Asa's reign, and Judah and Israel were at war throughout the entire forty-one years (1 Kings 15:16).

Around that time, another particularly wicked king arose, this time in the Northern Kingdom. King Ahab took the north back into pagan idolatry, as "Ahab, who sold himself to do evil in the eyes of the LORD . . . behaved in the vilest manner by going after idols, like the Amorites the LORD drove out before Israel" (1 Kings 21:25–26). God sent the prophet Elijah to Ahab with a warning, saying, "I am going to bring disaster on you. I will wipe out your descendants . . . because you have aroused my anger and have caused Israel to sin" (1 Kings 21:21–22). Here, not only was Ahab found guilty of idolatry himself, he was further condemned for leading his nation away from God.

Israel's back-and-forth dalliance with idolatry and subsequent disobedience continued into the next century, until the Southern Kingdom of Judah finally turned away from idols completely during the reign of King Hezekiah. Scripture says that Hezekiah "did what was right in the eyes of the LORD, just as his father David had done. He removed the high places, smashed the sacred stones and cut down the Asherah poles" that were used in idol worship (2 Kings 18:3–4). During this time, the Israelites began burning incense to the bronze serpent that God had commanded Moses to make many generations earlier to heal the people. Confusing the object itself for the power behind it, the people began worshipping the artifact rather than the God Who worked through it. Hezekiah, however, took the serpent and broke it into pieces as a symbol of ending the national idolatry for good (2 Kings 18:4).

God blessed Hezekiah for his faithfulness in rooting out the idolatry from the Southern Kingdom, and, as we've seen time and again throughout biblical history, that blessing came in the form of protection from foreign enemies and continued enjoyment of the land. This divine protection became clear only four years into Hezekiah's reign when Assyria began a campaign to conquer the Holy Land. After three years of fighting in the north, the Northern Kingdom fell and the people were taken captive "because they had not obeyed the Lord their God, but had violated his covenant—all that Moses the servant of the Lord commanded. They neither listened to the commands nor carried them out" (2 Kings 18:12).

After Israel's fall in the north, King Sennacherib of Assyria turned toward Judah and laid siege on Jerusalem (2 Kings 18:13–17). Sennacherib's general began taunting the people of Jerusalem, saying:

> On whom are you depending, that you rebel against me? . . . [I]f you say to me, "We are depending on the Lord our God"—isn't he the one whose high places and altars Hezekiah removed, saying to Judah and Jerusalem, "You must worship before this altar in Jerusalem"? . . . Has the god of any nation ever delivered his land from the hand of the king of Assyria? . . . Who of all the gods of these countries has been able to save his land from me? How then can the Lord deliver Jerusalem from my hand?" (2 Kings 18:20–22, 33, 35)

The Assyrians believed themselves to be invincible and immune to any "god" their enemies worshipped. They were wrong.

When Hezekiah heard about the enemy general's taunting, he went to the Temple to pray to God. In his prayer, he recognized the connection between God's blessings and God's purpose for the nation:

> "It is true, Lord, that the Assyrian kings have laid waste these nations and their lands. They have thrown their gods into the fire and destroyed them, for they were not gods but only wood and stone, fashioned by human hands. Now, Lord our God, deliver us from his hand, *so that all the kingdoms of the earth may know that you alone, Lord, are God.*" (2 Kings 19:17–19, emphasis added)

God answered Hezekiah's prayer, as described in 2 Kings 19:35: In the middle of the night, an angel of the Lord killed eighty-five thousand of the Assyrian army outside Jerusalem. Because of this,

Sennacherib and his army were forced to retreat to Nineveh, and Jerusalem was unharmed. Soon thereafter, Sennacherib was killed by his own sons while worshipping a false god.

This story powerfully demonstrates how God supernaturally preserved the Jewish people and their possession of the Holy Land when they obeyed and worshipped Him—even when the northern half of the kingdom failed to do so. It also demonstrates that His purpose in doing so was that "all the kingdoms of the earth may know" that He is the Lord God (2 Kings 19:19). Further, this incident shows that occupation and enjoyment of the land God gave to the Jewish people is a separate issue from their ownership of the land. When God's chosen people obeyed God, they were able to occupy and enjoy the land He had given them. When they were disobedient, God allowed them to be driven out of parts of the land, thereby temporarily depriving them of their ability to occupy and enjoy the land that they owned until they recognized their sin, repented of it, and sought anew the face and favor of God. This is a key point that we'll discuss at length in the next chapter.

By the time of Zedekiah's reign in the Southern Kingdom a century later, the pendulum had swung back toward disobedience, leading to one of the greatest tragedies in Jewish history. Jeremiah chapter 52 describes in painful detail how King Nebuchadnezzar of Babylon engaged in a two-year siege of Jerusalem, culminating in the complete destruction of the Temple of Solomon and much of the city itself. To the horror of the Israelites:

> [Nebuzaradan, Nebuchadnezzar's commander of the imperial guard,] set fire to the temple of the LORD, the royal palace and all the houses of Jerusalem. Every important building he burned down. The whole Babylonian army, under the commander of the imperial guard, broke down all the walls around Jerusalem. (Jer. 52:13–14)

While catastrophic for the Jewish people, this destruction should not have come as a surprise. During the Temple's construction centuries earlier, God had promised Solomon:

"As for this temple you are building, *if* you follow my decrees, observe my laws and keep all my commands and obey them, [*then*] I will fulfill through you the promise I gave to David your father. And I will live among the Israelites and will not abandon my people Israel." (1 Kings 6:12–13, emphasis added)

Here we see that critical "if-then" statement. While God promised to "live" in the Temple among the people, that promise was on the condition of the Israelites' continued faithfulness and obedience to His commands. Now, in the time of Zedekiah, the people's disobedience had grown so great that God allowed the Temple to be overtaken and destroyed and His people to be taken into captivity, demonstrating the severe consequences of disobedience.

While most of the nation was carried off into Babylonian captivity, it is important to note that not *all* the Israelites were removed from the land. Jeremiah 52:16 tells us that, although most of the city's inhabitants were removed, "Nebuzaradan left behind the rest of the poorest people of the land to work the vineyards and fields." Here, we see again that a faithful remnant remained in the Land of Promise—even when most were exiled. Despite the greatest tragedies, the Jewish people have always had *some* presence in the land.

> **Despite the greatest tragedies, the Jewish people have always had *some* presence in the land.**

Years before this Babylonian invasion and the Temple's destruction, Jeremiah had warned the people of Israel that their possession of the Holy Land would be taken away and that they would suffer great destruction because of their disobedience to God's commands:

And though the LORD has sent all his servants the prophets to you again and again, you have not listened or paid any attention. They said, "Turn now, each of you, from your evil ways and your evil practices, and you can stay in the land the LORD gave to you and your ancestors for ever and ever. Do not follow other gods to serve and worship them; do not arouse my anger with what your hands have made. Then I will not harm you." . . . Therefore the LORD Almighty says this: "Because you have not listened to my words . . . [t]his whole country will become a desolate wasteland, and these nations will serve the king of Babylon seventy years." (Jer. 25:4–6, 8, 11)

True to Jeremiah's prophecy, it was seventy years before a group of Israelites returned to Jerusalem to rebuild the Temple (2 Chron. 36:20–21). This second Temple stood for four centuries, but it, too, was eventually destroyed, this time by the Romans.

HOPE FOR THE NATION

Through these ups and downs over the centuries of Israel's kingdom history, we see how the Israelites' obedience resulted in peace and abundance in the land and how their disobedience led to tragic consequences, resulting in conflict in or temporary exile from the land. Despite the consistent disobedience of Israel, the destruction of the Temple, and the scattering of its people, hope was not lost. Even in their darkest hour, it was always possible for the children of God to repent and regain enjoyment and control of the land.

EZEKIEL AND THE VALLEY OF DRY BONES

The prophet Ezekiel gives us tremendous insight into God's enduring commitment to Israel, despite their disobedience: "The hand of the LORD was on me [Ezekiel], and he . . . set me in the middle of a valley; it was full of bones. . . . I saw a great many bones on the floor of the valley, bones that were very dry" (Ez. 37:1–2). There, God spoke to Ezekiel and asked the prophet if the bones could be brought back to life. Ezekiel answered, "Sovereign LORD, you alone know" (Ez. 37:3). With this, God commanded Ezekiel to prophesy to the bones so that the bones would "hear the word of the LORD" and live (Ez. 37:4–5).

Ezekiel did as the Lord instructed, and reported:

So I prophesied as I was commanded. And as I was prophesying, there was a noise, a rattling sound, and the bones came together, bone to bone. I looked, and tendons and flesh appeared on them and skin covered them, but there was no breath in them. Then he said to me, "Prophesy to the breath; prophesy, son of man, and say to it, 'This is what the Sovereign Lord says: Come, breath, from the four winds and breathe into these slain, that they may live.'" So I prophesied as he commanded me, and breath entered them; they came to life and stood up on their feet—a vast army. (Ez. 37:7–10)

This prophecy of Ezekiel has tremendous meaning for the Jewish people as a message of hope. The bones represented Israel. God revealed to Ezekiel:

Then he said to me: "Son of man, these bones are the people of Israel. They say, 'Our bones are dried up and our hope is gone; we are cut off.' Therefore prophesy and say to them: 'This is what the Sovereign Lord says: My people, I am going to open your graves and bring you up from them; *I will bring you back to the land of Israel.* Then you, my people, will know that I am the Lord, when I open your graves and bring you up from them. I will put my Spirit in you and you will live, and *I will settle you in your own land.* Then you will know that I the Lord have spoken, and I have done it, declares the Lord.'" (Ez. 37:11–14, emphasis added)

> **I will put my Spirit in you and you will live, and *I will settle you in your own land.***

Here again we see that God doesn't just promise to bring Israel back to life; He promises to return the Israelites to their land. Again and again, we see the people stray from the Lord's commands, but He continually offers them the chance to return to the land He has given them.

GOD'S ENDURING FAITHFULNESS

God has tied His faithfulness into the very existence of Israel, saying through the prophet Jeremiah that the nation of Israel will exist as long as the laws of nature remain, the expanse of outer space remains unquantifiable, and the depths below the earth's crust remain unexplored (Jer. 31:35–37).

> **God has tied His faithfulness into the very existence of Israel.**

Jeremiah goes on to explain that God has promised that Israel will always have a ruler of the line of David, and that He will cause the Israelites to return to their land (Jer. 33:25–26).

Well after David's death, the prophet Ezekiel spoke God's words describing the future king in the line of David:

> My servant David will be king over them, and they will all have one shepherd. They will follow my laws and be careful to keep my decrees. *They will live in the land I gave to my servant Jacob,* the land where your ancestors lived. *They and their children and their children's children will live there forever, and David my servant will be their prince forever.* I will make a covenant of peace with them; it will be an *everlasting covenant.* I will establish them and increase their numbers, and *I will put my sanctuary among them forever.* My dwelling place will be with them; I will be their God, and they will be my people. Then the nations will know that I the LORD make Israel holy, when my sanctuary is among them forever. (Ez. 37:24–28, emphasis added)

This future king described here is the Messiah, who would return to free and save Israel once and for all. Christians obviously believe this passage refers to Jesus, while Jews believe it points to a future coming Messiah. What's important for us to note here is that the Messiah will usher in an era of Jews dwelling in their land, undisturbed, forever. This is the ultimate fulfillment of God's covenant promise to Abraham.

FAITHFULNESS AND HOLINESS

Israel's history shows God balancing His faithfulness to an imperfect nation with His holiness. If Israel ceases to exist, God is not faithful. But if He permits the nation to disobey His laws, then He is not holy. Because it would be against His nature to do so, God could not break His covenant promises (2 Tim. 2:13). God did punish Israel, but He always left a remnant—many times members of the Tribe of Judah, from which David and ultimately Jesus descended (2 Kings 17:18; Jer. 39:10; Matt. 1:1–17). The nation of Israel will always exist simply because God is faithful to His Word. But as we'll explore in depth in the next chapter, the Israelites must obey His decrees to be able to participate in the purpose of the nation of Israel and occupy and enjoy the land they were given. And as we've seen, that's where they've gotten into trouble in the past.

> **The nation of Israel will always exist simply because God is faithful to His Word.**

KEY TAKEAWAYS

1. Despite the fact that, throughout their history, the Jewish people have been driven from their land time and time again, there has always been a Jewish remnant dwelling in the land.

2. Even during times of conquest or captivity, the Jewish people have never at any point in history lost their ownership of the land.

5

THE NATURE OF THE COVENANT

"You yourselves have seen ... how I carried you on eagles' wings and brought you to myself. Now if you obey me fully and keep my covenant, then out of all nations you will be my treasured possession. Although the whole earth is mine, you will be for me a kingdom of priests and a holy nation."

—EXODUS 19:4–6

Civilizations throughout history have had a distinct pattern that occurs repetitively over the course of centuries. Kingdoms rise and fall, nations are built only to collapse centuries later, and people groups appear and then fade from the annals of time.

The civilizations of the Middle East have been no exception. In fact, the entire region from Mesopotamia in the east to Egypt in the west has always been a particularly tumultuous part of the world. Mesopotamia consisted of the area between the Tigris and Euphrates Rivers and was known for its rich agricultural societies. The region stretched from the Persian Gulf and the Zagros Mountains in the east, up north through modern-day Iraq and into Asia Minor, west toward Syria, and south toward the Levant, ending at the Arabian Desert in the south and Nile River in Egypt. Two factors made Mesopotamia such a ripe target for conflict: its fertile land and the fact that it was geographically indefensible, which made it difficult for nations that conquered it to maintain control of the region for long.[1]

As a result, throughout its history, Mesopotamia changed hands over and over again: from the Assyrians to the Babylonians, to the Persians, to the Greeks, to the Romans, and then to the Muslims.[2] One of the longest-lasting civilizations in the world, Egypt, survived for a remarkable three thousand years due to its strategically defensible and isolated location, but even it was eventually conquered by a stronger nation, Greece.[3] Greece later succumbed to the inevitable pattern of civilizations when it fell to the Roman Empire, and the Roman Empire, in turn, collapsed centuries later.[4]

This rise and fall of civilizations seems to be a constant cycle over the course of time, with one notable outlier: the Jewish people. The Jews have supernaturally existed for more than three millennia, while their enemies have fallen and disappeared, one by one. I say "supernaturally" because, as we discussed in the previous chapter, we're viewing the course of Jewish history from the perspective of the Jewish people. This is what the Jewish people believe, and, honestly, it is hard to laugh that off from a historical perspective. The fact that the Jewish people exist at all in the modern age after so many powerful kingdoms have risen and fallen over that same span of time is, some would argue, miraculous.

> The fact that the Jewish people exist at all in the modern age after so many powerful kingdoms have risen and fallen over that same span of time is, some would argue, miraculous.

The Jews can trace a continual existence all the way back to the life of Abraham more than 3,700 years ago. They have never ruled a massive empire, nor have they ever been able to boast of a vast population relative to other civilizations. Instead, their history has been a troubled one of dispersion, discrimination, and decimation.[5] The Jews have, therefore, defied the inevitable pattern and ending of other civilizations, even while those who dominated them over time have fallen prey to it. In their persistent presence in the world and in their enduring connection to the land of Israel, we can see echoes of

God's covenant with Abraham from so long ago. Remember the two important aspects of the covenant: the people and the land. Let's see how that's played out over thousands of years.

THE NATURE OF THE COVENANT

Today, many people believe that Jews no longer hold a special place before God and that the covenant God made with them is no longer valid. Some Christians believe God's covenant has been transferred to the Christian church through Christ's death and resurrection; Muslims, on the other hand, believe that Jews have been cursed by God and that they no longer hold any special place before Him due to their disobedience. Muslims further believe that Islam has replaced both Judaism and Christianity and that Muslims are now the vehicle of God's message to the world. Yet, the Bible tells us that God's covenant with the Israelites was not for a finite term. Rather, it was an everlasting and eternal covenant—an unending relationship between God and His chosen people, the Jews. If the covenant is everlasting, then modern Jews still remain in that covenant relationship with God, the same covenant He first established with Abraham. By exploring the nature of God's covenant with His chosen people, we can better understand the lasting implications and determine if the Jews, in fact, have been replaced.

> **The Bible tells us that God's covenant with the Israelites was not for a finite term. Rather, it was an everlasting and eternal covenant—an unending relationship between God and His chosen people, the Jews.**

ETERNAL AND ONE-SIDED COVENANT

From the earliest stages of the covenant's formation, God made known that His covenant would be everlasting. God said to Abraham, "All the land that you see *I will give to you and your offspring forever*" (Gen. 13:15, emphasis added). He further said, "I will establish my covenant as an *everlasting covenant* between me and you and your descendants after you for the generations to come, to be your God and the God of your descendants after you" (Gen. 17:7, emphasis added). God gave the Holy Land to Abraham and his descendants as an unconditional gift for the faith and obedience that Abraham had already displayed. The promise of a gift does not require the recipient of the gift to give anything in return. Abraham did not have to do anything in order to receive the land. This fact is evidenced by the formal ceremony of the covenant.

We touched on this briefly in Chapter 3, but let's dig deeper into the process and meaning of the covenant ceremony in Genesis chapter 15. When Abraham asked God how he would know that God would give him the land, God told Abraham to bring "a heifer, a goat and a ram, each three years old, along with a dove and a young pigeon," cut them in half (except the birds), and lay the halves opposite each other (Gen. 15:9–10). At night "a smoking firepot with a blazing torch . . . passed between the pieces," and God said to Abraham, "To your descendants I give this land . . ." (Gen. 15:17–18).

Dividing the animals in half and walking between them was, as attorney Sandra Teplinsky says, "used in Abraham's day to formalize a legal covenant" as a promise unto death.[6] When both covenanting parties walked between the pieces, each party took "solemn oaths to perform their duties. If only one party passed through the bodies, however, only that one party undertook to perform covenant duties."[7] That is, if only one of the two parties walked between the pieces, that party was the only one with any legal obligation to the covenant. This party, therefore, took *full responsibility* for the covenant. Since only God walked between the bodies of the animals, only He assumed a legal obligation (i.e., to give the land to Abraham and his descendants). Abraham (and his descendants) were under no obligation to perform any covenant duties to receive the land. The land is theirs.

ISRAEL'S RESPONSIBILITY: A HOLY NATION

Although God clearly gave the land to Abraham's descendants as an eternal covenant, God gave them the land for a specific purpose. The purpose of the covenant was to make Israel a holy nation, setting it apart from all others, and to bless other nations through it so that they might come to know God, His laws, and how to follow Israel's example.

> **The purpose of the covenant was to make Israel a holy nation, setting it apart from all others, and to bless other nations through it so that they might come to know God, His laws, and how to follow Israel's example.**

Throughout the Bible, the Jews are consistently referred to as God's *chosen* people.[8] They were chosen to create a holy nation that God would use to bless others. Deuteronomy 14:2 states that the Israelites were chosen "[o]ut of all the peoples on the face of the earth . . . to be his treasured possession." Exodus 19:5–6 explains that God established His covenant with them to create "a kingdom of priests and a *holy* nation" (emphasis added) for all the other nations to emulate. Israel, then, would be an example to the rest of the world of what a holy nation should be. Through Israel's example, the other nations of the world would be blessed (Gen. 22:18).

These passages show that, while God's covenant promise to give them the Holy Land forever was an eternal and one-sided covenant, the Israelites were also expected to use the land for its intended purpose: to keep it a holy nation by obeying God's law. If they failed to do this, they would not lose *ownership* of the land (as that had been promised and secured by God), but they would temporarily lose *possession and enjoyment* of the land. This important point—the issue of possession and enjoyment versus ownership—is something we'll discuss in more detail and with many historical examples later in this chapter.

As a sign of entering into the covenant and the obedience that accompanied the act, God required Abraham and his male descendants to be circumcised:

Then God said to Abraham, "As for you, you must keep my covenant, you and your descendants after you for the generations to come. This is my covenant with you and your descendants after you, the covenant you are to keep: Every male among you shall be circumcised. You are to undergo circumcision, and it will be the sign of the covenant between me and you. . . . My covenant in your flesh is to be an *everlasting* covenant. Any uncircumcised male . . . will be cut off from his people; he has broken my covenant." (Gen. 17:9–11, 13–14, emphasis added)

Circumcision was not merely an outward act. It was a symbolic statement of obedience on the part of the Israelites. As such, there was an internal element to it as well, a circumcision of the heart as described in Deuteronomy 10:16: "Circumcise *your hearts*, therefore, and do not be stiff-necked any longer" (emphasis added). Deuteronomy 30:6 continues, "The LORD your God will *circumcise your hearts* and the hearts of your descendants, so that you may love him with all your heart and with all your soul, and live" (emphasis added). Later, the prophet Jeremiah reminded Israel to "[c]*ircumcise yourselves to the LORD*, circumcise your hearts, you people of Judah and inhabitants of Jerusalem, or my wrath will flare up and burn like fire because of the evil you have done . . ." (Jer. 4:4, emphasis added).

This circumcision of the heart was God's way of telling His people to follow Him and keep His commandments. From the very beginning of the covenant with Israel, God meant for His people to not simply go through outward rituals but also to focus internally on their own hearts. So He commanded the Israelites to obey Him through physical circumcision, an outward symbol, and also to obey Him internally through circumcision of their hearts, by adhering to His law. Without the latter, the former meant little. And when the people failed to attune their hearts to God and remain faithful to their covenant responsibility, the price they paid was the peace and their continued presence in the land.

OWNERSHIP VERSUS POSSESSION AND ENJOYMENT OF THE LAND

Any attorney knows that, in the courtroom, the opposing counsel will often jump up and shout "Objection!" to call a piece of evidence into question. I have to confess that one of my favorite parts of a trial is making evidentiary objections. In this case, as for the legitimacy of Israel as a Jewish state, maybe you're already standing up with an objection. I understand that. Even if you accept the biblical testimony and deep Jewish belief that God promised the land of Canaan to Abraham and his descendants, it is reasonable to look back on the scope of history and ask, "Well, what about the Babylonian Captivity or the sacking of Jerusalem by Rome? Clearly the Jewish people haven't *held* the land for four thousand years. Does that mean the covenant is over?" The answer is an emphatic no!

> **Clearly the Jewish people haven't *held* the land for four thousand years. Does that mean the covenant is over? The answer is an emphatic no!**

The many times throughout history during which the people of Israel have been attacked, conquered, removed, or otherwise held captive do not indicate that God's covenant with them has come to an end. Instead, as we've seen already, it indicates that the Jewish people's enjoyment and possession of the land—not their ownership of the land—is dependent on their continuing faithfulness to God's commandments. Basically, we're saying that the land has always belonged to them according to God's covenant promise, even when they've been forcibly removed from the land or another nation has laid claim to it. It's a matter of ownership versus possession, which deserves some attention here.

FIGHTING REPLACEMENT THEOLOGY

First, let's deal with the question: *Has God removed His blessing from the Jewish people and given it to someone else?* That is a matter of some debate among the three great monotheistic faiths in the world. While the Bible tells us that God's covenant was eternal and everlasting, the Quran does not consider the covenant eternal. This is a key point on which the Quran differs from the Bible. You'll remember from Chapter 3 that the Quran teaches that Allah made a covenant with the children of Israel to make them a special people—a vehicle of his message to mankind—and gave them the Holy Land. Judaism, Christianity, and Islam all agree on that point. However, the Quran goes on to assert that Allah withdrew his blessings from the children of Israel because of their disobedience. This is where Judaism, Islam, and even some parts of Christianity go in vastly different directions.

The Quran teaches that Allah first chose the children of Israel as a special people for his message and sent them his word, the Torah. In this, Allah made a covenant with them, but they ultimately disobeyed and broke the covenant. Then Allah sent his message, the Gospels, to Christians, who Muslims believe also disobeyed and broke the covenant. Finally, Allah sent his final word, the Quran, to the final prophet, Muhammad, and his Muslim *ummah*, the new chosen people. Through this process, says the Quran, Allah effectively replaced Jews with Muslims as his holy people.[9]

To be fair, the Quran's view that Muslims have replaced the children of Israel is similar to the replacement theology held by some Christians. Proponents of replacement theology, as summarized by Christian apologist Matt Slick, believe that the "Christian church has replaced national Israel regarding the plan, purpose, and promises of God."[10] As such, the promises God originally made to Israel are fulfilled in the Christian church. Replacement theology teaches that the Christian church, instead of the Jews, now makes up God's chosen people and that the Mosaic Covenant has been replaced by the new covenant.[11]

To be blunt, this view is simply not biblical. If replacement theology is valid, then God is not true to His word. He promised to give the Holy Land to the Jews forever. He said that His covenant was everlasting. He alone took the full responsibility for the covenant. If God gave the Holy Land to the children of Israel forever, they own the land for eternity. Although at times—as a result of their disobedience—the children of Israel have been displaced temporarily from the land, they still hold the title to it according to God's eternal promise.

POSSESSION CONDITIONED UPON OBEDIENCE

Let's next dig further into this matter of ownership versus possession, which we mentioned briefly in the previous chapter. God is not a liar, so how should we reconcile God's eternal, unconditional gift of the land to Abraham's descendants with the fact that they've been forcibly removed from the land so often throughout history? As we've seen, it comes down to an issue of obedience. You'll remember that God gave Israel the land for a purpose, and that purpose was to be a holy nation, a shining light to bless all nations. The people accomplished this purpose by keeping the nation holy through their faithfulness and obedience to God's law. If the children of Israel failed to keep the land holy, the purpose of the covenant would be defeated, and they would temporarily lose possession and enjoyment of the land.

This expectation of obedience and its connection to God's covenant with the children of Israel was made public when God first brought the entire nation into His promise. Through Moses, God said on Mount Sinai:

> "You yourselves have seen . . . how I carried you on eagles' wings and brought you to myself. Now *if* you obey me fully and keep my covenant, *then* out of all nations you will be my treasured possession. Although the whole earth is mine, you will be for me a kingdom of priests and a holy nation." (Ex. 19:4–6, emphasis added)

Here, we see that God is clearly making an "if–then" statement: *If* the people obey, *then* God will make them a treasure among nations. As such, it's reasonable to assume that, if they *do not obey*, God will *remove* their enjoyment of His promises and possession of the land for a season.

Leviticus 18:24–28 is even more revealing in its direct connection between obedience and possession of the land, as God proclaims, "Do not defile yourselves in any of these ways. . . . *Even the land was defiled;* so I punished it for its sin, and the land vomited out its inhabitants" (emphasis added). Here, God warns the Israelites that defiling the land through disobedience would cause the land to literally spit them out. This warning became even clearer a few chapters later:

> But if you will not listen to me and carry out all these commands, and if you reject my decrees and abhor my laws and fail to carry out all my commands and so violate my covenant . . . *I will scatter you among the nations* and will draw out my sword and pursue you. Your land will be laid waste, and your cities will lie in ruins. (Lev. 26:14–15, 33, emphasis added)

So, the Israelites' safety in their land was at risk if they were disobedient. That's obvious in the passage. But don't miss the subtle nuance in the last part of that passage. God warns them that "*your* land" and "*your* cities" would be endangered. That is a clear recognition of ownership, even though it was in the context of God exercising His judgment over disobedience. This is further cemented in God's warning in Deuteronomy 5:33: "Walk in obedience to all that the LORD your God has commanded you, so that you may . . . *prolong your days in the land that you will possess*" (emphasis added).

By being circumcised and then later promising at Mount Sinai to obey God's commandments, the Israelites (i.e., each descendant) assumed the covenantal duty of obedience in order to enjoy continuous possession of the land. If they disobeyed, they would find themselves in foreign lands or ruled by their enemies. Yet, if they repented, turned back to God, and followed His laws again, they would regain possession of the land because of God's eternal promise. He said:

> But if they will *confess their sins* and the sins of their ancestors—their unfaithfulness and their hostility toward me, which made me hostile toward them so that I sent them into the land of their enemies—then when their uncircum-

cised hearts are humbled and they pay for their sin, *I will remember my covenant with Jacob and my covenant with Isaac and my covenant with Abraham, and I will remember the land.* (Lev. 26:40–42, emphasis added)

This passage is rich with the key words we've been entrenched in throughout this discussion: obedience, repentance, covenant, land. These concepts are a drumbeat throughout Scripture that we cannot ignore.

There were many acts outlined in the Law that could have been considered disobedience. Such things included murder, stealing, coveting, adultery, disrespecting the Sabbath, failing to tithe, disregarding cleanliness, performing sacrifices, and more. However, at the top of the list—the most important law that God consistently emphasized to His people—was the command to not worship any other gods.[12] This was nonnegotiable for God, and He outlined this standard at Mount Sinai when He first spoke to the nation through Moses:

"You shall have no other gods before me. You shall not make for yourself an image in the form of anything in heaven above or on the earth beneath or in the waters below. You shall not bow down to them or worship them; for I, the LORD your God, am a jealous God, punishing the children for the sin of the parents to the third and fourth generation of those who hate me, but showing love to a thousand generations of those who love me and keep my commandments." (Ex. 20:3–6)

If the Israelites violated this command, the land would be defiled, and the Israelites would lose their possession and enjoyment of it.

As an added measure against the worship of other gods, God further warned His people not to listen to the voice of false prophets (Deut. 13:1–5). Coupled with this ban on idol worship was the express command prohibiting interreligious marriages:

Do not intermarry with them. Do not give your daughters to their sons or take their daughters for your sons, for they will turn your children away from following me to serve other gods, and the LORD's anger will burn against you and will quickly destroy you. (Deut. 7:3–4)

The Lord reminded Israel of this command through Joshua after the Israelites defeated all the tribes of Canaan and settled in the land:

"So be very careful to love the LORD your God. But if you turn away and ally yourselves with the survivors of these nations that remain among you and *if you intermarry with them and associate with them*, then you may be sure that the LORD your God will no longer drive out these nations before you. Instead, they will become snares and traps for you, whips on your backs and thorns in your eyes, *until you perish from this good land, which the LORD* your God has given you. Now I am about to go the way of all the earth. . . . But just as all the good things the LORD your God has promised you have come to you, so he will bring on you all the evil things he has threatened, until the LORD your God has destroyed you from this good land he has given you. If you violate the covenant of the LORD your God, which he commanded you, and go and serve other gods and bow down to them, the LORD's anger will burn against you, and you will quickly perish from the good land he has given you" (Josh. 23:11–16, emphasis added).

Some throughout history have tragically and wrongfully said this passage is about racial or ethnic mixing, but that is not the case. It is a matter of spiritual mixing. In other words, the main issue was not about interreligious marriage itself; it was more about the fact that such marriages would cause the Israelites to violate the first and most important commandment, "You shall have no other gods before me" (Ex. 20:3). Unfortunately, as we saw in the previous chapter regarding King Solomon, Israel frequently disobeyed this solemn command, as well as the other commands God had given them. And, as a result, that disobedience often cost them possession and enjoyment of the land that God had given them.

INDIVIDUAL DISOBEDIENCE AND NATIONAL CONSEQUENCES

While only the disobedient individuals were outside the covenant's terms, often the disobedience of a few individuals caused negative consequences for the entire nation. We see this play out in Numbers chapters 13 to 14 when Moses sent spies into the Promised Land once they first reached the outskirts of the region. He picked twelve spies to survey the land and report back. Of those twelve, only two, Joshua and Caleb, came back excited about the beautiful region and certain that God would give them the land. The other ten came back terrified of the Canaanites they saw there. They described them as giants that would surely destroy the Israelites. They spread fear and doubt among the people until the entire nation began to grumble. They even begged to be taken back to Egypt as slaves!

God's response to this faithless disobedience was hard but just: "Because they have not followed me wholeheartedly, not one of those who were twenty years old or more when they came up out of Egypt [except Caleb and Joshua] will see the land I promised on oath to Abraham, Isaac and Jacob—" (Num. 32:11). In this, God punished the entire generation that disobeyed Him, not allowing them to personally experience the glory of the Promised Land. He made them wander in the desert for forty years until the entire generation had died out. Even though they were standing on the very doorstep of the Promised Land, the Israelites would not begin to take possession of the land for another forty years because of their disobedience. In effect, they were denied possession and enjoyment of the land before they even got there.

NATIONS RISE AND FALL BASED ON THEIR TREATMENT OF ISRAEL

While Israel's continual cycle of blessing and discipline is interesting in itself, it is perhaps even more interesting to trace the well-being of *other nations* throughout history through the lens of how they've treated Israel. Those empires and nations that treated the Jews well have historically prospered, while those who harmed and attempted to destroy the Jews have met disaster and destruction.[13] That, I believe, is no coincidence. It is the visible, verifiable outworking of the Lord's promise to Abraham when He called him to leave Harran for the Promised Land: "I will bless those who bless you, and whoever curses you I will curse; and all peoples on earth will be blessed through you" (Gen. 12:3). You can trace the pattern of blessings and curses stemming from this promise from the very beginning of Jewish history to this very day. Both great and small nations have experienced the blessing, and even the most powerful have not escaped its curse.

THE CYCLE IN SCRIPTURE

We see this cycle repeat throughout biblical history, starting with the earliest example, Egypt. As we saw in Chapter 3, Egypt experienced amazing prosperity during the time of Joseph. Due to Joseph's wise administration, Egypt was apparently the only nation in the region that avoided the ravages of starvation during the crippling famine of the time (Gen. 41). Historical records confirm that Egypt was the most powerful nation in the region during Joseph's time.[14] But, as we've seen, a new pharaoh arose who "knew not Joseph" and grew concerned about the rapid population growth of the Israelites in Egypt (Ex. 1:8–10, KJV). This new dynasty instituted four hundred years of enslavement, oppression, and murder of the Jews. Ultimately, though, God sent ten plagues to torment the Egyptians in response to Pharaoh's refusal to release the Israelites from bondage. The plagues—culminating in the death of all the Egyptians' firstborn—

led to the emancipation of the Jewish slaves (a large part of Egypt's workforce) and the destruction of Pharaoh's charioteers in the Red Sea. Ultimately, these were all consequences of Egypt's abuse of the children of Israel and a national humiliation for the once-mighty Egyptian empire. [15]

Later, great empires including Assyria and Babylon fell after attacking and enslaving the Israelites. Assyria conquered the northern ten tribes and then Babylon overran Assyria. Then, after Babylon sacked Jerusalem and took the residents into captivity, it fell to the Persians.[16] This clear cycle of nations abusing Israel and facing dire national consequences as a result is not only in keeping with God's covenant promise to Abraham, it's also in line with the consistent warnings of Israel's prophets. Jeremiah, for example, recorded this clear warning:

> This is what the LORD says: "As for all my wicked neighbors who seize the inheritance I gave my people Israel, I will uproot them from their lands and I will uproot the people of Judah from among them. But after I uproot them, I will again have compassion and will bring each of them back to their own inheritance and their own country. And if they learn well the ways of my people and swear by my name, saying, 'As surely as the LORD lives'—even as they once taught my people to swear by Baal—then they will be established among my people. But if any nation does not listen, I will completely uproot and destroy it," declares the LORD. (Jer. 12:14–17)

This prophecy is not only a warning to Israel's enemies, it's also a promise to Israel itself. It's an affirmation of God's promise to both protect the people of Israel and to return them to their homeland. Again we see the evidence of God's covenant with Abraham in His protection of the people and the land.

THE CYCLE OUTSIDE OF SCRIPTURE

Events taking place outside of a biblical context after the fall of Jerusalem to the Roman Empire in the first century A.D. display the same pattern. Rome itself—one of the most successful and powerful political and military entities to ever exist—eventually fell apart, while the tiny nation of Israel it sought to stamp out—though scattered and spread out over much of the known world—has endured to the present day.

FIFTEENTH-CENTURY SPAIN

Let's jump forward almost fifteen centuries to see the cycle continue beyond ancient times. In 1492, Spain was a great European power. It had been a relatively comfortable home for the exiled Jews for hundreds of years, and yet, in 1492, Spain expelled the Jewish people.[17] Holland welcomed many of the Jews exiled from Spain.[18] The diverging histories of the two countries at this time exemplify the Genesis 12:3 model. Less than a hundred years later, in 1588, Spain suffered the defeat of the Spanish Armada by the British and the onset of the Spanish economic crisis of 1588–1598.[19] In contrast, the Dutch—having welcomed the Jewish exiles during this time—experienced what's known as the Dutch Golden Age (1580–1670), followed by a tremendous expansion of the Dutch empire in the seventeenth century through colonialism during the height of Jewish commercial enterprise in the country.[20]

ENGLAND'S RISE AND DECLINE

Holland wasn't the only country to experience a time of enormous growth following their generosity toward the Jews. Britain, in fact, rose to the status of a world superpower following their readmission of Jews under Cromwell and William III in the mid-1600s. England's power continued to grow for three hundred years until World War I. Then, after giving Jews the right to return to their homeland in 1917, Britain halted Jewish emigration to Palestine at the worst possible time—the onset of the Holocaust. This led to the horrific arrest and extermination of millions of Jews. Britain survived World War II, but, as with many nations that had brought harm to Israel throughout history, it sustained heavy damage and lost much of its influence in the years following.[21]

Following the war, Israel's most vocal supporter, the United States, replaced Britain as the leading superpower in the West. And the German Third Reich, possibly the Jews' most unrelenting and murderous persecutor, was of course obliterated by World War II, leaving Germany itself completely devastated.

So not only has Israel survived despite all odds when other nations, no matter how wise, powerful, prosperous, or advantaged, have invariably declined and eventually disappeared from the world stage, it is also possible to draw a direct correlation between the fate of many of those nations and the way they have treated the Jews. The promise of Genesis 12:3— "I will bless those who bless you, and whoever curses you I will curse"—is therefore to be taken seriously, not only by the Jews, but by all nations. That biblical admonition is not, as we have seen, empty words or a vacant promise from an ancient scroll. It remains vital and in force, and its consequences have been felt in our own lifetimes. Those who ignore it do so at their own peril.

GOD'S FAITHFULNESS TO HIS PROMISE

History and Scripture have shown us that the eternal nature and purpose of the covenant are intertwined. God's covenant is eternal, but the Israelites' disobedience in refusing to fulfill the covenant's purpose could lead to punishment and, as a result, to losing enjoyment of the land. However, even during periods when the Israelites lost their enjoyment of the land, they never lost ownership of it. As we'll see throughout this book, there has always been a continued presence of

Jews in Israel even during the times when the Israelites were overrun or taken into captivity.

In Leviticus, God said to Moses:

> "[I]f they will confess their sins and the sins of their ancestors . . . then when their uncircumcised hearts are humbled and they pay for their sin, I will *remember my covenant with Jacob* and *my covenant with Isaac* and *my covenant with Abraham*, and *I will remember the land. . . .* Yet in spite of this, when they are in the land of their enemies, *I will not reject them or abhor them so as to destroy them completely, breaking my covenant with them.* I am the LORD their God. But for their sake *I will remember the covenant with their ancestors* whom I brought out of Egypt in the sight of the nations to be their God. I am the LORD" (Lev. 26:40–42, 44–45, emphasis added).

Here, God makes it clear that, although the Israelites may forget Him, He will *never* forget them and *never* break the covenant. Notice how He not only says He would remember the covenant but specifically says He will remember the land. The land is always tied to the covenant.

Scripture is filled with similar promises. In Deuteronomy 4:31, Moses said to the Israelites: "[God] will not abandon or destroy you or *forget the covenant with your ancestors, which he confirmed to them by oath*" (emphasis added). In Deuteronomy 4:40 he continued: "Keep his decrees and commands, which I am giving you today, so that it may go well with you and your children after you and that you may live long in the land the LORD your God gives you for all time."

Later, when God renewed His covenant with the Israelites in Moab, God said: "I am making this covenant, with its oath, not only with you who are standing here with us today in the presence of the LORD our God *but also with those who are not here today*" (Deut. 29:14–15, emphasis added). Once again, God revealed the everlasting nature of the covenant, underscoring that it was meant for all *future* generations of Israelites, not just those who were there at that time.

In Judges 2:1, God again said: *"I will never break my covenant with you . . . "* (emphasis added). Although the book of Judges is filled with examples of the nation's disobedience and the subsequent consequences, God made it clear that His covenant would always remain in place.

In addition to these more explicit references in Scripture, the very existence of the Jewish people and all of the supernatural events that occurred from the very beginning—leading up to the establishment of the Jewish State in 1948 and beyond—shows that God's covenant is everlasting, eternal, and unbroken. As I said earlier, it's a miracle that the Jewish people exist today at all! And yet, because the covenant is never-ending, God has continuously kept His nation alive and distinct from other people groups. The children of Israel have certainly made mistakes over such a long history, and those mistakes have cost them dearly. They continually experienced the beauty and richness of their land, only to be removed for a season due to their disobedience. However, while other nations, peoples, and empires have fallen, dispersed, and even completely disappeared, the nation of Israel (i.e., the Jewish people) remains alive and well today just as it was millennia ago when God first made His everlasting and eternal covenant with Abraham.

KEY TAKEAWAYS

1. God's covenant with the Israelites was not for a finite term; it was an everlasting and eternal covenant.

2. The purpose of the covenant was to make Israel a holy nation so that, through Israel, other nations might come to know God.

3. Although Israel's disobedience cost them their presence in and enjoyment of the Promised Land at times, they never lost rightful ownership of it.

SECTION III

THE HISTORICAL AND ARCHAEOLOGICAL EVIDENCE

History (noun): a chronological record of significant events (such as those affecting a nation or institution) often including an explanation of their causes.[1]

Archaeology (noun): the scientific study of material remains (such as fossil relics, artifacts, and monuments) of past human life and activities; remains of a culture of a people.[2]

6

SUPPORTING THE BIBLICAL HISTORY

Ever since scientific archaeology started a century and a half ago, the consistent pattern has been this: the hard evidence from the ground has borne out the biblical record again and again—and again. The Bible has nothing to fear from the spade.[3]

—PAUL L. MAIER

When I'm preparing and presenting a case before a judge or jury, I'm always focused on a narrative. The story is important. All too often, in fact, the way you *frame* the evidence can be more important than the evidence itself. It would be easy to bring in an endless string of expert witnesses to drone on and on about facts and figures, but all the facts in the world won't help you if the jury falls asleep. That's why you always need to put the facts in context, showing the jury how the puzzle pieces fit together into the bigger narrative you're telling.

In an average criminal case, for example, the jury would hear all the relevant details arranged in a compelling sequence from start to finish as it pertains to the crime. The scope of those details would maybe span one night or a day. For example, the accused left his home at 8:00 p.m., arrived at the victim's home at 8:24 p.m., was seen speeding away at 8:47 p.m., was pulled over by the police on a routine traffic stop at 9:01 p.m., and so on. For more complex cases, the narrative may get bigger to paint a picture of the series of events for a week or maybe a month. The reason attorneys like me do this is to give the jury a clear, progressive flow to the facts. We need to show how one piece of evidence leads into the next, then to the next, then to the next. The result is a clear, undisputed, unbroken narrative that leads the jury to make the right decision.

When we apply this to our case for the Jewish people's enduring presence in the Holy Land, things get much more complicated. In this case, the series of events doesn't span one evening, week, or month; the events span thousands of years. The lands we know as modern Israel (including Judea and Samaria, also called the West Bank, and the Gaza Strip)—and indeed all of the Middle East, including Syria, Lebanon, Jordan, Iraq, Egypt, Turkey, and the Arabian Peninsula—have been occupied by mankind since time immemorial. It is a place where a person practically cannot throw a rock without hitting a previously undiscovered archaeological site. And every new discovery has the potential to change, expand, or explain all the discoveries that came before it. Such change is routine the Middle East.

Lawyers deal with facts and evidence, framing the vast amount of information into a narrative that attentive listeners can understand in order to present a case for truth. When looking at archaeology and ancient history, we have a wealth of credible sources to draw from, including the Bible, archaeological sites, scrolls and inscriptions, coins from lost civilizations, ancient writings, and more. For example, we have the well-documented works of the great Jewish historian Josephus, as well as significant, extensive archaeological corroboration of those written accounts.

With all of this in mind, and in light of all the credible sources we have to draw on, it is my goal in this section to set forth a clear evidentiary record of the Jews in Palestine. Running through four thousand years of history and archaeology is no easy feat, however, and presenting a complete history of the Jewish people in full detail is well beyond the scope of this book. So, instead of going into excessive detail on every century, power struggle, captivity, rebellion, war, and empire, I'm going to instead try to provide enough detail and supporting evidence to tell a compelling narrative that will walk you through the key moments of the Jews' long history in the land. By providing the evidence and facts, along with the

> **By providing the evidence and facts, along with the different interpretations by experts, I will establish that the Jewish people have had a constant presence in the Land of Promise—Israel— for almost four millennia.**

different interpretations by experts, I will establish that the Jewish people have had a constant presence in the Land of Promise— Israel—for almost four millennia.

SEARCHING FOR ABRAHAM

In the previous section of this book, we spent a lot of time going through the biblical history of the Jewish people and how Scripture shows them intimately connected to the land. Now, as we transition into the historical/archaeological evidence, let's see how the Bible's account is verified by reliable extra-biblical sources and archaeological discoveries. As we begin, I'll admit that specific archaeological references to the Jews and Israel as a people are hard to come by until the time of King David. However, we can still see some historical basis for much of what we see in the early Genesis and Exodus accounts and beyond.

CULTURAL HISTORY

Biblical and extra-biblical sources indicate that the Jewish people have resided in Palestine since approximately 2200 B.C. None of the other contemporary groups from that time—the Amorites, Hittites, Hivites, Perizzites, Canaanites, Philistines, or Gergesenes— still exist.

As we saw in the previous chapters, the Jewish people trace their heritage back to Abraham, who, the Bible says, was promised the land of Israel by God Himself. We've already seen that Jews, Christians, and Muslims all agree on this point. The world of Abraham was the world of the Fertile Crescent, stretching from Lower Mesopotamia at the end of the Persian Gulf, through Upper Mesopotamia between the Tigris and Euphrates Rivers, and down through the eastern Mediterranean coastal strip to the Nile River.[4]

While archaeology has not yet uncovered extensive historical evidence of Abraham himself, the record does confirm much of early Genesis's account of life in the land. Many of the practices and stories we see in Genesis are consistent with the ancient letters, accounts, and laws recovered from Harran in modern-day Turkey, thereby lending credibility to the Genesis account.[5] For example, Genesis tells of how both Abraham (Gen. 12:10–16; 20:1–2) and Isaac (Gen. 26:7–8) presented their wives as their sisters rather than spouses. This is consistent with a cultural practice of giving wives legal status as sisters from that time.[6]

Evidence from the Bronze Age (3300 B.C.–1200 B.C.)

Palestine of the Middle Bronze Age (circa 2200–1570 B.C.) is described in some detail in a group of Egyptian texts, referred to as the Execration Texts, which were written around 2000–1750 B.C.[7] The earliest archaeological evidence from these texts includes references to Jerusalem, Ashkelon, Beth Shan, Rehob, and Byblos. These cities still exist in our time and include Israel and even modern-day Lebanon. Stone inscriptions from around that same time found in southern Egypt represent the earliest example of a complex alphabetic script adapted from Egyptian hieroglyphs, proving that Semitic speakers—including Jews—lived and worked in Egypt as early as the Egyptian Middle Kingdom circa 2050–1640 B.C.[8]

Researchers have unearthed around twenty thousand cuneiform tablets dating back to 1800 B.C. that have given a compelling picture of life in the region during that time. Tel el-Hariri, the ancient Amorite city of Mari, has yielded a gold mine of particularly insightful letters that detail extensive contact between Canaan and northern and southern Mesopotamia during the late nineteenth and early eighteenth centuries B.C.[9] The personal names, language, and customs used in the so-called Mari Letters directly reflect the customs and culture of the Patriarchal Age (time of Abraham, Isaac, and Jacob) and align with the biblical record.[10]

One Mari tablet, referring to the "men of Ki-na-aḫ-um," contains the earliest known use of "Canaan" as a geographical term. The tablets also describe the prominence of the city of Hazor, which correlates to Joshua's reference to Hazor as "the head of all these kingdoms" in Joshua 11:10: "At that time Joshua turned back and captured Hazor and put its king to the sword. (Hazor had been the head of all these kingdoms.)"[11] Another especially revealing Mari tablet (Mari, II, No. 131) refers to "the Hapiru of the land" ("Habiru" in other texts), which may be an early reference to the Hebrew people.[12]

A similarly important find was a record of the alphabet, dating to around 1300 B.C., which was found at Izbet Sartah in the coastal plain north of Mount Carmel. This book bears the largest inscription of a twenty-two-letter West Semitic alphabet, which some scholars consider "early Hebrew."[13] This provides strong evidence to an Israelite presence in Canaan well before 1270 B.C.

In A.D. 1896, the German Egyptologist Wilhelm Spiegelberg published an inscription commemorating Pharaoh Merneptah's victory over the Libyans (1213–1204 B.C.).[14] In a few lines toward the end, the inscription also refers to Israel:

The princes are prostrate, saying: "Mercy!"
Not one raises his head among the Nine Bows.
Desolation is for Tehenu; Hatti is pacified;
Plundered is Canaan with every evil;
Carried off is Ashkelon; seized upon is Gezer;
Yanoam is made as that which does not exist;
Israel is laid waste, his seed is not;
Hurru has become a widow for Egypt!
All lands together, they are pacified;
Everyone, who was restless, he has been bound [emphasis added].[15]

This is the first known reference to the name Israel, which is historically significant. Commenting on the Merneptah inscription, historian Niels Peter Lemche explains that, although exact details regarding Israel's defeat at the hands of Merneptah cannot be precisely determined, the important point is that it references Israel and indicates some sort of political, geographical, or ethnic

> **This is the first known reference to the name Israel, which is historically significant.**

relationship between this Israel and the later kingdom of this name in the Iron Age (c. 1200 B.C.–500 B.C.).[16] Later evidence establishes the presence of the kingdoms of Judah and Israel.

This reference to Israelites in the region at that time lines up with other archaeological evidence from the Hill Country, which shows the remains of six hundred to seven hundred villages that appeared during the Late Bronze Age (1570–1200 B.C.) in the exact locations where the Bible indicates the Israelites initially settled.[17] These villages show a simple way of life. Many of these dwellings were abandoned after a generation or two, which may indicate further migration by the Israelites as they settled Canaan based on their allotments to each tribe.[18] Each of the twelve tribes of Israel was given jurisdiction over a particular portion of Israel. Joshua 13–21 describes in detail the boundary lines and property for each tribe.

Following the death of Joshua (c. 1390 B.C.), the time of the Judges, or *shophetim*, was ushered in according to the biblical record. These Judges were periodically raised up to deliver Israel from local oppressors.[19] At different times, the Israelites were oppressed by a number of different rulers and tribes, such as the Philistines and the Midianites.[20] This picture of Israel during the time of the Judges fits their designation in the previously mentioned Merneptah Victory Stele.

Remarkably, throughout the time of the Judges, Egyptian texts shed some light on the historical geopolitical circumstances in the Holy Land at the time. The Amarna Letters, found at Tell el-Amarna, the abandoned capital of Amenhotep IV and Akhenaton (1352–1336 B.C.), consist of 382 letters written on tablets in cuneiform to and from the pharaoh and his Canaanite vassals.[21] These letters from Byblos, Tyre, Megiddo, Pella, Gezer, Hebron, Jerusalem, Gaza, and Ashkelon clearly indicate that Canaanite groups still controlled these cities.[22] Some letters pleaded for the pharaoh's assistance against troublemakers—including the 'Apiru—indicating that Egyptian control existed but may have been weak at this time.[23] It may well be that the troublemaking 'Apiru (also Hapiru and Habiru) is a reference to the Hebrews.[24]

Other letters vividly characterize the "atmosphere of mutual suspicion and treachery" that prevailed between the vassal kings.[25] The kings who *are not* mentioned, however, may be even more interesting than those who are. The kings of the areas that Israel is believed to have conquered by this time—including Jericho, Bethel, Gibeon, and Hebron in the central Hill Country and Rift Valley—are absent from the Amarna Letters.[26] If Israel had already conquered these areas, there would be no Egyptian vassal kings to communicate with, lending some credence to Israel's growing conquest. While these letters do not offer any direct correlation to the biblical actors and events, they do testify to the political conditions during the very time in which the Israelites were beginning to settle the land.

KING DAVID, NEHEMIAH, AND CAPTIVITY

Many critics over the centuries have questioned whether specific biblical figures mentioned in the Hebrew Bible ever actually existed at all. And, as we've seen, the names of specific individuals up through the Bronze Age have not yet been uncovered by archaeology. However, starting with David—one of the most significant figures in Israel's history—we can begin to

> However, starting with David—one of the most significant figures in Israel's history—we can begin to see historical verification of not only nations, cultures, and customs but of individuals and specific conflicts, as well.

see historical verification of not only nations, cultures, and customs but of individuals and specific conflicts, as well.

THE HOUSE OF DAVID

Up until just twenty-five years ago, theologians, historians, and archaeologists hotly debated the very historical existence of King David. If he was such a central figure, critics argued, why had we never found any extra-biblical verification that kings named David or Solomon ever actually ruled in Israel? That debate ended in the summer of 1993, when the name "House of David" was first uncovered on an artifact discovered at the biblical site of Tel Dan in northern Israel. The critical excerpt was found on part of a black basalt monument that had been broken and reused in a later period as a building stone. The inscription, written in Aramaic, the language of the Aramaean kingdoms of Syria, related the details of an Aramaean king's invasion of Israel. It is widely presumed that it tells the story of the assault of Hazael, king of Damascus, on the northern kingdom of Israel around 835 B.C. In the inscription, Hazael boasts about his enemies, whom he defeated in battle: "[I killed Jeho]ram son of [Ahab] king of Israel, and [I] killed [Ahaz]iahu son of [Jehoram king] of the House of David. And I set [their towns into ruins and turned] their land into [desolation]."

The inscription, clearly including the phrase "House of David," a reference to the ruling dynasty of the Southern Kingdom of Judah, is strong evidence that David did indeed exist—so much so that historians Israel Finkelstein and Neil Asher Silberman, in their book, *The Bible Unearthed: Archaeology's New Vision of Ancient Israel and the Origin of Its Sacred Texts*, state that the debate has moved beyond the question of David's existence. Later finds near the City of David, including what many assume to be David's actual palace and at Khirbet Qeiyafa (Elah Fortress), have been viewed by some archaeologists and paleographers as confirmation of the existence of a centralized and powerful Israelite kingdom in the early tenth century B.C.[27] Scholars assume that an Israelite fortress of this scale establishes the existence of a strong, centralized Israelite kingdom at the time of David.[28] Moreover, the extensive ongoing archaeological excavation in the portion of Jerusalem south of the Temple Mount, commonly known as the City of David, uncovers more and more new evidence practically every day. These new findings support the biblical account concerning ancient Israel around the time of King David and his successors.[29]

French scholar André Lemaire has additionally suggested that a similar reference to the House of David can be found on a famous inscription of Mesha, king of Moab, from the ninth century B.C.[30] This artifact, commonly known as the Mesha Inscription, was discovered at Dhiban in Transjordan in 1868. The inscription appears in Moabite in line 31 of the text with the same meaning as the Tel Dan inscription, referring to David as the founder of the dynasty of Judah.[31] A third inscription has also been found in Egyptian, which mentions a region in the Negev called "the heights of David" named after King David.[32]

The genuineness of the Mesha inscription has never been disputed in any serious way, and it is a critically important piece of evidence regarding Israel's status in the Iron Age. The inscription has been dated to the middle of the ninth century B.C. because of its reference to King Omri of Israel and his son (unnamed but presumed to be Ahab). This mention of the Omri dynasty is an unparalleled reference to Israel and its political aspirations in the area we know as the Transjordan.[33]

EVIDENCE OF OTHER ISRAELITE KINGDOMS AND ACTIVITY

Beyond these key inscriptions referring to the House of David, a significant collection of small-scale inscriptions—seals, stamps, letters, inventories, burial inscriptions, and commemorative inscriptions—provide evidence of the existence of ancient Israel. These pieces, dating from the tenth century B.C. to the sixth century B.C., give some insight into life in the divided kingdoms of Israel and Judah. The evidence here additionally indicates that, although writing was known in the region, literacy was extremely rare, which likely explains why most excavation sites in the region have failed to locate any written material.[34]

Niels Peter Lemche, whose work influenced much of this chapter and who, like many scholars, approaches Jewish history and historical figures with skepticism, provides a detailed list of twenty-seven Near Eastern inscriptions referring to the kingdoms of Israel and Judah, proving that such a people clearly existed.[35] Most significant, the numerous inscriptions he lists detail ancient Israel's devastating defeats and exiles by both the Assyrians and Babylonians.[36]

Moreover, archaeological and historical data have confirmed particular events from the Old Testament. Although Lemche is generally skeptical regarding the Old Testament, he notes that there is a general harmony between the biblical narratives of 2 Kings and ancient Near Eastern documents. They agree, for example, that Hezekiah ruled before Manasseh. In inscriptions, Sennacherib mentions Hezekiah, while his successors Esarhaddon and Ashurbanipal name Manasseh as the son and successor of Hezekiah.[37] Therefore, it is clear from the archaeological evidence that ancient Israelite kingdoms existed, were ruled by kings—many of whose specific identities have been confirmed—and that the Israelite kingdoms were conquered and exiled from what then became known as Palestine.

BABYLONIAN CAPTIVITY AND NEHEMIAH'S WALL

Israel's conquest and subsequent captivity at the hands of Babylon in the sixth century B.C., as recounted in the Old Testament books of Nehemiah and Ezra, is a key point in Jewish history. Archaeological and historical evidence reveals important traits about the history of Israel and the Jewish people during that time.

The capture of Jerusalem is mentioned in the "Chronicle Concerning the Early Years of Nebuchadnezzar," a tablet in cuneiform from Mesopotamia that states:

> [Rev.11'] In the seventh year [598/597], the month of Kislîmu, the king of Akkad [Babylon] mustered his troops, marched to the Hatti-land,
> [Rev.12'] and besieged the city of Judah and on the second day of the month of Addaru he seized the city and captured the king.

[Rev.13'] He appointed there a king of his own choice, received its heavy tribute and sent to Babylon.[38]

Other archaeological evidence shows the destruction of the Babylonian conquest occurred primarily in and around Jerusalem, while other areas, such as Benjamin, continued to build during the Persian period.[39] Though many of the Jewish people were taken into captivity, a sizable Jewish population remained in Palestine and the land was not resettled by a foreign group under Babylonian or Persian rule.[40] This is a fundamentally important point in our case for Israel's enduring presence in the land. Even during one of Israel's greatest tragedies and exiles, the Holy Land was never entirely without a Jewish population.

> **Even during one of Israel's greatest tragedies and exiles, the Holy Land was never entirely without a Jewish population.**

While removed from their land during the nearly six decades of captivity in Babylon, it's important to note that the Jewish exiles maintained their national and religious identity. This is evidenced by a series of clay cuneiform tablets that were found in modern-day Iraq, dating from 572 B.C. to 484 B.C. The inscriptions describe life in three Jewish settlements in Babylonia, including one named "al-yahudu" or "Judahtown" or "Village of Judea."[41] Most of the tablets are simple agricultural, commercial, and inheritance records written in Akkadian cuneiform.[42] Together they reveal insight into the impact of the exile on one family across three generations. It appears that the first generation experienced deportation and exile, while the second and third generations grew up as the first Jewish communities formed in Babylon. Later this family appeared to grow successful and engaged in business with other families.[43]

An opponent of Nehemiah, called Sanballet in Nehemiah 2:10, is mentioned in Aramaic papyri found in Elephantine, Egypt.[44] This, of course, lends credence to the details of Nehemiah's biblical account. These papyri are a collection of the letters from the Jewish outpost in Elephantine (southern Egypt) to Jewish leaders in Jerusalem, some of which date to 407 B.C. Their content shows a Jewish religious and civil structure in both Elephantine and Jerusalem at the time that worked together to make certain requests of the Persian leaders after Babylon's fall to Persia.[45] Again, this shows Jews living throughout the land, this time in the period following the Babylonian exile.

Scholars debate the archaeological evidence of the wall the Bible says Nehemiah built around Jerusalem following the exile (Nehemiah chapters 1–7). However, even some historians who are skeptical or even outright dismissive of the biblical account, such as Israel Finkelstein, will admit that:

> archaeologists have accepted the description of the recon-struction of the wall in Nehemiah 3 as an historical fact, and have been divided only about the course of the fortifications. The minimalists restricted them to the City of David, and the maximalists argued that the description included the southwestern hill . . . [46]

Regardless of the exact date or size of the wall's construction, the wall clearly emerged, and it evidences an active Jewish community in Jerusalem even after the Babylonian Exile.

From the time of the first Jewish return until the time of Nehemiah (roughly 515–445 B.C.) there is almost no mention of Judah or a particular governor over Judah in the records available. Starting around the time of Nehemiah and thereafter, however, there is a sudden increase in archaeological and historical references to Judah as a political entity. We can see some evidence for this in the coinage found in the region dating from the periods before and after Nehemiah. The Persian Empire, which had overtaken the Babylonians and assumed control of the region, allowed local officials to mint coins for local business. Before Nehemiah, the only coinage found at the time appears fairly generic and heavily influenced by Persian and other regional (pagan) symbols and names. However,

> **Starting around the time of Nehemiah and thereafter, there is a sudden increase in archaeological and historical references to Judah as a political entity.**

archaeology has unearthed a large number of seal impressions containing the inscription "Yehud" (Aramaic for "Judah"), dating to the late fifth century B.C. Some of the newer seals and coins are written in Aramaic, but many of the later impressions are written in Hebrew. The later silver coins also began to emerge with the name "Yehud" written on them, primarily in Hebrew.[47]

The reintroduction of the term "Yehud" ("Judah") on official seals and coins suggests that after a time of being controlled from Samaria or another local center of government in the early Persian period, Judah became its own independent province under the authority of Persia. The continued emphasis of the local Jewish term "Yehud" and the revival of the Hebrew script are evidence that the people in the land strove to maintain continuity with their roots and the preexilic Jewish kingdoms.[48]

ALEXANDER THE GREAT, SUCCESSOR EMPIRES, AND THE ROMANS

Starting with the rise of Alexander the Great, the control of the region can be compared to a game of hot potato, with rule changing hands every few generations. Control of the region changed amid political power struggles and takeovers as new world powers rose and fell. While a detailed history of these ups and downs would be interesting, it would definitely be beyond the scope of this book. Instead, I'll try to stick to facts as they pertain directly to proving the continuing Jewish presence in the land during the last few centuries before the time of Christ. Buckle up, though, because this is going to be a quick race through several centuries.

ALEXANDER THE GREAT

The works of the famed first-century Jewish historian Josephus provide a full account of Alexander the Great in Palestine.[49] His relationship with the Jews and the priesthood in Jerusalem is a particularly interesting story. A great Greek ruler, Alexander's conquests ended

Persian control of Palestine in 332 B.C. After defeating the Persian king Darius's army in a series of battles, Alexander captured Damascus and Sidon and began the siege of Tyre. During the siege, Alexander sent an emissary requesting supplies to the Jewish high priest in Jerusalem, who refused. Alexander became enraged and determined that, after conquering Tyre, he would march on Jerusalem to make an example of the high priest.

When the high priest heard that Alexander was marching toward Jerusalem, he ordered the people to make supplications and offer sacrifices to God in the hope of divine protection. That night the high priest had a dream that he should take courage, adorn the city, open the gates, and command the people to wear white and greet the king. When Alexander arrived and saw the city in this manner, he held his army back and entered Jerusalem to talk with the high priest.

Asked why he relented, Alexander said that he had seen this happen in a dream when he was still in Macedonia. After recounting his dream, Alexander went with the priests and offered a sacrifice to God according to Jewish custom. Then the priests showed Alexander the Book of Daniel, which revealed how the Persian Empire would be conquered by his hand. The following day Alexander granted that the Jews could live according to their religious customs throughout his empire and that any volunteer who wished to join his army could do so. Many Jews joined Alexander's army and all the surrounding Jewish cities greeted Alexander with splendor.[50]

ALEXANDER'S SUCCESSORS

When Alexander the Great died in 323 B.C., his kingdom was divided among his generals or aides.[51] Two of Alexander's generals were Ptolemy and Seleucus, who eventually shared control of Palestine, which they called Coele Syria. These generals' heirs later fought for control of the region in the six Syrian Wars (274 B.C.–168 B.C.), during which time the Jews in Palestine enjoyed a level of self-governance and autonomy.[52] The Jews paid tribute to the Ptolemaic pharaohs of Egypt during most of that time, but in return were shown a fair degree of religious tolerance by their Egyptians rulers.[53]

After several years of mostly peaceful relations with the Ptolemaic pharaohs of Egypt and the Hellenistic Seleucid dynasty that later supplanted them in Palestine, things took a dark turn. In 169–168 B.C., Hellenistic king Antiochus IV of the Seleucid dynasty invaded Egypt. Historian Josephus recounts that, on his return, Antiochus plundered Jerusalem, slaying anyone who opposed his rule. Satisfied, Antiochus left Jerusalem but returned two years later—this time pretending that he desired peace—and was let into the city. His peaceful ploy was a trick: After looting the Temple, Antiochus forbade the Jews from sacrificing according to their custom. He pillaged the rest of the city, enslaved about ten thousand citizens, demolished the city walls, and built a citadel overlooking the Temple manned by loyalists, after which he departed Jerusalem.[54] Affirming the Josephus account, this citadel was discovered in Jerusalem by archaeologists in 2016.[55]

RISE OF THE MACCABEES

For reasons that still puzzle us today, Antiochus IV decided to forcibly convert the Jews from Judaism to paganism.[56] According to Josephus, a Greek official commanded the priest Mattathias to offer a sacrifice to an idol, a clear violation of God's command against idolatry and an act of sacrilege. When Mattathias refused, another Jew attempted to sacrifice in his place. Outraged over the attempted sacrilege, Mattathias and his sons killed both the offending Greek official and the Jewish man who attempted to make the idolatrous sacrifice. Afterward, Mattathias and many villagers fled into the desert to live in caves. The Greek generals heard of this and pursued the group, nicknamed the Maccabees (Hammers), and their followers, burning many of them in the caves during the Sabbath.[57]

This harsh treatment only emboldened the Jewish survivors, who made Mattathias their ruler. He decreed that Jews could fight on the Sabbath if it was absolutely necessary and subsequently led a large army to destroy the idols, kill those who broke Jewish laws, and circumcise everyone who had not been already.[58] This was, some believe, not only a revolt against foreign oppression but also a type of

Jewish civil war between traditionalist Jews and those favoring Hellenism.

Historian Robert Doran recounts that, upon recapturing Jerusalem, the Jews under the Maccabees purified the Temple and relit the menorah—a rededication now celebrated in Judaism as the festival of Hanukkah, which is another one of my family's favorite Jewish celebrations. The holiday is celebrated with the lighting of the menorah in every Jewish home. The symbolism is a poignant reminder of God's work among and faithfulness to the Jewish people. Shortly after taking back control of Judea, Mattathias died, and his son Judas took control of the army. Upon hearing of the defeats at the hands of the Maccabees and worried about their growing power, according to Doran, King Antiochus IV gathered an army to crush the Jewish rebels. Around 168–167 B.C., Antiochus captured the Temple and destroyed the walls surrounding Mount Zion.[59]

> Upon recapturing Jerusalem, the Jews under the Maccabees purified the Temple and relit the menorah—a rededication now celebrated in Judaism as the festival of Hanukkah.

The Hasmonean Dynasty of Judah

These and other conflicts dominated the region for another twenty years—well after the death of Antiochus—until the Hasmonean kingdom of Judah finally gained full independence in 143–142 B.C. They were given a letter relinquishing them from the obligation to pay tribute and were recognized by the Roman Senate in 139 B.C. The Hasmoneans immediately expelled all Greek garrisons from their territory and appointed Simon, the second son of Mattathias, as both leader and high priest of Judea.[60]

During the reconquest, the Hasmoneans established new settlements, which were recently discovered in archaeological digs. Migdal is perhaps the most significant archaeological find in the Galilee region, because it reflects the Hasmoneans' interest in the economic possibilities surrounding the Galilee region. It is likely that the Hasmonean rulers encouraged Jewish migration into the Galilee region based on archaeological evidence such as Hasmonean olive presses and a large quantity of Hasmonean coins.[61]

Simon's reign over the Hasmonean kingdom came to an abrupt end in 135 B.C. when he was assassinated at a banquet. Subsequent conflicts over leadership and land managed to expand the borders from the Lake of Galilee in the north to the Negev in the south and from the Mediterranean in the west well into what is now considered Transjordan in the east.[62] These power struggles within the Judean Hasmonean kingdom persisted until 63 B.C., when Pompey took Jerusalem on behalf of Rome, thereby ushering in the period of Roman rule.[63]

ROME AND KING HEROD

The Romans greatly reduced the territory of the Hasmonean state, leaving only the regions with a dense Jewish population to the Hasmoneans. The area was further divided into two separate units: Judea proper with Idumea and Perea in the south, and Galilee in the north. The two parts of the country were separated by a chain of Greek townships and by Samaritan territory, whose inhabitants were hostile to the Jews. On the west, Judea was barred from the Mediterranean coast and also lost territorial control of Jaffa and its surroundings.[64] Other land divisions were attempted throughout the expected Roman and Judean power struggles of the ensuing decades, but nothing of consequence lasted until the rise of King Herod.

Herod rose to power during the last quarter of the first century B.C. Beginning as a governor over Judea, Herod gained further status by successfully backing the winning sides in inner turmoil in Rome and was counted on by Roman figures such as Cassius and Antony. Furthermore, in a wise power play, Herod became engaged to a Hasmonean princess, which gave him a degree of standing with many Jews who were still loyal to the former Hasmonean ruling family.[65]

Herod, often referred to as Herod the Great, was an apt ruler. By the year 25 B.C., Herod had won for himself a sizable kingdom, covering Palestine and some of the area east of it. He continued to back winning sides in Rome and, in the final stage of the Roman civil war, none of Herod's troops were engaged on the side of Antony and Cleopatra against Octavian. When Octavian emerged victorious, he confirmed Herod's large domain and the title "king."[66]

Throughout this unending turmoil in the Holy Land, the Jews were dispersed throughout the ancient world. In fact, no other minority was as spread out throughout the provinces of both Rome and Persia as the Jews.[67] Literary evidence of Jewish presence throughout the Roman Empire comes from several sources, including the Greek geographer Strabo and, of course, Josephus, among others.[68] As for when the Jews arrived in Rome, historical evidence clearly shows that the Jews were present in Rome by at least the first century B.C. The Roman Senate passed a decree banning their ceremonies in A.D. 19, and inasmuch as they could hardly have arrived and had their religious rites banned the next day, it is a fair inference that they had been present in large numbers for a long time by that point.[69]

> In fact, no other minority was as spread out throughout the provinces of both Rome and Persia as the Jews.

The Great Revolt

Throughout the first half of the first century A.D., some Jews had started to adopt Roman culture and Roman authority, which in turn, gave the Roman government the confidence to entrust them with the local government. Their governance infuriated less affluent Jews, creating a schism between the Jewish social classes.

However, everything changed in A.D. 66 when the Roman government interfered in the Jewish sacrifices. The Romans demanded that the high priests offer a daily sacrifice to the emperor and stop offering a sacrifice to the Jewish God. The Roman procurator, Gessius Florus, had also looted the Temple treasury.[70] Against this background of political and religious tension, Eleazar, a son of the Jewish high priest, Ananias, and governor of the temple, convinced those who officiated over the sacrifices to not perform them in honor of the Roman emperor or to receive any offerings from foreigners.[71]

Despite efforts to soften the perception of their rebellious actions and affirm their loyalty to key Roman authorities, tensions were too high to be stopped on both sides. The initial violence of the Great Revolt started in Caesarea between Jews and Syro-Greeks and led to the annihilation of the Roman garrison in Jerusalem.[72] An attempt by Roman consul Cestius Gallus to put down the Jewish rebellion was defeated in A.D. 66.[73]

With their patience at an end, the Romans sent their general Vespasian to begin the final military campaign against the Jews. Assigned to the region by Emperor Nero, Vespasian and his son, Titus, entered Galilee in A.D. 67 and began the conquest of Israel. After Nero died, the Roman Empire went through a succession struggle, out of which Vespasian emerged as victor and emperor. Vespasian appointed Titus to take his place on the campaign against the Jews, and it was Titus who ultimately took and sacked Jerusalem in A.D. 70.

The siege of Masada, in A.D. 73–74, is regarded as the last battle of the Great Revolt. After the destruction of Jerusalem, a group known as the Zealots established themselves in the stronghold of Masada in the Judean Desert.[74] At 1,300 feet above sea level and with twenty acres within its walls, Masada was not an easy fortress for the Romans to take. The Zealots were able to fend off the Romans in this stronghold for three to four years before the fortress was final captured.[75] When it became apparent that the Romans were going to take the fortress, the Zealot leader Elazar Ben-Yair convinced those at Masada that committing suicide was better than surrendering to the Romans.[76]

THE END OF AN ERA

The crushing finale of the Jewish Revolt marked the end of the Jewish State until modern times.[77] From A.D. 70 until 1948, the Jewish people had no land to officially call their own. As turbulent and chaotic as the Jewish State's first two thousand years were, however, it only served to prepare them for the warfare and conflict of the following two thousand years, which we will discuss next.

We have examined a huge amount of ancient history in this chapter, and we still have plenty of history left to unpack. What's important for us to note here, though, as we bring the B.C. era to a close and enter into the Christian era, is that the history, records, and archaeology have shown a consistent presence of the Jews in the Holy Land from the time of Abraham through the first century A.D. Even during massive upheavals such as the Babylonian Captivity or the Roman siege of Jerusalem, we see evidence of a Jewish population enduring in the region. The land is their home, and it has never been without some Jewish presence since the time of Abraham.

> **The history, records, and archaeology have shown a consistent presence of the Jews in the Holy Land from the time of Abraham through the first century A.D.**

KEY TAKEAWAYS

1. Strong historical and archaeological findings support the history of the Jewish people as outlined in the Bible.

2. Artifacts and historical records outside the Bible verify the existence of an Israelite kingdom in the Promised Land.

3. Even during the Babylonian Captivity, one of Israel's greatest tragedies and exiles, the Holy Land was never entirely without a Jewish population.

7

LIFE UNDER MUSLIM RULE

revolution (noun): a fundamental change in political organization; especially the overthrow or renunciation of one government or ruler and the substitution of another by the governed.[1]

Al Qaeda. Hamas. ISIS. These are names that have become synonymous with terror, murder, genocide, and other atrocities too horrible to describe. Over the past two decades, the world has seen radical Islamic violence played out on a global scale. Every week, it seems, we see pictures and videos of smoking rubble or innocent victims who were gunned down while going about their normal lives. We've seen it in New York, London, and Paris. We've seen it at an Orlando nightclub and at a Minnesota shopping mall. And certainly we've seen it all over the Middle East. I've already told you how my son Jordan was almost killed by a Hamas rocket that was part of a brutal strike against Israel. Muslim terrorists are targeting civilians, schools, hospitals, malls, business centers, roads, and of course soldiers, seeking to kill as many Jews, Christians, and other "infidels" as possible—all in the name of Allah. With so much terror going on in the world today, it can be hard to imagine a time in history when Jews and Muslims actually lived and worked together in relative harmony. But it happened, albeit for a brief period of time.

> With so much terror going on in the world today, it can be hard to imagine a time in history when Jews and Muslims actually lived and worked together in relative harmony. But it happened, albeit for a brief period of time.

In the previous chapter, we did a mad dash through the first two thousand years of Jewish history, from the time of Abraham all the way up to the Romans' destruction of the Jerusalem Temple in A.D. 70. Now, as we shift our focus to all the ups and downs of the Christian era, we can slow down a bit to examine a few key points in Israel's history. Control of the Holy Land has changed hands numerous times over the past two thousand years, with each transition causing new challenges for the Jews in the region. As I've said before, the complete history of the Jewish people in general is a fascinating study, but it is well beyond the scope of this book. So we'll stick to just what we need to make our case.

In this chapter and the next, we will touch on the four main conquests in the region over the last two millennia and take a look at how those four different ruling groups—Arabs, Christian Crusaders, Mamluks, and Ottomans—treated the Jewish inhabitants in the area. And, of course, we'll also zero in on key records, letters, and other historical evidence that will prove the Jews' continuing, unbroken presence in the Land of Promise. For now, let's take a look at how the Holy Land first fell under Muslim rule and what that meant for the Jews who lived there.

THE RISE OF ARAB RULE IN THE HOLY LAND

When we left off in the previous chapter, Rome had come into Jerusalem and utterly crushed the Jews in A.D. 70, ushering in a period of almost nineteen centuries in which the Jewish people had no state to call their own. After A.D. 70, the Romans held Jerusalem for several decades before any real threat arose to challenge their rule. Then a series of revolts began that set the stage for something we have a hard time imagining today: an active military cooperation between Jews and Muslims.

THE BAR KOKHBA AND GALLUS REVOLTS

Roman rule of Jerusalem faced its first credible threat since the Great Revolt in A.D. 132 when Jewish leader Simon Bar Kokhba led a revolt that resulted in the Jews holding Jerusalem for three years, A.D. 132–135.[2] The Roman emperor Hadrian ultimately re-took Jerusalem through extreme measures, executing Bar Kokhba and bringing the revolution to an end. In retaliation for the revolt, Hadrian banned all Jews from Jerusalem (but not the entire Holy Land).[3] He also made a significant change that still holds true today, more than eighteen centuries later. Whereas the Roman world knew the land as Iudaea (Judea) prior to A.D. 135, Hadrian renamed it Palestina (Palestine) after the Bar Kokhba revolt to sever all out-ward signs of the region's ties to the Jews.[4]

Roman rule remained relatively unchallenged for more than two centuries afterward until the Gallus revolt of A.D. 352, which be-gan what is now known as the Byzantine period.[5] Here, Jewish lead-ers rose up against the newly appointed Roman Caesar of the East, Gallus. The revolt didn't last long and happened without rabbinic support, and it resulted in Rome destroying a couple of cities and establishing a permanent garrison in Galilee.[6]

The Byzantine period—which refers to the eastern portion of the Roman Empire from A.D. 330 to 1453—saw Jews, Christians, and pagans living together throughout Palestine. Over time, as the Christian church spread, the Christian population became the ma-jority. Relations between Jews and Christians seem to have been friendly, and a vibrant Jewish community continued to exist.[7] Yet each group appears to have lived in its own villages.[8]

The political landscape changed yet again in A.D. 614 when the Sassanian (Persian) Empire took Jerusalem from the Byzantines.[9] According to Christian sources, the Jews assisted the Persian conquest, which caused trouble for them down the road. When the Byzantines reconquered Palestine from the Persians in A.D. 629, it became apparent that their former relatively friendly relationship with the Jews had come to an end. Because the Jews had supported the Persian conquest, the Byzantines sought to exact revenge on the Jews.[10] This harsh treatment set the stage for a historically ironic situation years later when the Jewish people welcomed and supported the Arab Muslims in their conquest of the Byzantines to gain control of the Holy Land.

> **This harsh treatment set the stage for a historically ironic situation years later when the Jewish people welcomed and supported the Arab Muslims in their conquest of the Byzantines to gain control of the Holy Land.**

EARLY ISLAMIC CONQUESTS

Almost everywhere, especially in Palestine, the Jews helped the Arab Muslims when they came and conquered, and the Arab Muslims regarded the Jews as their allies.[11] Because the Jews were treated quite badly by the Byzantines, they welcomed change. Such change came when the caliph Omar conquered Palestine sometime between A.D. 636 and 640.[12] This ended Byzantine rule in Palestine.

Later Jewish writers indicate that, while conditions under Omar and the Muslims were harsh, things were not as bad as they had been under the Byzantine Christians. According to a letter from the Rabbinites in Jerusalem written between 1051 and 1062, the Jews in Jerusalem were able to obtain some concessions from the Arab conquerors because they had given valuable aid to the Arabs during the conquest. These concessions included the ability to visit Jerusalem without interference, pray at the Temple spot, and buy the Mount of Olives for the Jewish community to use for prayers and festivals. Large numbers of Jews came and settled in Jerusalem after the Arab conquest, and more visitors and pilgrims came as well.[13]

There were some negative results from Muslim rule, of course. For starters, Omar compelled the Christian bishop Sophronius to point out the exact Temple location. Omar, in turn, built the famous Dome of the Rock on that precise location.[14] We'll see more on that later. During this period, Jews, like other non-Muslims, were labeled *dhimmi* (people of the *dhimma*, a code that protected non-Muslims) and, therefore, subjected to special taxes and restrictions.[15] For instance, under Muslim law, the testimony of a Jew or Christian was invalid when put against the testimony of a Muslim. These restrictions reflected the Muslim view that non-Muslims should abide by the *dhimma* out of gratitude to the ruling Muslim authorities who permitted them to live and enjoy the ruler's protection. The severity and enforcement of the *dhimma* restrictions depended on the sultan and the local rulers.[16]

It's helpful to explain what some of these restrictions were to understand how the Muslim rulers treated the Jews and what the Jews were subjected to. For example, another restriction placed on Jews in Palestine was that they had to pass Muslims on their left side, because that was the side of Satan. Jews had to yield the right of way and step off the pavement to let Arabs go by. Above all, Jews had to make sure not to touch Arabs in passing, because this could provoke a violent response. Additionally, Jewish buildings and activity had to be placed out of sight of Muslims, so synagogues were placed in humble, hidden places, and the sounds of Jewish prayer were carefully muted.[17]

A major shift during the Arab rule was that the prosperity of the Roman and Byzantine times was gone forever. All of Palestine suffered a decline in living standards under Arab rule. Also during this time, Arabic—a language previously rare in Palestine—began to supplant the Aramaic and Greek of the Jews and Byzantines.[18]

THE ABBASIDS' RISE TO POWER

In the A.D. 740s, Palestine and the Muslim world experienced another tremendous political upheaval that culminated around A.D. 749–750 when the Abbasids sacked the Umayyad capital of Khurasan. The Abbasids, like most Muslims in the region, saw the Umayyads as wealthy outsiders and rejected their secular view and rule. With the help of many foreign, non-Arab converts to Islam, the Abbasids ousted the Umayyads and ushered in a new caliphate more directly based on the Islamic faith and prophetic succession of Muhammad. Because so many foreigners had contributed to the Abbasid conquest, many historians believe that the Islamic culture saw a shift away from Semitic influence and toward more Iranian views.[19] As such, the Abbasids shifted power from the west in Syria to the east in Iraq.[20]

Beginning with the leadership of Abu' l-'Abbās (from whom their name Abbasid is derived), the Abbasids enjoyed a long reign from A.D. 750 to 1258.[21] It was under the Abbasids that Arabic became widely spoken in Palestine as well as its primary written language.[22]

Jews Under the Abbasids

We only have indirect information on the Jews in Abbasid Palestine. We can assume that the Abbasids, as well as the subsequent caliphates, treated the Jews in Palestine the same as they treated Jews in Baghdad and Cairo, places for which we have sources about the Jews in the seventh and eighth centuries.

The Abbasids did not physically persecute the Jews and, on the whole, they were treated the same if not better than Christians (who were themselves treated quite well).[23] There is a consensus among historians that the Jewish existence under the Abbasids was superior to what they experienced under both the Byzantines and the Persian Sassanids.[24] While still recognized as nonbelievers and categorized as *dhimmi*, they possessed a special status as "people of the book" that elevated them above pagan groups and, at least in theory, prevented Muslims from directly harming them.[25] In addition to their protected status, the Jewish population was relatively small, so the Abbasids did not view them as a threat to their rule.[26]

Jewish Prosperity

Under Abbasid rule, Jews and Christians held an equal place within society. Up until the mid-800s, Jews, Christians, and recent converts to Islam translated various works into Arabic that were originally written in Greek. In fact, the first translation of the Old Testament into Arabic was completed by Sa'īd al-Fayyūmi (Saadia Gaon, A.D. 882–942), and this is the same version all Arabic-speaking Jews use to this day.[27]

Jews and Christians enjoyed respected positions outside of academia as well. For example, records indicate that in A.D. 985 most of the money changers and bankers in Syria were Jews, while most of the clerks and physicians were Christians. There are also accounts of Jews serving in government positions throughout the capital of Baghdad and various provinces during the reign of al-Mu'tadid (A.D. 892–902).[28] Perhaps more surprisingly, when the Abbasids took power from the Umayyads, a Jew was commissioned to plot out a city plan for the new capital at Baghdad.[29]

So we can see that by the A.D. 900s, the Jews in Palestine thrived in prestigious fields such as international banking and commerce, and they oftentimes worked directly under the caliphs and other Muslim rulers. Many Jews obtained immense wealth, and they often supported their poorer Jewish brothers.[30] Within the prosperity of the initial Abbasid dynasty, a sort of renaissance occurred among the Jews in Palestine. During the A.D. 700s and 800s, the main parts of the Masora, the text of Jewish traditions based on the Hebrew Scripture, were finished, mainly in Tiberias, and much of the Masoretic text of today is their work.[31] A tremendous amount of Hebrew poetry was written, and the Jewish Talmud was completed as well.

Although some Jews occupied high places in Abbasid society, many others did not socially integrate, and some Abbasid rulers passed discriminatory legislation.[32] There was also internal strife among the Muslim rulers in the Levant, resulting in civil wars, and although all people groups suffered from such conflict, the Christians and Jews were the primary victims.[33] However, despite this political instability, Arab sources describe Palestine as a fertile and prosperous region of the empire.[34] Trade flourished, as did industry and agriculture, and there was a growing demand, probably from the court at Baghdad, for dyeing, weaving, and glasswork.[35]

THE FATIMID PERIOD

In opposition to the Abbasid dynasty, the Fatimids, founded by Sa'īd ibn-Husayn, rose to power in A.D. 909 in Tunisia and captured Egypt by A.D. 969.[36] From this period until roughly 1250, when the Fatimid dynasty fell, control of Palestine went back and forth between the Fatimids, Abbasids, Crusaders, and Turks.[37] Fortunately for history, the Fatimid period is extremely well-documented by the Cairo Geniza documents. Historians have been able to determine with great certainty what life was like for Jews living under the Fatimids, not only in Cairo and Egypt, but also in Palestine. Unlike the Abbasid period, there are plentiful specific examples and stories for study, not just general overviews.

THE FATIMIDS' TREATMENT OF JEWS

Most Fatimid rulers exercised tolerance for Jews and Christians, and Jews even rose and prospered within the Fatimid court. They worked as bankers, government officials, and physicians to Muslim rulers, and in other prestigious positions. However, as we see in modern times, Fatimid rulers who were more religiously motivated and zealous in their Muslim faith persecuted Jews and Christians throughout their lands. Jews within Palestine, though, faced a far harsher existence than their brothers elsewhere in the Fatimid empire.

Palestine was politically unstable due to numerous rebellions, insurrections, and warfare between the various Muslim factions and dynasties, and the Jewish people were constantly stuck in the middle. From A.D. 996 to 1021, Jews were forced to wear black robes, ride only on donkeys, and wear a yoke with bells around their necks if in a public bath.[38] In 1009, an order to destroy all churches and synagogues throughout the empire was issued, but it is unclear if this decree was ever carried out.[39]

An insurrection took place in 1024–1029 that, as historian Jacob Mann explains, was particularly bad for the Jews of Palestine when three Muslim rebel leaders conspired to take over portions of Palestine and Syria. The Jews suffered tremendously as these leaders' armies pillaged, plundered, and raided various towns and villages. While the entire population—both Jewish and non-Jewish—suffered, some forms of oppression were reserved only for the Jews. One of the rebel leaders, Hasan, extorted greater sums of money from the Jews and even burned the city of Ramlah, taking away four hundred wagonloads of men and supplies. For a time, the Palestinian Jews were left completely undefended. The evidence of the dire situation is found in letters to Jewish leaders in Egypt pleading for assistance against the rebel armies. One such letter says: "Be gracious unto us, our brethren, the house of Israel, for punishment has afflicted us." Even Jerusalem was not safe from such extortion.[40] Again, this record of persecution leaves no doubt that the Jewish community resided in Palestine during this period.

JERUSALEM DURING THE FATIMID ERA

The Jewish population in Jerusalem was small, but the city was a major center for Jewish spiritual worship and debate.[41] We can see the condition of Jerusalem at this time by seeing it through the eyes of three different Jewish groups, each one operating in and near Jerusalem during the eleventh century.

First, as Jacob Mann explains, the Rabbinites were a sect that settled in Jerusalem and created an academy there led by a religious leader called the Gaon (literally "genius"). Although this academy frequently moved between Jerusalem and other cities, Jerusalem remained the center. The Rabbinites relied tremendously on outside support, which greatly diminished during the revolt of 1024–1029 discussed above. Also, pilgrimage to Jerusalem, the main source of income for the Jerusalem Rabbinites, largely dried up. The Rabbinites were forced to plead for even more outside assistance, as seen by the various letters sent from Jerusalem to the surrounding communities.

A letter from Tyre to Aleppo talks about the "deplorable conditions" within Jerusalem during this period. Another letter from the Rabbinites in Jerusalem to Ephraim ben Shemarya, head of the congregation in Fustat, talks about the heavy tax burden. The Rabbinite community was unable to pay their share of these taxes, and, as a result, several Jews were tortured and killed. Jews regularly had to sell their homes and precious family possessions in order to meet the tax levy.

The Jewish people were often caught between the Fatimid armies coming from the south to restore order, the rebels within Palestine, and the invading armies coming from the north. These crises caused the Jewish population there to rely on their fellow Jews in Egypt for assistance in order to survive. Furthermore, the roads leading into Jerusalem were treacherous, creating a dangerous journey for pilgrims trying to access the religious center. The hazards were compounded as travelers and citizens alike faced the constant threat of being robbed.[42]

The second notable Jewish group during this time, the Karaites, also had an important settlement in Jerusalem. They had their own academy that became prestigious within the Jewish community and drew many famous scholars who worked in such fields as the Bible, the Hebrew language, law, philosophy, and theology.[43]

The third group within Jerusalem was the Mourners for Zion. They are first found in a collection of Judaic texts, lamenting the destruction of the Temple and praying for its restoration and the coming of the Messiah.[44] They emphasized the importance of the Temple within Jewish society and Judaism, and they looked forward to the day when the Temple would be rebuilt by the Messiah. The Mourners' spiritual theology became known as "practical Kabbalah," a kind of spiritual mysticism that has made a small comeback in recent decades, notably among some celebrities.[45]

JEWS, CHRISTIANS, AND MUSLIMS WORKING TOGETHER

There is no doubt that history has shown a long line of Jewish abuse at the hands of Arab rulers. This animosity has been true since the days of Isaac and Ishmael. However, it is interesting to look back on pockets of history that show a glimmer of hope that Jews and Arabs could peacefully coexist. Seeing Jews and Muslims ride into battle together against a common enemy is practically unimaginable today, and yet there it is, in the history of Palestine. We have seen it here in the early Arab conquests, and we'll see it again in the next chapter with the greatest battle either nation had ever faced: the Crusades.

KEY TAKEAWAYS

1. Despite changes in rulers over time, the Jewish presence in the land of Israel continued through the beginning of the Christian era and up through the Middle Ages.

2. At times, there was active cooperation between the Jewish and Muslim communities against common foes.

8

CONTINUED BATTLES AND CONQUESTS IN THE HOLY LAND

conquest (noun): The subjugation and assumption of control of a place or people by military force.[1]

Although the Jewish people had faced nearly insurmountable obstacles and terrible persecution for almost three thousand years already, little could prepare them for the violence, mourning, massacres, and constant upheaval that the second millennium would bring. Wave after wave of new conquerors arrived on their shores, seeking to add Palestine to their respective empires. From 1099 until the twentieth century, however, there were three main groups that impacted the Jewish people most: the Crusaders, the Mamluks, and ultimately the Ottomans, who would reign until the First World War. Before we leave our review of the historical evidence of the Jews' persistent presence in the Holy Land, we need to catch up on the last one thousand years of Jewish life. We'll start with one of the most tragic periods in Jewish history: the Crusades.

THE CRUSADES

When I say the word "Crusades," certain images may immediately spring into your head. This time period has become completely clouded in myth as a result of the literature and poetry of the Romantic era and the modern condemnation of the Crusades as a bloody, brutal, gritty attempt at colonization that cost many people—especially Jews—their lives. We need to look past the tales of romantic medieval chivalry and imperialistic unrighteous conquests. The truth is far more complicated, as historian Thomas F. Madden shows in his overview of recent histories on the Crusades.[2]

CRUSADER CONQUEST OF JERUSALEM

The Crusades began when Western Christendom sought to regain control of the Holy Land from Muslim rule. Beyond lore, this had a great effect on the Jewish people. Aside from the various massacres that took place throughout Europe, once the Crusaders got to the Holy Land, they took Ramlah in 1099. This became the first Palestinian town to fall into Crusader hands. They reached Jerusalem with their army of forty thousand on June 7 of that year.[3] As the Crusaders approached Jerusalem, the Fatimid ruler of the city, Iftikhar ad-Dawla, drove out all Christians—including the Arab Christians—from the city, but he allowed the Jews to stay.[4] In fact, as had happened in the past, Jewish troops fought alongside the Muslim troops during the siege of Jerusalem.[5]

The Crusaders first tried marching around the city barefoot and blowing their horns, hoping it would fall like Jericho. When this failed, they began siege operations and finally took Jerusalem on July 15, 1099.[6] Upon entering the city, the Crusaders proceeded to slaughter most of the city inhabitants, including women and children. Sources report a gruesome scene, with mounds of heads, hands, and feet filling the streets and squares of the city.[7] According to one account, a group of Jews attempted to escape the slaughter by retreating to their chief synagogue. However, because the Jews had aided the Muslims in the defense of the city, the Crusaders burned the synagogue to the ground.[8] It is estimated that sixty-five to seventy thousand people perished in the Crusader conquest of Jerusalem.[9] Many—but not all—of the remaining Jewish community dispersed.[10]

JEWISH RESISTANCE AND DEFEAT

When a small Crusader army arrived at the city of Tiberias, Jewish fears were confirmed by the massacre that ensued.[11] Historian Steven Runciman recounts that when the Crusaders later reached Haifa (a mostly Jewish city), the Jewish inhabitants decided to fight. They defended against the first assaults successfully, even sinking one Venetian ship among the squadron of ships trying to sail into the harbor. Their weapons were provided by the Muslims, and both fought side by side as they had at Jerusalem. However, in the final assault, the Crusaders stormed the main defense tower, took the city, and once again massacred most of the inhabitants. The only survivors were those who successfully fled.[12]

Historian James Parkes alleges that, of all the local peoples, the Jews probably suffered the greatest proportional loss during these campaigns. During the initial Crusader conquest, the Jews had flocked to large towns and cities for refuge and security. However, while the Crusaders mostly spared small towns, large towns and cities often suffered horrific massacres. Almost the entire Jewish populations of Jerusalem, Acre, Caesarea, and Haifa were wiped out, and the Jews fled from Ramlah and Jaffa.[13]

LIFE UNDER CRUSADER RULE

The Crusaders and merchants of these times were financially successful, and a vital society formed.[14] From the beginning of their rule, the Crusaders had to pay careful attention to the rights of the local population; otherwise, they could not maintain control over the land.[15] It is important to note for the purposes of this book that while the Jewish population decreased dramatically, it did not disappear entirely. There were small communities of Jews to be found throughout Palestine, notably in the Galilee.[16]

The rule of the Crusader Baldwin I—later named king of Jerusalem—in the early 1100s was also quite tolerable to both the Jews and Muslims.[17] Baldwin allowed some synagogues and mosques, permitted Muslims and Jews to swear on the Quran and Torah in law courts, gave Jews and Muslims access to the courts for complaints, and did not criminalize intermarriage between Christians and Muslims.[18]

While both Christian and Islamic rulers saw the Jews as law-abiding subjects, historian Paul Johnson noted a particular pattern in the treatment of Jews during the Crusades: Both Christian and Muslim rulers treated the Jews favorably whenever a strong ruler was in place. However, trouble came during times of religious enthusiasm, when fundamentalist priests intimidated the ruler or, worse still, turned him into a zealous convert. Interestingly, when trouble did arise during these waves, most Jews responded without force or violence, having given up such conduct in the second century. Instead, Johnson notes, the Jews protected themselves through nonviolent means.[19]

One way they protected themselves was to engage in professions that made them useful. Many Jews were doctors, for example, and treated not only ordinary citizens but also the wealthy and those in power.[20] Saladin, the great Muslim conqueror, was attended by multiple Jewish doctors who were known for their medical brilliance. One of Saladin's family physicians was the Jewish scholar and philosopher Moses Maimonides, who is a good example of the many Jewish physicians who were in high positions or enjoyed great influence.[21] There were also Jewish bankers serving the Crusader nobility, and many grew quite prosperous.[22] By putting themselves into such valuable and high positions, the Jews hoped to insulate themselves from waves of persecution, and it did work to a certain degree.[23]

> By putting themselves into such valuable and high positions, the Jews hoped to insulate themselves from waves of persecution, and it did work to a certain degree.

The Jewish community remained close-knit during this period.

Because education was so important to the Jewish people, most Jewish communities were centered around the school and synagogue.[24] We cannot overlook the influence of fear in their close ties, however.[25]

THE MAMLUK CONQUEST

Even though the Crusader period was a chaotic time and filled with constant warfare, Palestine fared fairly well economically. According to one scholar, commerce and agriculture flourished; justice was administered in a hundred baronial and commercial courts; and Syrian Christian, Jewish, and Muslim peasants went about their business in safety.[26] When the Crusader kingdoms fell, however, things changed. In the ensuing period, Palestine was constantly ravaged by wars, famines, and plagues—often the result of Muslim infighting. In fact, the conflict between Muslim factions led to the long reign of a surprising faction: the Mamluks.

THE MAMLUKS' RISE TO POWER

Considering the length of their eventual rule, it is especially interesting to see where the history of the Mamluks began. The name "Mamluk" actually comes from the word for slave in Arabic.[27] The Mamluks started as slave soldiers in Egypt used by Muslims to fight *each other.*[28] Because the Quran prohibits Muslims from fighting with other Muslims, the Mamluk slaves were captives taken from many different areas, ethnicities, and nationalities.[29] As slaves, they were used as soldiers and bodyguards for their Muslim masters.[30]

In 1249, after the death of the latest ruler of the Ayyubid dynasty, al-Malik as-Salih Ayyub, the Mamluks rose up, murdered the heir apparent, and successfully installed one of their own as sultan.[31] Their initial empire consisted only of Egypt, but they later expanded their empire to the east and controlled portions of Palestine and Syria.[32] There were forty-seven Mamluk rulers over 267 years, making the average rule only six years.[33] And, understandably due to their history, almost all of the rulers were either former slaves or the offspring of slaves.[34] By 1375 the Mamluks pushed out the last of the Crusader kingdoms in the Levant, and the only Crusader kingdoms that remained were on the islands of Rhodes and Cyprus.[35] Additionally, the Mamluks stopped the advancing Mongols and prevented their spread farther west.[36]

MAMLUK RULE IN PALESTINE

The Mamluks, in expanding their empire into Palestine and Syria, destroyed most of the rich coastal cities and other areas, many of which remained desolate until the end of the nineteenth century.[37] Trade, coming predominantly from Spain and the city-states of Italy, shifted from the coastal cities of Palestine to Egypt. As a result, trade in Palestine severely stagnated, with only a few trading ships per year going to Acre, Jaffa, and Ramlah.[38] Some historians estimate that the populations of Syria, Egypt, and Palestine fell by as much as two-thirds under Mamluk rule, whose instability affected all populations, not just the Jews.[39]

After the coastal devastation, the Jews, who had begun returning to the coast under the Crusaders, moved once again, heading inland to the hills and country.[40] Lydda, Ramlah, Acre, and Gaza were the only coastal cities to have small Jewish communities; the others completely disappeared.[41] Over time, however, there was a Jewish movement back toward the coast.[42] Between the communities in the hills and the few remaining in coastal cities, even though conditions were harsh and their numbers had diminished, the Jews retained their enduring presence in Palestine.

The Jewish population in Jerusalem was almost completely wiped out by 1267, though, when physician and scholar Rabbi Moses ben Nahman Girondi arrived there. Nahman went to work immediately, helping rebuild the old synagogues and establishing a rabbinical college, which drew more Jewish families and students to Jerusalem from the surrounding countryside.[43] When Nahman first arrived, he found only two Jewish families living in Jerusalem.[44] Within a century, there were hundreds of Jews there.[45] Additionally, Jewish presence in the cities of Safed, Acre, Ramlah, and Sarafand increased.[46] Despite a general population decline, the Jews seemed to have actually increased their numbers in Palestine during this time while doing well economically.

JEWISH LIFE UNDER THE MAMLUKS

A great deal of historical consensus exists over how the Jews were treated under the Mamluks, who were often harsh. C. E. Bosworth notes that the worst periods came in 1301, 1321, and 1354. Mamluk sultan an-Nasir (1285–1341), for example, was harsh toward both Christians and Jews. He reinstated many discriminatory laws from other Mamluk rulers that had existed in previous centuries.[47]

James Parks explains that both Jews and Christians lost many shrines, churches, and synagogues to the Muslims. Not all were outright destroyed, however. Many of the Jewish and Christian holy sites were deemed important to Islam and were taken before the Mamluks ever assumed power. The Church of Saint Anne in Jerusalem, for example, became a mosque after Saladin captured the city during the Crusade era. However, many more Jewish and Christian sites were taken under Mamluk rule and converted into Muslim shrines as symbols of conquest. The Jewish rabbi, Rabbi Jacob, who visited Palestine from Paris in the late 1200s, found Muslim shrines on the altar of Elijah on Carmel; the tombs of the patriarchs at Hebron; the tomb of Moses' father-in-law, Jethro, at Kfar Hittin; the tomb of Jonah at Kfar Kanah; Samuel's tomb outside Jerusalem; and even the tomb of the first-century rabbi Gamaliel at Jabne.[48]

Sultan Barsbay (1422–1438), one of the more inefficient and draconian of the Mamluk rulers, took even more from Christians and Jews. He deprived non-Muslims of their offices in government and enforced dress regulations on them.[49] Barsbay, however, was far from being the only Mamluk ruler to take such measures. Some of his predecessors had taken similar actions, as did subsequent sultans, such as Jaqmaq and Khushqadam.[50] Yet, despite this oppression and instability under the Mamluks, there was a steady trickle of Jewish immigrants into Palestine during the 1400s. Some of these immigrants came from North Africa and other Islamic countries, but many more Oriental Jews (Sephardim) came from as far as Spain and Portugal.[51]

The mass expulsion of Jews from Spain in the 1490s, which we mentioned briefly in Chapter 5, caused many of these Sephardim to migrate back to the Promised Land. *The Handbook of Palestine* notes that many were men of wealth or intellect. Within a generation, there were about ten thousand Jews living in Palestine, and the leadership of these communities came from the wealthy and learned Sephardi. The population in the growing city of Safed began to rival even that of Jerusalem.[52]

LIFE FOR THE JEWISH PEOPLE UNDER OTTOMAN RULE

Despite the persistent threats of the Mongol horde, the Khwarizmians, and other conquering forces, the Mamluk rule was not decisively defeated once and for all until the Ottoman Turks set their sights on the Mamluk empire in the early sixteenth century. This ushered in the Ottoman Empire, which would rule for more than four hundred years, until the end of the First World War.

OTTOMAN GOVERNMENTAL STRUCTURES

The Ottoman Empire expanded its power throughout the 1500s, conquering its competitors, Mamluk Egypt and the Byzantine Empire.[53] From this point until the end of World War I, the basic outlines of Turkish governance remained relatively the same. When the Muslim Turks conquered Palestine, Syria, and much of the Middle East, they split the area into various administrative districts. They administered Palestine, Lebanon, and Syria together under the name of Syria with the capital in Damascus.

The Turkish sultan exercised loose control over non-Muslim subjects through the millet system. "Millet" comes from the Arabic word *millah*, meaning religion or nationality.[54] Members of religious minorities were classified as *rayah*, meaning "herd," and fell under the banner of a millet. Then each minority religious group centralized its supreme authority in the hands of one man who represented his people and resided in Istanbul.[55] The Arabs had developed this system to preserve order in a religiously and ethnically diverse society by isolating minorities to avoid contact between them.[56] With the millet system, Christians and Jews created their own schools and law courts, as well as other institutions.[57]

The pasha, or governor of a region, was often sent directly from Istanbul, the capital of the Ottoman Empire.[58] The pasha bought his position to enhance his personal prestige and as a financial investment in future tax revenue. The position could be quite lucrative, as it included the right to farm out taxes in the region.[59]

The role of the provincial pasha was to maintain military forces in the region, collect taxes, and, from those taxes, provide for his own salary and expenses.[60] Landowners in the province were able to continue to enjoy their estates as long as they paid taxes and provided a number of troops for the empire.[61] And while the pasha *supervised* the local Ottoman troops and enforced order, he did not pay their salaries. Instead, the Ottoman treasury paid the troops directly to try to maintain the loyalty of the soldiers.[62] Turnover was a constant issue for the pashas in Syria, which administered Palestine. In Damascus, for example, there were 133 different pashas in a single 180-year period (1517–1697).[63]

Unlike the pasha, the mufti, a Muslim religious leader, often held his position for decades, and he was often appointed by the sultan from the locality in which he served.[64] The role of the mufti was to analyze religious sources like the Quran and Hadiths and issue fatwas, or legal opinions.[65]

The Ottoman feudal system—in which a peasant was given land in return for serving a ruler—exacerbated corruption and its impact on the local inhabitants.[66] Tax farming, for example, put a significant burden on Palestinian peasants. In this practice, a person bought from the Ottoman government the right to collect taxes from a village. While the tax farmers were required to pay the government a specific amount, they could demand sums over and above that amount. When they did so, peasants were generally helpless to resist. Living conditions deteriorated significantly for the peasants of Palestine in the seventeenth and eighteenth centuries, and the disruptive nature of the tax farm appears to have been one of the primary causes.[67]

The Ottomans divided Syria (the *pashalik*, or jurisdiction, of Damascus) into five districts: Gaza, Jerusalem, Nablus, Lajjun, and Safed.[68] Other nearby *pashaliks* were Aleppo, Tripoli, and later Sidon (which included Galilee).[69] The same people groups—including the Jewish community—who were present before the Ottoman conquest continued to inhabit Palestine during this time.[70]

JERUSALEM AND PALESTINE IN THE CALIPHATE

Under Ottoman rule, the sultan claimed the title of caliph, asserting his position as the leader of the entire Muslim community around the world and the successor to Muhammad. Even today, the title of caliph has special meaning in the Muslim world. For instance, Abu Bakr al-Baghdadi calls himself the caliph of his self-proclaimed Islamic State. Due to the mixing of government and faith in Islam, Jerusalem was of significant importance to the Ottomans, and maintaining possession of it became one of the Ottoman Turks' primary concerns. The Ottoman military always kept the bulk of its small Palestine force in Jerusalem to hold the city, and it bolstered this force with soldiers raised from the local population.[71]

> Under Ottoman rule, the sultan claimed the title of caliph, asserting his position as the leader of the entire Muslim community around the world and the successor to Muhammad.

Some of the early sultans also concerned themselves with the poor of the city as well as maintenance of the Al Aqsa Mosque and the Dome of the Rock. For instance, in the 1520s and 1530s, soon after the conquest of the region, Suleiman the Magnificent rebuilt and renovated parts of Jerusalem still damaged from the wars following the Crusades, improved the water supply by constructing wells, and renovated the Dome of the Rock, specifically the cupola and ceramic tiles on its wall. Due to these renovations and playing off his name, Suleiman was hailed as the "second Solomon" in some inscriptions.[72]

SEPHARDIC IMMIGRATION TO PALESTINE

As we've already seen, many Sephardic Jews—those emigrating from Spain and the Iberian Peninsula—immigrated into Syria. Most Sephardic Jews coming into Palestine settled near Safed, but Jerusalem was another frequent destination. These immigrants fared better in Safed because the land and villages of Galilee sustained them, whereas the fewer Jerusalem villages could not.[73] By 1600, this population growth resulted in as many as thirty thousand Jews in Safed, which had become an influential center of rabbinical learning for the Jewish diaspora.[74] A high point in the region was in 1577, when Eliezer Ashkenazi and Abraham ben Isaac Ashkenazi began operating a Jewish printing press in Safed. Eliezer had worked as a printer in Eastern Europe and brought his craft to Palestine. The first book printed was a commentary on the book of Esther called *Lekah Tov*, or *Good Doctrine*.[75]

The growing population and focus on education did not help Safed escape the challenges of the region, however. Both Safed and nearby Tiberias were successively sacked by Bedouin and Druze raiders.[76] Two Christian visitors to Safed in the early 1600s reported that, for the Jews, life there was the poorest and most miserable that one can imagine, between insecurity, generally high Ottoman taxation, and the additional taxes specifically imposed on Jews.[77]

> **Two Christian visitors to Safed in the early 1600s reported that, for the Jews, life there was the poorest and most miserable that one can imagine, between insecurity, generally high Ottoman taxation, and the additional taxes specifically imposed on Jews.**

The Jewish presence in Safed nearly came to an end in the late 1600s when the Jewish community there was massacred and much of the town destroyed by the Bedouin and Druze. It was reported that only one Jew escaped death.[78]

THE RISE OF AN ANTI-JEWISH SULTAN

Even during the time of Safed's prominence as a Jewish center, Jerusalem remained an important city for Jewish learning within Jewish circles. Furthermore, Jerusalem became an increasingly important Jewish gathering point during Galilee's periods of volatility, which were fairly common.[79] Such problems were compounded for Jews in Palestine and throughout the Ottoman Empire when Murad III, the first avidly anti-Jewish sultan, took power.[80]

Murad III issued multiple decrees against Jews and other non-Muslim minorities during his twenty-one-year reign (1574–1595). At his worst, the impulsive Murad III was so enraged by seeing wealthy Jews in Istanbul that he ordered the execution of all Jews. Thankfully, this order was never carried out, as Solomon ben Nathan Ashkenazi, a Jew who served as an important Ottoman diplomat, was able to intervene.[81]

Instead, as historian Elli Kohen explains, Murad III contented himself with enforcing decrees forbidding Jews from displaying outward signs of wealth. For instance, in 1577 he forbade Jews and other *rayah* (non-Muslims) from wearing white or red sandals, silk, or fine clothing. Two years later he banned the use of turbans by Jews or other non-Muslims and required that these groups wear a red hat. In 1576 he ordered that one thousand Jews move from Safed to Cyprus to boost the economic and political stability of the island, although it is unclear whether this order was ever carried out.[82]

Following the sultan's lead, Muslims in the area frequently persecuted the Jewish community in Jerusalem. Joan Peters explains that Jews were often taken by angry mobs and even blamed for droughts in the countryside. Often the Jews could only escape this violence by paying off the mobs using money borrowed at

> **Following the sultan's lead, Muslims in the area frequently persecuted the Jewish community in Jerusalem.**

high interest rates from Muslim lenders, who threatened even more violence if the Jewish borrowers were unable to repay the loan.[83]

Then, in 1586, the authorities closed the Jerusalem synagogue originally built in the time of Moses ben Nahman Girondi in the thirteenth century. Between the closing of the synagogue and the exorbitant taxation aimed at Jews, many Jews decided to settle in Hebron, Gaza, or Tiberias in the late 1500s.[84] Yet, though their numbers were dwindling, a Jewish presence remained in Jerusalem.

Then, during the following reign of Murad IV as sultan (1623–1640), things took an even worse turn for the Jews in the region. Ibn Barouk purchased the pasha governorship from the sultan. His time in power ushered in a period of particularly bitter persecution for the Jewish community, and Ibn Barouk had many of the Jewish leaders arrested and subjected to fines.[85] Despite the persecution, banditry, general lawlessness, and relentless taxation, the Jews remained in Hebron, Gaza, Ramle, Nablus, Safed, Acre (Akko), Sidon, Tyre, Haifa, Irsuf, Caesarea, El Arnish, and many other Galilean villages. Observers at the end of the seventeenth century noted that Jews had to pay a high price to continue living under Turkish rule.[86] Jesuit father Michael Naud noted that the Jews "prefer[red] being prisoners in Jerusalem to enjoying the freedom they could acquire elsewhere."[87] This shows once again the Jewish community's continued desire to maintain a presence in Jerusalem even under arguably unbearable conditions.

> **Jesuit father Michael Naud noted that the Jews "prefer[red] being prisoners in Jerusalem to enjoying the freedom they could acquire elsewhere."**

A Time of Desolation

"Desolation" is a word often associated with Palestine from 1500–1800. The exact causes and extent of the despair are sometimes debated, but desolation is the region's defining feature for that time. Poor administration, extraordinarily high taxation, unscrupulous pashas, and anti-Jewish abuse and persecution all worked together—along with other factors—to create a harsh way of life for not only the Jews but the entire population of Palestine during Ottoman rule. Mark Twain, upon visiting Palestine during this time, wrote, "Palestine sits in sackcloth and ashes. Over it broods the spell of a curse that has withered its fields and fettered its energies. . . . Palestine is desolate and unlovely." [88]

As a result, whereas the Roman Middle East may have contained 40 million to 45 million people and a fifth of the world's total population by 1700, the entire population of Syria was only 1.5 million—fewer than one hundred thousand of whom lived in Palestine. [89] Yet despite all of this, history—even a history of abuses and misery—shows a continual Jewish presence throughout Palestine.

THE EVIDENCE OF HISTORY

We have covered four thousand years of history in these last six chapters, and yet we have only scratched the surface. Again, the goal of this section has been to prove through biblical texts, historical records, and archaeological evidence the continued, unbroken existence of a Jewish community in Palestine from the time of Abraham to today. I said at the beginning of this section that I wanted to create a narrative, a story to show the flow of history from one era to the next. I believe we have done that. While I didn't give a decade-by-decade review of every aspect of Jewish history, I am confident that the record we've outlined in these chapters has shown the continual presence of Jews in the Holy Land

> **Regardless what they have faced over these four millennia, a faithful remnant remained.**

up through the modern period—often despite incredible obstacles and against all odds. Regardless what they have faced over these four millennia, a faithful remnant remained.

At this point, we have traced the history of the Jews from Creation; into the Abrahamic Covenant; through the Exodus; into and out of Babylonian captivity; throughout the reign of the Israelite kings; through the reigns of Alexander, the Romans, the Arabs, the Crusaders, the Mamluks, and more; and now to the rule of the Ottomans, which lasted until the First World War. Now, as we enter into the more recent history from the last century, it's time to take off our biblical and historical lenses and approach the evidence from a new perspective: the law. By reviewing the legal defense for the Jewish State of Israel, we'll see how both history and the law are on Israel's side against the modern anti-Israel movement.

KEY TAKEAWAYS

1. The Jewish people survived countless regime changes in the Holy Land, often by putting themselves in valuable positions under different rulers.

2. Rather than fleeing to safer areas, many Jews chose to stay in Jerusalem and its surrounding areas despite the harsh treatment they endured there.

3. History has shown an unbroken four-thousand-year Jewish presence in the Holy Land from the time of the Exodus to modern times.

SECTION IV

THE LEGAL EVIDENCE

On the 29th November, 1947, the United Nations General Assembly passed a resolution calling for the establishment of a Jewish State in Eretz-Israel; the General Assembly required the inhabitants of Eretz-Israel to take such steps as were necessary on their part for the implementation of that resolution. This recognition by the United Nations of the right of the Jewish people to establish their State is irrevocable.

This right is the natural right of the Jewish people to be masters of their own fate, like all other nations, in their own sovereign State.

—THE DECLARATION OF THE ESTABLISHMENT
OF THE STATE OF ISRAEL, MAY 14, 1948

9

WORLD WAR I AND THE DREAM OF A JEWISH NATION

Palestine is our unforgettable historic homeland. . . . Let me repeat once more my opening words: The Jews who will it shall achieve their State. We shall live at last as free men on our own soil, and in our own homes peacefully die. The world will be liberated by our freedom, enriched by our wealth, magnified by our greatness. And whatever we attempt there for our own benefit will redound mightily and beneficially to the good of all mankind.

—THEODOR HERZL, *DER JUDENSTAAT*[1]

'**ve been blessed with a long and rewarding career in law going back** several decades. In all of that time, though, I truly feel that some of my most important work has taken place over these last several years as I have fought tooth and nail for the State of Israel. We at the ACLJ have worked with and in Israel for a long time, but that work got much more serious in 2009 when I was asked to lead a team defending Israel's legal position at the International Criminal Court (ICC) at The Hague. The Palestinian Authority was trying to bring Israeli government officials and military officers up on charges before the ICC, accusing them of war crimes for actions that took place during Operation Cast Lead in the Gaza Strip. The Palestinians knew they wouldn't succeed; it was just another in a long line of attacks against Israel. But this one deserved a powerful, even overwhelming response.

I was contacted by Israel's minister of justice, Yaakov Neeman, and the deputy foreign minister, Danny Ayalon, and asked to put together a legal team to fight these absurd charges. It was the first real, significant lawfare challenge against Israel in an international court, and Israel's response needed to be hard, swift, and decisive. The ACLJ took on the challenge, and we assembled a team of some of the greatest legal minds from around the world. In a matter of weeks we met together for the first time in our ACLJ offices in Strasbourg, France. I will never forget sitting at that conference table and looking across at such giants as former U.S. attorney general John Ashcroft, counsel of state for France François-Henri Briard, and former executive director of the European Court of Human Rights Hans Christian Kruger. We also had two or three military lawyers from the U.S., an English barrister, and Canadian and Polish international law experts, among others. We had convened in Strasbourg to lay out a strategy to fight these charges against Israel. It also struck me at the time that this wasn't just a collection of political conservatives. Rather, our group consisted of people from all political stripes and nationalities. We had people from the left, the right, and down the center. We weren't there to discuss politics. We were there to discuss the law—and its justification for Israel's right to defend itself from attacks.

The Israelis sent their representatives to join us as well, and they were impressed by the caliber of lawyers that we had assembled. We had legal experts from Poland, Germany, Great Britain, France, Canada, and of course the United States. It was an impressive group. We sat together at that conference table for four days, mapping out our strategy and ultimately putting together what we called our "initial document." From that first meeting, we produced a strong letter to the ICC prosecutor challenging both the Palestinians' allegations against Israel as well as their right to raise them before the ICC. Over the next six months we submitted hundreds of pages of documents to the ICC refuting the allegations against Israel and citing the applicable law that supported Israel and its actions. We responded in depth to every charge leveled against Israel. We weren't going to pull any punches. We were there to win. We had decided that if we could win that case, we could get one tribunal out of the way and move on to the next. So we sat in the Office of the Prosecutor of the ICC with all of our prepared material and presented the outline of our case. It became apparent to the prosecutor at that point that we were going to provide serious pushback to every allegation, and he decided to set up an NGO roundtable. That was a gathering that would comprise four legal and political representatives from Israel's side (led by me), four representatives from the Palestinian side, and the prosecutor and many of his assistants. From that exchange, he ultimately issued a ruling.

The meeting consisted of eight hours of oral arguments, and it represented well over ten thousand pages of documentation from both sides combined. After deliberation, those ten thousand pages of briefs resulted in a two-page decision: Israel prevailed. The ICC found, as we knew they would if they followed the law, that the Palestinian Authority did not have state status and, therefore, was unable to bring charges up to the international court. We realized at the time that this was just the first of many upcoming battles, and we were focused on knocking them out one by one.

So far in this book, we've carefully reviewed the biblical and historical evidence in support of Israel as a Jewish state. Now, in this section, we're going to catch up on the last century of Israel's history and change our perspective a bit to examine the legal support for Israel's right to exist. Starting in the late twentieth century, Israel's biggest fights changed from conquests to courtrooms. That's why our meeting in Strasbourg was so important: It was the first time such an incredible collection of legal minds from around the world had gathered to connect all the dots and officially spell out why the law supported Israel. Our research is still being used to fight these battles in smaller arenas across the world. Being prepared to fight the legal battles of the twenty-first century and beyond will ultimately determine Israel's fate as a nation, and we're going to be ready. But first let's see how we got here.

A LONG HISTORY OF
EUROPEAN ANTI-SEMITISM

As the Ottoman Empire exercised power over the Jews in Palestine throughout the nineteenth century, Europe was awash in competing philosophies and beliefs. In czarist Russia and Eastern Europe, it was a time of political unrest often punctuated by anti-Semitic pogroms, organized massacres of Jewish people with the intention to eliminate them from the face of the earth.[2] My own family fled Russia due to these pogroms against the Jewish communities. In Central and Western Europe, it was a time of political upheaval and nationalistic fervor.[3] Western nations were undergoing widespread changes as the old political, social, and economic orders were being replaced by a new, freer, and more democratic order. The Industrial Revolution was under way, causing massive social disruptions. Political revolutions erupted throughout Europe in 1848.[4] For European Jews, the period was a time of both fear and great hope. The Jews of Russia and Eastern Europe were obviously fearful of the horrific pogroms directed against them by virulent anti-Semites. And the Jews in more liberal Western European societies were hopeful that full Jewish inclusion and acceptance might finally be possible. However, that hope wouldn't be realized for a long time.

THE ALBERT DREYFUS AFFAIR OF 1890

The idea of Jewish assimilation was almost completely shattered by the Albert Dreyfus affair in 1890s France.[5] A country considered by many at the time to be one of the most tolerant, egalitarian, and sophisticated societies in the world, France's vaunted republican values should never have encouraged, much less permitted, what happened to French army captain Alfred Dreyfus.

Captain Dreyfus was the only Jewish officer serving on the French general staff in the French army. He was from a wealthy Jewish family from Alsace that was totally committed to full assimilation into French society, making this whole affair that much more tragic. While Captain Dreyfus was serving on the general staff, officials discovered that someone had provided French military secrets to the German military attaché in Paris. Dreyfus was accused of selling those secrets. Accordingly, the French military leadership convened a court-martial that tried and convicted Captain Dreyfus of treason based on forged evidence from a known anti-Semite.[6] Upon his conviction, Captain Dreyfus was publicly humiliated and stripped of his rank and military decorations before being sentenced to solitary confinement on Devil's Island for the remainder of his life.[7]

A few valiant French officers recognized the injustice and called for Captain Dreyfus's exoneration and release.[8] However, even when it became clear that Dreyfus was, in fact, innocent, things shockingly got worse. Rather than face the humiliation of admitting they had convicted the wrong man, senior French military officials chose to cover up the whole affair, even though it meant leaving the innocent Dreyfus in prison while the man they *knew* was guilty walked free.[9] So, *based on the same false evidence,* a second court-martial was convened and reconvicted Dreyfus, while another tribunal intentionally acquitted the real traitor.[10]

Despite their pious claims of faithfulness to the principles of justice and the rule of law, French military leaders knowingly manipulated the French military justice system to avoid embarrassment to themselves, and the army knowingly kept the innocent Dreyfus in prison instead. It took decades for the wrong to be righted and for Captain Dreyfus to finally be exonerated.[11]

THE BIRTH OF ZIONISM

As these troubling events were taking place, a growing number of European Jews were coming to the realization that, in order to be safe and secure as a people, Jews would need to establish a state of their own. They began dreaming of a state populated and governed by Jews—something they hadn't known since the biblical time of Israelite kings.

Seeing the writing on the wall, Austrian journalist Theodor Herzl, the father of the Zionist movement—the goal of which was to establish a Jewish nation—laid the groundwork for what would ultimately lead to the modern State of Israel.[12] Herzl authored the famous pamphlet *Der Judenstaat* (*The Jewish State*), and called an 1897 meeting of interested Zionists in Basel, Switzerland.[13] This meeting would become the first Zionist Congress, and its purpose was twofold: to create the World Zionist Organization and to declare Zionism's goals, the first of which was "to create for the Jewish people a home in Eretz Israel, the land of Israel, secured by law."[14]

At the same time, non-Jewish groups, primarily in Great Britain, were taking a growing interest in the Jewish people. Specifically, they were looking at the Bible's promises that the Jews would one day return to the Holy Land.[15] As a result, key British Christian leaders—both in and out of government—allied themselves with the Jewish Zionists.[16] Among these leaders were Winston Churchill and Arthur Balfour, the author of the Balfour Declaration, which would first provide formal UK support for the establishment of a Jewish state. These events set the stage for the movement to reestablish a home for the Jewish people in Palestine, a movement that would continue to grow throughout the First and Second World Wars.

DEVELOPMENTS DURING AND AFTER WORLD WAR I

To appreciate what led to Israel's historic founding in 1948, we must first understand what happened in Europe in the decades preceding it: the two largest global wars in human history. Following the assassination of Austria's Archduke Franz Ferdinand and his wife in Sarajevo by a Serbian nationalist on June 28, 1914, the political situation in Europe quickly devolved into turmoil. As one provocative act followed another, no one was able to stop the rapid descent into war, leading to the inevitable outbreak of the First World War.[17]

In response to the archduke's assassination, the Austro-Hungarian Empire issued a wholly demeaning ultimatum to Serbia.[18] The terms of this ultimatum would have severely diminished Serbian sovereignty and independence by permitting Austria-Hungary to exercise a veto on Serbian government decisions and personnel appointments. Serbia rejected the terms and immediately sought help from its traditional ally, czarist Russia.[19]

Over the ensuing weeks, different nations quickly took sides. As Russia raced to support Serbia, the German Reich affirmed its strong support for Austria-Hungary.[20] Russia in turn reached out to Great Britain and France.[21] Two opposing coalitions emerged:

- Allied Powers: the British Empire, France, czarist Russia, Italy, Japan, and ultimately the United States (though explicitly as an "Associated" Power).

- Central Powers: the German Reich, the Austro-Hungarian Empire, the Ottoman Empire (which ruled Palestine at the time), and Bulgaria.

Once the nations were aligned and the battle lines set, the world went to war. While this discussion could go in a hundred different directions at this point, we'll stick to the details as they pertain *to Israel.*

CONFLICTING PROMISES

Because critical British supply routes during the war passed through the Mediterranean Sea and via the Suez Canal, the Red Sea, and the Indian Ocean, the British military was engaged in the Middle East as well as Europe. The Ottomans' potential disruption of sea routes to India inspired Britain to encourage an Arab uprising against the Ottomans in the hopes of removing Ottoman forces from the region. In return, the British promised to support the creation of an independent Arab state following the Ottomans' defeat.

The Anglo-Arab negotiations are enshrined in the Hussein-McMahon letters between Hussein bin Ali, the sharif of Mecca, and Sir Henry McMahon, the British high commissioner in Cairo.[22] However, as was common at the time, Britain was having one conversation with the Arabs while having an entirely different conversation with France and Russia about how best to divide the Ottoman territories after the war.

While the British were openly supporting the Arabs in 1916,

Britain, France, and Russia met secretly and agreed to divide the Arab territories among themselves.[23] These negotiations were enshrined in a document known as the Sykes-Picot Agreement, after the English and French negotiators of the deal.[24] The Sykes-Picot Agreement did not draw actual boundary lines but simply established general zones over which each country would maintain influence.[25] According to the agreement, France would control the area that would eventually become Lebanon and Syria, Britain would control Mesopotamia (Iraq) and Jordan, and Russia would control the Turkish straits, Turkish Armenia, and Persian Azerbaijan. Palestine was to be placed under international control.[26]

THE BALFOUR DECLARATION

By the fall of 1917, Britain's forces were split between Western Europe and their joint campaign with the Arab military to drive Ottoman forces away from the Suez Canal and out of the Arabian Peninsula. On November 2 of that year, a letter was issued from the United Kingdom's foreign secretary Arthur Balfour to Lionel Walter Rothschild, 2nd Baron Rothschild. The impact of this letter was so great that it reached the Zionist Federation of Great Britain and Ireland and was published a week after its writing. Known as the Balfour Declaration, it declares:

> His Majesty's Government view with favour the establishment in Palestine of a national home for the Jewish people, and will use their best endeavours to facilitate the achievement of this object, it being clearly understood that nothing shall be done which may prejudice the civil and religious rights of existing non-Jewish communities in Palestine, or the rights and political status enjoyed by Jews in any other country.[27]

Although the Balfour Declaration was a solely aspirational British statement of policy when issued, the declaration has turned out to be one of the most significant political documents of the twentieth century.

The stated goal of the Balfour Declaration—the creation of a Jewish national home in Palestine—was ultimately adopted by the international community of nations in the post–World War I period. It was incorporated into international agreements that ended the war, thereby enshrining the declaration's aims in binding international law. These agreements provided the foundation for reconstituting and reestablishing a Jewish state in the Jews' ancient homeland, and they continue to serve as internationally recognized and binding legal underpinnings for the territorial claims of the modern Jewish State of Israel. To be clear, though, they did not *create* the Jewish people's right to their homeland; they merely *recognized* it in binding legal fashion.

After World War I

Europe was thoroughly devastated by the time the 1918 armistice was agreed to, finally ending World War I. Both sides were exhausted. Their countries and citizens had been torn apart by four years of war, and much of the continent had been destroyed. Cities and towns were reduced to rubble, and both winners and losers of the war were left facing significant political upheaval. The following events were among the postwar fallout:

- A revolution in Russia had swept away the czarist regime and resulted in the creation of a Bolshevik, Communist dictatorship.[28]

- The German Empire had also been destroyed. The German kaiser had abdicated his throne and sought political asylum in the Netherlands, leaving his country in shambles and in danger of a Communist revolution.[29]

- The Austro-Hungarian Empire had been subdivided into a number of independent states, based primarily on ethnicity.[30]

- The Ottoman Empire had been soundly defeated, had lost the majority of its non-Turkish territories, and was threatened with foreign military occupation of significant portions of Anatolia (Asia Minor, including most of modern-day Turkey).[31]

•   France had been devastated by the war, which, on the Western Front, had been fought primarily on French soil. France lost more than 1,385,000 who were killed in action, and its treasury was bankrupt.[32]

•   Great Britain was reeling from its vast number of war casualties and economic losses.[33]

Considering the widespread havoc the war had wreaked on Europe, the victorious Allied Powers were in no mood for leniency or for offering an outstretched hand to their former foes. Despite President Woodrow Wilson's attempts to mitigate the drive for revenge via his famous Fourteen Points, the treaties that resulted from the various peace conferences were harsh on the nations that had lost the war.[34] The treaties demanded all manner of reparations, with no consideration for the fact that the defeated nations had suffered as much—if not more—than the victors and were simply incapable of meeting such demands. Many historians and experts point to these demands as one of the root causes of World War II.

TREATY OF SÈVRES

The peace agreement negotiated between the Allies and the Ottoman Empire was known as the Treaty of Sèvres, named for the French city where it was signed.[35] Although signed by representatives of the Ottoman sultan, the treaty was so harsh and punitive that the Ottomans never ratified it. In fact, its terms were so severe that Ottoman army officers rose in revolt against its signatories, which resulted in their overthrowing the sultan and driving foreign forces out of what then became the modern state of Turkey.[36] The victorious Turkish forces demanded the renegotiation of the Treaty of Sèvres, and it was ultimately replaced by the Treaty of Lausanne, which confirmed that

Turkey renounced all claims to its prior non-Turkish territories.[37] Nevertheless, the Treaty of Sèvres still played a critical role in how the region was divided, as we'll see below.

THE MANDATES

One of the key issues following the First World War was determining what to do with the former territories belonging to the defeated Central Powers. The newly formed League of Nations, an international organization founded in 1920 to maintain world peace, took up the charge. Article 22 of the Covenant of the League of Nations called for the creation of a series of mandates under the auspices of the league to assume responsibility for those territories.[38] The system of mandates can be described as follows:

> The Mandate system implemented what was then a new principle in international affairs—the self-determination of peoples. At the same time, the European powers were not completely ready to surrender their traditional domination of international affairs, or the perceived benefits of colonialism. The resulting compromise was a new form of quasi-colonial rule, defined by Article 22 of the Covenant of the new League of Nations. Borrowing from the domestic laws of trust and guardianship, the Covenant described Mandates as a "sacred trust of civilization," and it committed the right to control the territories to the Mandatory powers . . . subject to the supervision of the League of Nations.[39]

Therefore, the mandate system was a quasi-colonial political system crafted by the League of Nations to allow the victorious Allied Powers to guide and shepherd former territories of the Central Powers toward eventual independence. The country appointed to carry out those responsibilities for each territory, or mandate, was referred to as the mandatory.

The Treaty of Sèvres is important because it established what the then-existing community of nations had envisioned for the three mandates created out of the non-Turkish territories of the former Ottoman Empire. The three mandates would become known as the mandates for Syria (including Lebanon), Mesopotamia (Iraq), and Palestine.

The mandates for Syria and Mesopotamia directed the mandatories to prepare their respective populations for independence. With respect to Palestine, the international community ruled that establishing a Jewish home in that territory would fulfill Jewish self-determination desires.

The third and fourth paragraphs of Article 22 describe the importance of adapting the mandates to the region and people being governed.[40] According to the fourth paragraph of Article 22 of the Covenant of the League of Nations, *"Certain communities* formerly belonging to the Turkish Empire have reached a stage of development where their existence as independent nations can be provisionally recognised subject to the rendering of administrative advice and assistance by a Mandatory until such time as they are able to stand alone."[41] Article 94 of the Treaty of Sèvres identifies those "certain communities" to be Syria and Mesopotamia. Article 95, which dealt solely with Palestine, explicitly did not include Palestine as one of the "certain communities." Palestine was a special case.

Mandates for Syria and Mesopotamia

Article 94 of the Treaty of Sèvres laid out what was envisioned for the mandates for Syria and Mesopotamia:

> The High Contracting Parties agree that Syria and Mesopotamia shall, in accordance with the fourth paragraph of Article 22,[42] Part I (Covenant of the League of Nations), be provisionally recognised as independent States subject to the rendering of administrative advice and assistance by a Mandatory until such time as they are able to stand alone.

Simply put, this means that Syria and Mesopotamia were deemed "ready" to be treated as independent states at the time, to be administered for a period by their respective mandatories.

Mandate for Palestine

Article 95 of the Treaty of Sèvres discusses the plan for Palestine and differs significantly from the language in Article 94. Article 95 reads as follows:

> The High Contracting Parties agree to entrust, by application of the provisions of Article 22, the administration of Palestine, within such boundaries as may be determined by the Principal Allied Powers, to a Mandatory to be selected by the said Powers. The Mandatory will be responsible for putting into effect the declaration originally made on November 2, 1917, by the British Government, and adopted by the other Allied Powers, in favour of the establishment in Palestine of a national home for the Jewish people . . .

Article 95 dealt solely with Palestine and did not include any reference to the "certain communities" mentioned in Article 22 of the League of Nations Covenant that could be provisionally recognized as an independent nation at the time. Instead, Palestine was to be developed so that it could support and sustain a national home for the Jewish people. That was the mandatory's principal obligation under the mandate, strongly suggesting that the Jewish homeland so envisioned would one day become a Jewish state.

The Anglo-American Treaty

Article 95 confirmed that the Balfour Declaration had been "adopted by the other Allied Powers," thereby establishing that the declaration was no longer simply an aspirational statement by the British government. Because it was adopted by the Allied Powers, the Balfour Declaration became accepted as an instrument of international law. Yet, because the United States had insisted that it be an Associated (as opposed to Allied) Power during the First World War, and because the United States never joined the League of Nations, the remaining Allied Powers felt it necessary to seek separate American approval of the Palestinian mandate. This was accomplished via the Anglo-American Treaty, which confirmed the United States' acceptance of the Balfour Declaration's goals. In this treaty, the U.S. affirmed the Jewish people's historical connection to Palestine, the appointment of Britain as the mandatory (governing authority) for Palestine, and the facilitation of Jewish immigration to Palestine.[43]

After the respective peace treaties were signed that formally ended the First World War—each of which incorporated the Covenant of the League of Nations—the principal Allied Powers met in San Remo, Italy, to draft the terms of the various mandates alluded to in Article 22 of the Covenant.[44] Once completed, the terms of the Mandate for Palestine were submitted to the League of Nations for approval, and the mandate was approved on July 24, 1922.[45]

ARTICLES OF THE MANDATE
FOR PALESTINE

Upon approval, the terms of the Mandate for Palestine explicitly required the mandatory to give priority to the Jewish people over any other population group in the area.[46] Yet, Article 25 of the mandate explicitly allowed the mandatory to "postpone or withhold" application of the mandate to territories *east* of the Jordan Rift Valley. The British did exactly that in September 1922, thereby disallowing Jewish settlement in approximately 77 percent of the mandate's territory.

BOTH SIDES UNHAPPY

The British placed one of the sons of the former sharif of Mecca in nominal leadership of the eastern area, which was renamed Transjordan. It appears that the British did this for two reasons: first, as an attempt to honor the agreement set forth in the Hussein-McMahon correspondence discussed above; and second, to meet Arab self-determination desires in Palestine. Both the Jews and the Arabs felt betrayed by this action—the Jews, because they lost more than three-quarters of the land they believed had been promised for their national home; and the Arabs, because they claimed the British had also promised them the territory west of the Jordan Rift Valley to the Mediterranean Sea as part of the Arab state to be created after the Ottomans' defeat.

The preamble to the mandate stated, "The Principal Allied Powers have . . . agreed that the Mandatory should be responsible for putting into effect the declaration originally made on November 2nd, 1917, by the Government of His Britannic Majesty [the Balfour Declaration], and adopted by the said Powers, in favor of the establishment in Palestine of a national home for the Jewish people." The clause also includes the original language that required "the civil and religious rights of existing non-Jewish communities in Palestine" to be protected. It is important to note that there was no mention of protecting the *political* rights of existing non-Jewish communities. That is a significant, telling omission. It confirms that political rights were originally reserved exclusively for the Jewish population of Palestine. The preamble further recognized "the historical connection of the Jewish people with Palestine and . . . the grounds for reconstituting their national home in that country." Note the reference to the "historical connection" the Jews have to the land, which we have discussed at length. Also noteworthy is the stated aim of "reconstituting" their national home, as opposed to creating it for the first time. In this, the mandate recognized that the Promised Land had historically been the Jews' national homeland.

As for the rest of the region, after Britain divided the original mandate into two parts, Jewish settlement in Transjordan was prohibited. The non-Jewish communities there ultimately inherited the political rights to the eastern 77 percent of the original mandate, thereby fulfilling their own self-determination rights.

EXCLUSIVE CLAUSES BENEFITING THE JEWISH PEOPLE

While non-Jewish communities gained political rights to 77 percent of the land following the British decision to implement the terms of

Article 25, the mandate included several exclusive clauses pertaining to the establishment of a Jewish national home that still applied to the remainder of the mandate west of the Jordan Rift Valley. Let's review the key excerpts to get a clear picture of the mandate's expectations for a Jewish state.

ARTICLE 2: CIVIL, RELIGIOUS, AND POLITICAL SAFEGUARDS

Article 2 of the mandate required that the mandatory place "the country under such political, administrative and economic conditions as will secure the establishment of the Jewish national home . . . and the development of self-governing institutions [as well as] for safeguarding the civil and religious rights of all inhabitants of Palestine, irrespective of race and religion." Note that the mandatory was only required to safeguard the *civil and religious* rights of *all* inhabitants, whereas Article 2 called for the Jews to be able to develop "self-governing [i.e., political] institutions." No non-Jewish Palestinian group was given any similar *political* authority.

ARTICLE 4: JEWISH ADVISORY AGENCY

Article 4 of the mandate required the mandatory to recognize "an appropriate Jewish agency . . . as a public body" to advise the administration of Palestine regarding "such economic, social and other matters as may affect the establishment of the Jewish national home and the interests of the Jewish population in Palestine." Article 4 even suggested that the World Zionist Organization be so designated. Nowhere in the Mandate for Palestine was there a similar call for creating or recognizing any agency or other public body on behalf of any other population group in Palestine.

ARTICLE 6: FACILITATING JEWISH SETTLEMENT

Article 6 of the mandate required the mandatory to "facilitate Jewish immigration under suitable conditions" and "encourage . . . close settlement by Jews on the land, *including State lands and waste lands* not required for public purposes." Once again, this type of advantage was not given to any other people or group.

Article 7: Palestinian Citizenship for Jews

Article 7 of the mandate called for a nationality law to be enacted and "to facilitate the acquisition of Palestinian citizenship by Jews who take up their permanent residence in Palestine." No other people group received such a benefit.

Article 11: Jewish Governmental Systems

Article 11 of the mandate instructed the mandatory to permit the Jewish agency referred to in Article 4 "to construct or operate . . . any public works, services and utilities, and to develop any of the natural resources of the country" wherever such activities "[were] not directly undertaken by the Administration." No other people group was given such opportunities. It is important to note that the activities mentioned here are part and parcel of what *governments* are required to do in a territory they govern. This reflects the fact that the Jews were viewed as the eventual political successors to the mandatory.

Article 25: Postponing Mandate Provisions

As noted above, Article 25 of the mandate is interesting in that it openly contradicted the underlying promise to facilitate the establishment of a Jewish home *in Palestine*. It permitted the mandatory, with the consent of the Council of the League of Nations, "to postpone or withhold application of such provisions of this mandate as [the Mandatory] may consider inapplicable to the existing local conditions" in the portion of Palestine "lying between the Jordan and the eastern boundary of Palestine." The British did in fact request and obtain permission to withhold application of key provisions involving the Jews in the eastern portion of Palestine.[47] By doing so, the mandatory limited its obligation to implement the terms of the Balfour Declaration to the 23 percent of the mandate lying to the west of the Jordan Rift Valley.

The 77 percent of the mandate lying to the east of the Jordan Rift Valley (Transjordan) was closed completely to Jewish settlement and instead was reserved solely for Arab development. This appears to be consistent with the British understanding of the Hussein-McMahon agreements, which asserted that purely Arab areas would become part of the promised Arab state following the defeat of the Ottomans. It also indicates Britain's recognition of its obligation to accommodate Arab self-determination desires.

However—and this is an important note—the British never sought permission from the League of Nations to *formally partition the original mandate into two separate entities*, and no such permission was ever granted.[48] Britain continued to treat Transjordan as part of the original mandate in its reports to the League of Nations until 1943, although it had entered into a formal agreement with Emir Abdullah in 1928 "that referred to Transjordan as an 'independent state.' "[49]

THE WEIZMANN-FEISAL AGREEMENT

The understanding that the territory west of the Jordan Rift Valley was to be given to and governed by the Jews was confirmed by His Royal Highness the Emir Feisal ibn Hussein in the 1919 Weizmann-Feisal Agreement.[50] Feisal, representing the Arab Kingdom of Hedjaz, and Chaim Weizmann, representing the World Zionist Organization, met together because they believed that establishing the Arab State and Palestine (referring to the Jewish territory west of the Jordan Rift Valley) as separate states would be beneficial to both parties. However, the wording of their agreement has been a point of contention among Jews and Arabs ever since.

ARAB SUPPORT FOR THE JEWISH STATE

Throughout the text, the Weizmann-Feisal Agreement distinguishes between "the Arab State" and "Palestine" and indicates that Palestine was to become a *Jewish*-ruled entity. Further, in the preamble to the agreement, the parties acknowledged "that the surest means of working out the consummation of [the Arabs' and the Jewish people's] natural aspirations [was] through the closest possible collaboration in the development of the Arab State and Palestine . . ." So, as early as January 1919, key Arab leaders agreed to the creation of a Jewish state in Palestine.

It is vitally important to note that there was a time, not even one hundred years ago, when Jews and Arabs in the Middle East both agreed on the fundamental right for a Jewish state to exist. When they met at Emir Feisal's camp on the Transjordan plateau, Weizmann told Feisal that the presence of a Jewish state would greatly benefit the Arabs. Feisal even wrote a letter to a member of the American Zionist deputation about the goodwill between Arabs and Jews, expressing "deepest sympathy [for] the Zionist movement."

British officer T. E. Lawrence—known to the world as Lawrence of Arabia—was a friend to both Feisal and Weizmann. As a liaison to the Arab forces, Lawrence was extremely pro-Arab yet sometimes wrongfully represented as anti-Zionist. Speaking in his autobiography of his interactions with Lawrence and Feisal, Weizmann wrote, "It was [Lawrence's] view—as it was Feisal's—that the Jews would be of great help to the Arabs, and that the Arab world stood to gain much from a Jewish Homeland in Palestine." [51]

The cordial relationship between these three is reflected in Article I of the Weizmann-Feisal Agreement, which reads as follows:

> The Arab State and Palestine in all their relations and undertakings shall be controlled by the most cordial goodwill and understanding and *to this end Arab and Jewish duly accredited agents shall be established and maintained in their respective territories.*

Article II was even more explicit that Palestine was to be a Jewish state:

> Immediately following the completion of deliberations of the Peace Conference, the definite *boundaries between the Arab State and Palestine* shall be determined by a commission to be agreed upon by the parties hereto.

Article III confirmed Emir Feisal's recognition of and agreement to implementing the terms of the Balfour Declaration in Palestine as the means to establish a Jewish state. Article IV reiterated Emir

Feisal's agreement to increased Jewish immigration into Palestine as well as to Jewish settlement of the land. The terms of this historic agreement are no doubt shocking to modern readers, but they demonstrate the hope that existed among many for the region at the end of World War I.

Emir Feisal later denied that he had acquiesced to the terms of the foregoing agreement.[52] However, in 2002, Muslim linguist and analyst Shibli Zaman—no friend of Zionists or their cause—reviewed the original document and wrote:

> I recently read over the little known Weizmann-Feis[a]l Agreement of January 1919 in which King Feis[a]l ibn Hussain agreed to full cooperation *between an independent Arabia and an independent Zionist State of Israel in Palestine.* . . . In spite of how disgusted one may be to read the Weizmann-Feis[a]l agreement . . . the agreement is 100% historically authentic.[53]

This is significant because it confirms that *in early 1919, even before the Mandate for Palestine had been drafted,* key Arab leaders had both understood and accepted what the Balfour Declaration and the then-future Mandate for Palestine were ultimately intended to accomplish—the creation and establishment of a "Zionist [Jewish] State of Israel."

THE STRUGGLE WAS FAR FROM OVER

As we've seen, the condition in the Middle East after World War I ended was still chaotic but seemingly moving toward a resolution. Britain had taken responsibility for Palestine as its mandatory. The Jewish people had received a parcel of land to begin building a new Jewish state, even though they received far less than they had hoped for or expected. The Arabs were also given a huge portion of the region to fulfill their right to self-determination and on which to establish a future Arab state. Zionist and Arab officials were discussing—even planning—how to move forward in a spirit of cooperation, while persons on both sides resented Britain's division of Palestine. It was a time of tension and resentment mixed with hope and planning. This discord stemming from the breakup of former Ottoman territories at the end of World War I led to much of the political enmity and turmoil in the Middle East today.

Even though Weizmann and Feisal were prepared to peacefully coexist and recognize each other's fundamental rights in 1919, the world was quickly and inexorably moving toward an unthinkable catastrophe for the Jewish people that would clearly demonstrate the need for a Jewish state more than anything else in history: the Holocaust and the fallout of World War II.

KEY TAKEAWAYS

1. When the Balfour Declaration was incorporated into the League of Nations' Mandate for Palestine, the Jewish people's right to reestablish a state in their ancestral homeland was recognized and sanctioned under international law.

2. Arab Palestinians were given 77 percent of the mandate territory in a region called Transjordan to fulfill their desires for self-determination and in which to develop an Arab state. The Jewish people were given rights to the remaining 23 percent.

10

HOW THE INTERNATIONAL COMMUNITY ESTABLISHED THE MODERN STATE OF ISRAEL

You ask me to repudiate the Balfour Declaration and to stop [Jewish] immigration. This is not in my power . . . and it is not my wish. . . . It is manifestly right that the scattered Jews should have a national centre, and a national home to be re-united, and where else but in Palestine, with which for three thousand years they have been intimately and profoundly associated?

We think it will be good for the world, good for the Jews, good for the British Empire, but also good for the Arabs who dwell in Palestine. . . . [T]hey shall share in the benefits and progress of Zionism.

—WINSTON CHURCHILL [1]

I've said earlier in this book that the case for Israel is not simply an emotional thing for me; it's a cause. When I am working on a case—*any* case—my client needs me to be calm, rational, and clinical. This is what a good lawyer does. However, I do have a personal connection to the nation of Israel. It's probably fair to say that *how* I go about the job is clinical, but *why* I'm such a strong advocate for the Jewish State is personal. And that really comes back to my family.

I'm only the second generation in my family to be born in America. All of my great-grandparents were emigrants from areas that were hit hard by the persecution and pogroms in the years leading up to World War I, which became more widespread in the lead-up to World War II. My father's family, including my grandfather Samuel (Schmulik) Sekulow, immigrated from Russia in 1914. They were Jewish people who barely survived economically during the deep discrimination of the time. Seeing the writing on the wall, most of my family got out before the Holocaust, but not all. Some members of my father's family tarried too long and paid the ultimate price. In fact, there's a plaque at our family cemetery in New Jersey that honors two hundred of my relatives on my father's side who were killed in the Holocaust. But, like I said, most of them got out. They were the fortunate ones.

On my mother's side of the family, most were members of the Austrian, Polish, and German Jewish communities. The first members of my mother's family to come to America arrived in 1904. Like my father's family and many Jewish families throughout Europe at the time, some emigrated before the Nazi regime; others did not. As a result, those who stayed in Germany and Austria were completely wiped out during the Holocaust.

We hear a lot about World War II and the Holocaust, but people sometimes forget that this is not ancient history. This isn't like reading about the Romans sacking Jerusalem in A.D. 70; this is my family. My parents were alive during that time. My relatives were right in the middle of it. Hundreds of my relatives died for no other reason than the fact that they were Jewish. So, yes, while I still have to be clinical in making the case, this is also quite personal for me. In fact, even though I have done legal work in Germany over the years, I couldn't bring myself to travel to Berlin until I was in my fifties. I had an aversion to it, a desire to stay away. And it is not at all because of the German people; it's because my family, like so many others, lost so much to the Nazi regime, and those scars run deep—even two generations later.

My grandfather was a Russian Jewish immigrant, who fled for his life and became a fruit peddler in Brooklyn, New York. But just two generations later his grandson gets to argue cases in front of the Supreme Court of the United States. That's amazing. That's how far we've come. And yet, as we have seen, violent anti-Semitism has reared its ugly head from time to time in world history. I personally hope and pray that my family and I never *need* a safe haven in the form of a Jewish homeland to run to, but I certainly want it to exist just in case we do. And I will always defend the Jewish homeland in every way I can.

> I personally hope and pray that my family and I never *need* a safe haven in the form of a Jewish homeland to run to, but I certainly want it to exist just in case we do.

I believe the world needs a Jewish homeland with set, secure boundaries that are recognized and respected by other nations—especially its Arab neighbors. So, now that we've reviewed the legal underpinnings for the existence of the Jewish State in the last chapter, let's take a look at where Israel's legal boundaries are—and why the Arab Palestinians reject them.

PALESTINE AFTER WORLD WAR II

We saw in the previous chapter that, although the Mandate for Palestine did not *require* the division of Palestine, Britain exercised its right as mandatory in 1922 to postpone or withhold application of the mandate to territories *east* of the Jordan Rift Valley. In doing so, Britain informally partitioned the land west of the Jordan Rift Valley for the Jews and assigned the land to the east to the Arabs. In reality, this meant that the Arabs got 77 percent of the original territory of the mandate, leaving only 23 percent for the Jews, the very people for whom the mandate was created in the first place. And, as we've seen,

Britain did this without getting official permission from the League of Nations. This arrangement lasted until the mid-1940s, when the divisions became official in the wake of World War II, which we will discuss in this chapter.

The Division of the Mandate for Palestine

In the years following the defeat of the Axis powers, the British economy was in shambles and its coffers virtually empty. In 1946, Great Britain formally divided the Mandate for Palestine when it recognized "the independence of the Hashemite Kingdom of Jordan" and terminated all British authority over the newly independent kingdom.[2] From that moment until British forces were removed from Palestine in 1948, the Mandate for Palestine consisted only of the territory west of the Jordan Rift Valley.

Even after releasing all responsibility as mandatory for what had become Jordan, Great Britain's postwar financial crisis made it difficult for Britain to bear the costs of its remaining obligations as mandatory in Palestine. Making matters worse, these costs were on the rise due to the growing animosity between Jews and Arabs in Palestine, which British forces had to quell. Accordingly, Britain notified the United Nations, the successor organization to the League of Nations, that it planned to withdraw all remaining British forces from Palestine no later than November 29, 1948.[3]

The Mandate Remained in Force

It's important to note that the British notified the UN because League of Nations mandates did not end with the dissolution of the league.[4] In fact, the UN Charter expressly recognized its responsibility for the mandates upon its formation. Regarding the responsibility for the mandates, the International Court of Justice (ICJ) concluded that such "obligations represent the very essence of the sacred trust of civilization. Their [primary purpose] and original object remain. Since their fulfillment did not depend on the existence of the League of Nations, they could not be brought to an end merely because this supervisory organ ceased to exist."[5]

In response to Britain's notification, the UN General Assembly (UNGA) formed the UN Special Committee on Palestine (UNSCOP) to devise a solution to the increasing violence in Palestine between different communities. UNSCOP ultimately proposed that Palestine be divided into three entities: a Jewish state, an Arab state, and an area around greater Jerusalem to remain under international control.

The terms of the UNSCOP proposal were ultimately set forth in UNGA Resolution 181, which was subsequently adopted by a majority of the UNGA membership.[6] The UN Charter does not grant the UNGA authority to compel compliance with its resolutions.[7] Nevertheless, had both Jewish and Arab Palestinians freely accepted the plan, the issues between them could have been resolved in 1948, thereby dissolving the Mandate for Palestine and bringing its terms to an end with two sovereign states. In fact, Jewish Palestinians did accept the plan. However, Arab Palestinians rejected it, and the UNSCOP resolution failed completely. Hence, the Mandate for Palestine continued in force, having never been dissolved, and according to Article 80 of the UN Charter the terms of the mandate continued to apply to the Jewish people in Palestine.[8]

The significance of Article 80 of the UN Charter is important to understand, but it may be difficult to follow. However, we can trace its significance through a few key conversations. First, in its 1971 Advisory Opinion on Namibia, the International Court of Justice noted the following with respect to Article 80, paragraph 1, of the UN Charter:

> The final words of Article 80, paragraph 1, refer to "the terms of existing international instruments to which Members of the United Nations may respectively be parties." The records of [the conference that drafted the UN Charter] show that these words were inserted in replacement of the words "any mandate" in an earlier draft in order to preserve "*any rights set*

forth in paragraph 4 of Article 22 of the Covenant of the League of Nations."⁹

Article 80 was unofficially known as "the Jewish people's clause" when drafted.[10] Eugene V. Rostow, undersecretary of state for political affairs under President Lyndon Johnson, noted:

> I am indebted to my learned friend Dr. Paul Riebenfeld . . . for reminding me of some of the circumstances which led to the adoption of Article 80 of the Charter. Strong Jewish delegations representing different political tendencies within Jewry attended the San Francisco Conference in 1945. Rabbi Stephen S. Wise, Peter Bergson, Eliahu Elath, Professors Ben-Zion Netanaya and A.S. Yehuda, and Harry Selden were among the Jewish representatives. Their mission was to protect the Jewish right of settlement in Palestine under the mandate against erosion in a world of ambitious states. Article 80 was the result of their efforts.[11]

As such, the UN, *by the terms of its own charter,* was—and still is—obligated to continue to protect the rights of Jews to settle throughout Palestine as set forth in Article 6 of the still-applicable Mandate for Palestine. The explicit right of Jewish settlement throughout the entire area remains fully intact.

> **The UN, *by the terms of its own charter,* was—and still is— obligated to continue to protect the rights of Jews to settle throughout Palestine.**

ISRAEL'S DECLARATION OF INDEPENDENCE

Following the Arab rejection of the UNSCOP plan, both sides readied themselves to deal with the withdrawal of British forces from Palestine. Jewish Palestinians prepared to declare, and then defend, as required, the independence of the newly proclaimed Jewish State of Israel. Arab Palestinians conspired with neighboring Arab states to attack and destroy the newly proclaimed Jewish State of Israel at its birth. Tensions in the region were high, and when the British accelerated their previously announced departure from late November to mid-May 1948, both the Jews and the Arabs knew what would happen next.

INDEPENDENCE AT LAST

Israel declared its independence on May 14, 1948, the night before British forces departed Palestine.[12] After Israel's first prime minister read their declaration of independence, Rabbi Yehuda Leib Maimon, leader of the Religious Zionist movement, read an ancient prayer, "Blessed are You, Lord our God, Ruler of the Universe, who has granted us life, sustained us and enabled us to reach this occasion."[13] The crowd responded with a chorus of "Amen."

> Israel declared its independence on May 14, 1948, the night before British forces departed Palestine.

The very next day, neighboring Arab armies invaded Palestine with the dual purpose of utterly destroying the newly proclaimed Jewish State of Israel and placing all of Palestine under Arab control. Yet, while they assisted and encouraged the invading Arab armies, Arab Palestinians did not declare a state of their own at that time.[14] In fact, the Palestinian Arab leaders waited until 1988—some forty years after Israel had declared itself a state—to declare their independence.[15] Even then, they had to do so from exile in Tunisia because they did not control a single square inch of territory in Palestine.

> The Palestinian Arab leaders waited until 1988—some forty years after Israel had declared itself a state—to declare their independence.

Israel's First-Year Expansion

Fighting between Jewish and Arab forces continued into 1949, when a series of armistice agreements was signed between Israel and neighboring Arab states. During the 1948–1949 fighting, Israel gained control of more territory than it would otherwise have been allocated had the UNSCOP plan been adopted. Israel ended up controlling approximately three-quarters of the territory of the Mandate for Palestine to the west of the Jordan Rift Valley.[16] The vast majority of the international community did not dispute Israel's rightful ownership of all the territory controlled by the new State of Israel at the time the armistice agreements were signed—thereby acknowledging that Israel was the victim of aggression and confirming that aggressors should pay a price for their unlawful conduct.

The international legitimacy of the State of Israel was confirmed when, on May 11, 1949, Israel was admitted as a full member of the United Nations. Despite Israel's entry into the UN, a state of war continued between Israel and its Arab neighbors. The Arab states had insisted that the lines separating Israeli and Arab armed forces at the time of the respective ceasefires be proclaimed armistice lines rather than internationally recognized national boundaries.[17] An armistice line is simply a "geographically defined line from which disputing or belligerent forces disengage and withdraw to their respective sides following a truce or cease fire agreement."[18] It does not signify a legal border. The Arabs demanded the lines be designated armistice lines because none of the Arab states wanted to convey any sense of national legitimacy to the Jewish State of Israel—something that the recognition of armistice lines as international boundaries would have done.

Further, for the next eighteen years, Egypt and Jordan held the territory *not* under Israeli rule under foreign military occupation. As belligerent occupiers, however, Egypt and Jordan had no sovereign authority over the territories they took over. This is due to the important principle under customary international law, *ex injuria jus non oritur*, or "illegal acts cannot create law."[19] In other words, a legal right or entitlement cannot arise from an unlawful act or omission. This principle suggests that any state that acquires land by nondefensive war or other aggressive action cannot claim any legal rights to the land it unlawfully acquired. The Palestinian Arabs in the West Bank and Gaza Strip lived under this foreign Arab military (Jordanian and Egyptian) occupation from the time the various ceasefires were declared in 1949 until Israel regained control over those territories as a result of the wholly defensive 1967 Six-Day War.

The term "West Bank" was used by Jordan to describe the territory it had illegally occupied on the west bank of the Jordan River after engaging in a war of aggression against Israel in 1948–1949. As authors Marc Zell and Sonia Shnyder explain:

> **The term "West Bank" was used by Jordan to describe the territory it had illegally occupied on the west bank of the Jordan River after engaging in a war of aggression against Israel in 1948–1949.**

> When . . . the [Kingdom of Jordan] conquered Judea and Samaria, [the kingdom] was no longer located exclusively across the Jordan on the river's east bank. Since referring to the western Palestinian territories as Judea and Samaria would have evoked a Jewish nexus to the areas and because the term Palestine was problematic for other reasons, the Jordanian bureaucrats invented a new name for the region, calling it the "West Bank."[20]

This is a name that endures today, and—even though it is a naming device designed to separate these regions from Israel—we'll use it here for the sake of clarity.

THE BORDERS OF ISRAEL

During the Jordanian and Egyptian occupation, Jewish residents of the West Bank and Gaza Strip were forced to flee from their homes. But because neither Jordan nor Egypt had any legal right under international law to the territories they occupied, the question remained: To whom did sovereignty over those territories belong?

"As You Possess Under Law"

Because of the confused nature of the situation involving Israelis and Arab Palestinians since the British departed in 1948, identifying Israel's legitimate sovereign borders can seem like a confusing task. Fortunately, there is a legal principle at play here that should help clarify things tremendously—for those willing to take an honest look at the situation.

Determining Israel's true borders largely falls on the international law principle *uti possidetis juris*, which means "as you possess under law."[21] This principle is used for determining territorial sovereignty for "newly created states formed out of territories that previously lacked independence or sovereignty."[22] Legal scholar and professor Steven R. Ratner explains that this principle "provides that states emerging from decolonization shall presumptively inherit the *colonial administrative borders* that they held at the time of independence."[23] As discussed below, the same principle applies to newly independent mandates.

The purpose for this is, as the International Court of Justice determined, to "prevent the independence and stability of new States being endangered by fratricidal struggles provoked by the challenging of frontiers following the withdrawal of the administering power."[24] That is, *uti possidetis juris* exists largely to protect newly formed states from conflicts arising from a dispute over its borders. The principle also requires the passage of the entire territory to the new and subsequent sovereign state, thereby preventing the existence of a territory without a sovereign.[25]

The doctrine is routinely applied even "when it conflicts with the [international law] principle of self-determination."[26] To this point, the International Court of Justice noted that "the maintenance of the territorial *status quo* . . . is often seen as the wisest course, to preserve what has been achieved by peoples who have struggled for their independence."[27]

APPLYING THE LAW TO ISRAEL'S BORDERS

The principle of *uti possidetis juris* has been consistently applied to states emerging from mandates as well.[28] This would clearly include the emergence of the Jewish State of Israel in May 1948. Not only was Israel the only state to emerge from the Mandate for Palestine upon the departure of the British, but Jewish settlements were scattered throughout Palestine, including in areas that were ultimately occupied by Jordanian and Egyptian armed forces. Pursuant to this principle of possession, then, the external borders of the mandate *at the time of Britain's withdrawal* on May 15, 1948, became the borders of the state that emerged. In this case, it was the Jewish State of Israel.

The borders of the mandate on May 15, 1948, were the present-day border with Lebanon, the borders with Syria and Jordan along the Jordan Rift Valley, and the present-day border with Egypt. Accordingly, this means that from the beginning, Israel's lawful borders always included the territories encompassing the present-day State of Israel, the so-called West Bank (Judea, Samaria, and east Jerusalem), and the Gaza Strip, thereby conveying to Israel sovereignty over all of these territories. Of course, Israel, like any other country, has the ability to negotiate its borders, and may cede sovereign territory to others under the right circumstances.

> From the beginning, Israel's lawful borders always included the territories encompassing the present-day State of Israel, the so-called West Bank (Judea, Samaria, and east Jerusalem), and the Gaza Strip, thereby conveying to Israel sovereignty over all of these territories.

THE FIGHT OVER THE WEST BANK AND GAZA STRIP

Despite this legal foundation, Arab Palestinians continue to label these areas "occupied Palestinian territories." The implication here is that these are Arab Palestinian territories that have been illegally occupied by Israel, but that's just not true under international law. Prior to Great Britain's withdrawal from Palestine, *all* inhabitants of Palestine were called Palestinians, so there were both Jewish and Arab Palestinians; today, *Jewish Palestinians* prefer to call themselves Israelis. Nonetheless, Arab Palestinians continually insinuate that Israelis are interlopers who are driving Arab Palestinians from their own country. When one recognizes that Israelis are *Jewish* Palestinians going by another name, this Palestinian hoax is exposed.

Arab Palestinians claim that these lands—the so-called occupied Palestinian territories—will form an eventual Arab state of Palestine.[29] Yet, their claims run counter to the principle of *uti possidetis juris*, which is binding on *all* nations and peoples. For a state or international body to ignore this familiar point of international law is tantamount to willfully ignoring binding precedent simply because they disagree with the outcome. The rule of law is not a light switch that is freely turned on and off but a developed framework of jurisprudence and norms that strive to avoid the kind of conflict that spawned the wars of the past and the deadly terror Israel faces daily. By applying fundamental legal principles like *uti possidetis juris*, the determination under international law is clear: the Arab Palestinians' claims to sovereignty over the West Bank, east Jerusalem, and the Gaza Strip have no basis in law.[30]

> **By applying fundamental legal principles like *uti possidetis juris*, the determination under international law is clear: the Arab Palestinians' claims to sovereignty over the West Bank, east Jerusalem, and the Gaza Strip have no basis in law.**

We've already noted that the West Bank and Gaza Strip territories were under foreign military occupation (by Jordan and Egypt) following the 1948–1949 Arab-Israeli War, which was a clear violation of customary international law.[31] Even though some Arab states and Israel were not members of the UN at that time, they were still bound by the customary legal principle *ex injuria jus non oritur*, "illegal acts cannot create law." So the extended eighteen-year occupation of parts of the mandate's territories by Jordan and Egypt did not grant them or anyone else rights to such land or interrupt Israel's sovereignty there. Rather, "the international law version [of *uti possidetis juris*] *disregards actual possession* and recognizes title on the basis of colonial [i.e., mandatory] administrative lines."[32] The principle operates as follows:

> Where the colonial [mandatory] administrative lines, and the exercise of colonial [mandatory] authority within those lines, were clear, the lines would serve as the boundaries of the new state *even where the new state did not actually possess the territory.* Therefore, a state that acquired territorial sovereignty over territory through *uti possidetis juris* would not lose sovereignty simply because another state possessed and administered part of that territory.[33]

Further, "the international law version [of *uti possidetis juris*] vests *absolute title*" to the territory previously ruled by the colonial power or mandatory in the state that actually emerges—which was unquestionably Israel in this case.[34]

Just to be clear, Israel is not the only illustration of this vital principle at work in modern history. The breakup of Yugoslavia serves as an excellent example showing which international law principle—*uti possidetis juris* or self-determination of peoples—supersedes the other when there is a conflict between the two. The Arbitration Commission of the European Conference on Yugoslavia found, "Whatever the circumstances, *except where the states concerned agree otherwise*, the right to self-determination must not involve changes to existing frontiers existing at the time of independence (*uti possidetis juris*) . . ."[35] This clearly means that *uti possidetis juris* supersedes the internationally recognized right to self-determination when the two are in conflict.

All of this comes down to what I believe is one clear, legally irrefutable finding: The recognition of Israeli sovereignty within the borders of the Mandate for Palestine as they existed on May 15, 1948—which includes the entire West Bank (as well as east Jerusalem) and the Gaza Strip—legally overrides under international law all Arab Palestinian counterclaims that their right to self-determination has been violated. Or, to put it simply, Israel has complete sovereignty over those territories, irrespective of Palestinian claims to the contrary.

WORKING TOWARD RESOLUTION

Over the years, successive Israeli governments have shown sympathy for Arab Palestinians' aspirations of self-determination and have been willing to accommodate them—*up to a point*. As we'll discuss more in the next chapter, Israel has expressed its willingness to negotiate face-to-face with Arab Palestinian leaders in an attempt to fulfill their desire for an independent state. Israel has made it clear that it would even be willing to cede portions of sovereign Israeli territory, but only to the extent that it can ensure the ongoing security and existence of the State of Israel as a Jewish state. To date, these negotiations have gone nowhere. And while Israel has long faced tremendous international pressure to make unilateral concessions, it is well documented that Palestinian Arabs' inflexibility, resistance, and enabling of terrorists to attack Israel have prevented any real progress toward a possible solution.[36]

KEY TAKEAWAYS

1. Israel declared its independence on May 14, 1948, the night before British forces departed Palestine. The neighboring Arab armies invaded Palestine the next day in an attempt to destroy the newly formed Jewish State and to place all of Palestine under Arab control.

2. Pursuant to the international law principle *uti possidetis juris* ("as you possess under law"), the external borders of the Mandate for Palestine at the time of Britain's withdrawal became the borders of the emerging State of Israel. This includes the territories encompassing present-day Israel, the so-called West Bank (Judea, Samaria, and east Jerusalem), and the Gaza Strip (from which Israel withdrew in 2005).

3. Even when other countries illegally and forcefully occupied parts of Israel, Israel never ceded title to the regions.

11

MODERN ISRAEL VS. THE ARAB WORLD

Our battle with the Jews is long and dangerous, requiring all dedicated efforts. It is a phase which must be followed by succeeding phases, a battalion which must be supported by battalion after battalion of the divided Arab and Islamic world until the enemy is overcome, and the victory of Allah descends.

—HAMAS CHARTER, PREAMBLE[1]

We've seen throughout this book that Israel has always faced an endless stream of enemies going back thousands of years. Especially since its inception as an internationally recognized sovereign state, Israel has faced war from its neighbors, as well as daily acts of terror against its territories and against Jews around the world. As I wrote in my previous books *Rise of ISIS* and *Unholy Alliance*, jihadists will use any political opportunity to achieve their number one goal: the destruction of Israel and the elimination of the Jewish people and their allies from the face of the earth. This constant pressure and atmosphere of threats and violence is practically a way of life for the nation of Israel, and it has been that way since its Declaration of In-

> **Jihadists will use any political opportunity to achieve their number one goal: the destruction of Israel and the elimination of the Jewish people and their allies from the face of the earth.**

dependence. Through it all, though, Israel has rightfully maintained its international legal right to exist—and it always will.

In the previous chapter, we examined the legal foundation for Israel's right to exist and its sovereign boundaries. Sadly, Israel's enemies have respected neither. Now, in this chapter, let's run through the major conflicts and territorial challenges that have occurred since the armistice lines were drawn in 1949 and see how the law remains on the side of the Jewish State.

POST-ARMISTICE TENSIONS

The 1948–1949 Arab-Israeli War did not go as well for the Arab aggressors as they'd hoped. In fact, as we've seen, the result of their yearlong war against Israel was the loss of even more territory to Israel than if they had agreed to the UN Special Committee on Palestine's original proposal.[2] Per their cease-fire agreements, the Arabs insisted that the lines separating the Arab and Israeli armed forces be designated armistice lines instead of internationally recognized boundaries. They did this for two reasons: first, to avoid giving any legitimacy to the Jewish State by recognizing international borders; and, second, to avoid making peace with Israel. And let's not forget that, for the next eighteen years, Egypt and Jordan occupied the Gaza Strip and the West Bank, respectively, even though they had no legal right to those territories. With such a tumultuous beginning, the decades that followed brought ceaseless conflict to the region.

Although, under *uti possidetis juris* ("as you possess under law"), Israel was sovereign over the Gaza Strip and the so-called West Bank, it did not exercise actual control of these territories. Neither did Arab Palestinians. Instead, foreign occupiers Egypt and Jordan held the territories, and at no time during their occupation did they seriously offer to relinquish control of the occupied territories to Arab Palestinians. In fact, Jordan even tried to annex the West Bank in 1950, but the vast majority of the international community rejected its efforts. Once again the legal principle *ex injuria jus non oritur*, or "illegal acts cannot create law," came into play. Put simply, Jordan could not and would not be rewarded for its clear wrongdoing.

Although the chief purpose of the armistice agreements was to halt hostilities between the signatories (Israel, Egypt, Jordan, Lebanon, and Syria), hostilities continued. Israel was attacked continually from neighboring Arab-controlled territory. Periodically, Israel counterattacked in an attempt to halt future Arab attacks on Israeli territory, but such efforts were only partially successful.

THE 1956 SUEZ CANAL CRISIS

Anti-colonialist fervor was increasing throughout the Arab world in the early 1950s. In 1955 and 1956, Egypt sought to flex its muscles against Western influence and meddling by striking Israel and asserting control over the Suez Canal. Egyptian president Gamal Abdel Nasser also blockaded the Straits of Tiran, which cut off Israel's access to the Red Sea and Indian Ocean from the Israeli port of Eilat on the Gulf of Aqaba. The blockade was clearly an act of war and violated the armistice agreement Egypt entered into with Israel in 1949.[3] When Nasser nationalized the Suez Canal, British and French leaders invited Israel to join them in drafting a plan to counter Nasser and respond to the Egyptian provocations. Britain and France wanted to regain their control of the Suez Canal, while Israel's principal goals were to capture the Sinai Peninsula in order to lift the blockade of the Straits of Tiran and to stop the fedayeen's, or Arab commandos', attacks from Egyptian-controlled territory on Israeli border settlements.[4]

The 1956 Suez campaign turned out to be a short-lived military success for Israel, but a colossal political failure that ultimately pitted traditional allies Great Britain and France against the United States.[5] The United States had been pursuing a foreign policy to end colonialism, and it believed actions by the British and French against Egypt represented the very colonial threat the United States was fighting against. The timing was poor, too, because the Suez Crisis occurred just as the United States was condemning the Soviets for their invasion of Hungary.

While the Egyptians had been soundly defeated militarily, they

TELWORTH

BIBLE

JITTERBUG

YELLOW PAD

FALSE TEETH

& ~~LUNCHARAC~~

LUNCH

on CARL ST

had won politically. President Nasser's prestige rose throughout the Arab world for having challenged and prevailed against Great Britain and France.[6] The UN ordered Britain, France, and Israel to remove their forces from Egyptian soil. The Israelis refused to comply until the UN established a peacekeeping force, the United Nations Emergency Force (UNEF), to ensure that Egypt did not again blockade the Straits of Tiran to the innocent passage of ships traveling to and from Israel's port of Eilat.[7]

THE SIX-DAY WAR

Relations in the Middle East remained tense in the decade following the Suez Crisis. Despite their political victory in 1956, the Egyptians continued to chafe over their military defeat by Israel. Accordingly, Arab states sought military aid from the Soviet Union, converting the region into an area of Cold War competition among the Great Powers. Throughout the decade, Israel continually faced violence and harassment from surrounding Arab-controlled territories, which ultimately led them back into war.

A Quick War with Significant Consequences

In early 1967, Egypt and Syria escalated tensions in the region by renewing calls for the destruction of the State of Israel.[8] Arab forces moved into position to attack Israel from the Sinai and the Golan Heights, and Nasser demanded that the UN withdraw its peacekeeping force in the Sinai. The UN acquiesced to Nasser's demand, and he reestablished the blockade of the Straits of Tiran.[9] Facing imminent attack from two directions, Israel struck preemptively on June 5, 1967, destroying Arab air forces on the ground and catching the Arab ground forces totally by surprise.[10] Israel warned Jordan that it would face an Israeli counterattack if it opened an additional front. Israel's warning went unheeded, and Jordan joined the fight. In six frenetic days, Israeli military forces utterly routed the Egyptian, Syrian, and Jordanian militaries.[11]

As a result of the so-called Six-Day War in June 1967, Israel gained control of the following territories:

- the Sinai Peninsula from Egypt

- the Gaza Strip from eighteen years of Egyptian military occupation

- the West Bank (including east Jerusalem) from eighteen years of Jordanian military occupation

- the Golan Heights from Syria.[12]

So, just as in the 1948–1949 Arab-Israeli War, Israel had been forced to fight a defensive war that ended in Israeli control of more territory than it had previously controlled. In 1967, this included territory that belonged to foreign aggressors outright (the Egyptian Sinai Peninsula and the Syrian Golan Heights) or had lawfully belonged to Israel but had been under unlawful military occupation (the Gaza Strip and the West Bank). In effect, in six days of intense combat, Israel reacquired sovereign Israeli territory that had been under unlawful foreign military occupation, and it acquired additional territory belonging to Egypt and Syria—a remarkable feat.

> Just as in the 1948–1949 Arab-Israeli War, Israel had been forced to fight a defensive war that ended in Israeli control of more territory than it had previously controlled.

I will point out again that this was a completely legal acquisition of territory under international law. And, in addition to the two legal bases we've already discussed, *uti possidetis juris* ("as you possess under law") and the continuing application of the Mandate for Palestine, Israel now had a third legal defense for its rights to the West Bank and the Gaza Strip. That new defense is the right of a state victim of aggression to take appropriate measures to defend itself, including the right to capture territory held by aggressors in order to ensure the victim state's security and to dissuade future aggression. Article 2 of the UN Charter forbids aggressive war, while Article 51 recognizes the right to individual and collective self-defense. When a victim state is prohibited from retaining control of territory captured in an act of self-defense against an aggressor state, the aggressor has little incentive to halt future attacks. This, in turn, encourages rather than dissuades future conflicts, which is in direct contradiction to the fundamental goals of the UN Charter.

UN Security Council Resolution 242

Following the Six-Day War, the United Nations Security Council (UNSC) adopted UNSC Resolution 242 in an attempt to resolve the Arab-Israeli conflict. The Resolution states, in pertinent part, as follows:

> *The Security Council . . . Affirms* that the fulfillment of Charter principles requires the establishment of a just and lasting peace in the Middle East which should include the application of both the following principles:
>
> (i) Withdrawal of Israeli armed forces from territories occupied in the recent conflict;
>
> (ii) Termination of all claims or states of belligerency and respect for and acknowledgment of the sovereignty, territorial integrity and political independence of every State in the area and their right to live in peace within secure and recognized boundaries free from threats or acts of force.[13]

There is a lot to unpack here, and I want to focus on four key takeaways as they relate to our discussion.

Takeaway #1: Intentionally Vague National Boundaries

First, note that the language in Resolution 242 requires that Israel withdraw "from territories" it occupied—not from "the" territories or "all the" territories it occupied. This is an important, intentional omission meant to keep the determination of Israel's national boundaries vague. Lord Caradon, then permanent representative of the

United Kingdom to the United Nations and chief drafter of Resolution 242, explains the omission:

> Much play has been made of the fact that we didn't say "the" territories or "all the" territories. But that was deliberate. I myself knew very well the 1967 boundaries and if we put in "the" or "all the" that could only have meant that we wished to see the 1967 boundaries perpetuated in the form of a permanent frontier. This I was certainly not prepared to recommend.[14]

So, by this omission, Resolution 242 abstains from committing to a clear definition of Israel's internationally recognized borders—including the previously occupied West Bank and Gaza Strip.

In addition to these two territories, Israel also captured the Sinai Peninsula from Egypt and the Golan Heights from Syria. These areas were also part of the "territories" to which Resolution 242 referred, and Israel has since returned the entire Sinai Peninsula to Egypt pursuant to the peace treaty between the two countries.[15] In fact, Israel has now returned roughly 94 percent of the territories it gained during the Six-Day War. Additionally, land exchanges were also made pursuant to the peace treaty with Jordan.[16] This demonstrates Israel's willingness to comply with the terms of Resolution 242 when Arab nations are serious about making peace.

Also, in this resolution the Security Council recognized Israel as a full-fledged member state subject to the provisions of the United Nations Charter. In contrast, there is no mention whatsoever of Arab Palestinians as either a population group or any sort of political entity, much less a state.

Takeaway #2: Requirement of Secure Boundaries
Second, note that Resolution 242 requires "secure boundaries." These did not exist prior to 1967. If they did, how does one explain the persistent attacks mounted against Israel from Arab-controlled territory? If, as some propose, the 1949 armistice lines—often wrongly referred to as the pre-1967 boundaries—were reestablished to serve as actual

borders, they would be indefensible and do more harm than good by inviting continued attacks against Israel. As such, they could hardly be considered "secure."

Takeaway #3: Respect of Sovereignty

Third, Resolution 242 calls for the termination of all "states of belligerency and respect for and acknowledgment of the sovereignty, territorial integrity and political independence of every State in the area." None of that occurred in the years immediately following the Six-Day War. In fact, shortly after that war ended, the Arab League met in Khartoum, and its members adopted the following common policy regarding Israel: "No peace with Israel, no recognition of Israel, no negotiations with [Israel]." [17]

Despite this belligerent policy, peace was ultimately negotiated with Egypt in 1979 and Jordan in 1994. Here again, it is important to underscore the fact that Israel has demonstrated its willingness to make the difficult decisions necessary to reach peaceful resolutions with its neighbors, when they are ready to reciprocate. This goes as far as implementing a painful decision to remove Israeli settlers and dismantle Israeli settlements when necessary, which Israel did in the Sinai Peninsula pursuant to the Egyptian-Israeli peace treaty of 1979.[18]

Takeaway #4: No Mention of Palestinians

Finally, note that Resolution 242 makes no explicit mention of Arab Palestinians. The resolution refers tangentially at best to the Arab Palestinian population. This potential reference is found where it mentions "achieving a just settlement of the refugee problem" as one of its additional goals for lasting peace in the region.[19] Nowhere else in the resolution is there any connection whatsoever to the Arab population of Palestine. This is no doubt due to the fact that there was no Arab State of Palestine at the time, because none of the belligerent parties in the 1967 war was Palestinian, and because no one (including the Arabs themselves) seriously believed that a Palestinian state was under consideration.

It is also noteworthy that, while the several states involved in the conflict—Egypt, Israel, Jordan, and Syria—were invited to address the United Nations Security Council in its deliberations, no Arab Palestinian representative or official was invited to address the council during the various debates that led to the adoption of the final language of Resolution 242.[20]

CONFUSION REGARDING THE WEST BANK AND GAZA STRIP

The sudden recapture by Israel of the West Bank and Gaza Strip led to a number of questions about how to classify these two territories, as well as how to deal with the areas' Arab inhabitants until the situation was resolved. Israel rightly rejected calling the areas "occupied" (a term from the "law of armed conflict" that connotes controlling land that belongs to a foreign sovereign), because doing so would contradict Israel's claim of sovereignty over them. By definition, a state cannot *occupy* its own territory.[21] Additionally, saying the territories were *occupied* by Israel "could be taken by some as acceptance of the cease-fire lines from 1949 as accepted international borders."[22] That was something Israel was not prepared to do in light of its continuing claims to those territories and because it was not required by UNSC Resolution 242 and successive legal resolutions dealing with the issue.

The international debate around whether Israel was the "sovereign" or "occupier" of the West Bank and Gaza Strip did not, however, impact Israel's commitment to treat the Arab inhabitants well. As such, Israel declared its intention to act *in accordance with* (not pursuant to) customary international law and the humanitarian provisions of the Fourth Geneva Convention. This intention seems consistent with the view of Israeli law professor Yehuda Z. Blum:

> The conclusion to be drawn from all this is that whenever, for one reason or another, there is no concurrence of a normal "legitimate sovereign" with that of a "belligerent occupant" of the territory, only that part of the law of occupation applies which is intended to safeguard the *humanitarian* rights of the population.[23]

So, regardless of how one viewed Israel's claim to the land, Israel held itself to higher standards of treatment than it was obligated to do under international law.

CONFLICTS FROM THE 1970s TO TODAY

Tensions remained high in the region for years following the Six-Day War. Egyptian and Israeli forces engaged in a war of attrition along the Suez Canal. Meanwhile, the Soviet Union massively rearmed the militaries of both Egypt and Syria.[24] This influx of arms came with a considerable emphasis on developing a sophisticated air defense umbrella over ground forces to counter the vaunted skill of the Israeli Air Force (IAF) and deny the IAF air superiority over future battlefields.[25]

1973 YOM KIPPUR WAR

Israel faced a surprise attack in 1973 when it least expected it: on the day of Yom Kippur, the holiest day on the Jewish calendar. Knowing that the entire State of Israel was shut down to observe the Day of Atonement, Egyptian and Syrian armed forces simultaneously attacked the State of Israel, kicking off the eighteen-day Yom Kippur War.[26] When the cease-fire finally went into effect, the Israeli military had rallied and decisively defeated both the Egyptian and Syrian forces. Israeli troops had trapped an entire Egyptian army east of the Suez Canal, and Israel Defense Forces (IDF) soldiers were on the west bank of the Suez Canal, just over sixty miles from Cairo.[27] Additionally, the IDF pushed the Syrian army completely out of the portions of the Golan Heights that the Syrians had taken back in the opening days of the war, advanced and conquered additional Syrian territory, and halted its attack approximately twenty-five miles from Damascus—well beyond what Israel had achieved in the 1967 war.[28] In response to the 1973 Yom Kippur War, the United Nations Security Council adopted Resolution 338, which essentially renewed the call for implementing the terms of UNSC Resolution 242, which called for Israeli withdrawal from territories it had captured in the

1967 War, an end to belligerency in the region, and the establishment of secure borders and recognition of sovereignty for Israel.[29]

THE INTERNATIONALIZATION OF THE ARAB-ISRAELI CONFLICT

The period following the Yom Kippur War led to an increased internationalization of the Arab-Israeli conflict. From 1973 to today, there have been several key altercations, declarations, and other moments that have led to where we are in the case for Israel today. I'm sure whole books could be written about each of these events, but for our purposes here, I'll just give a chronological thirty-thousand-foot view of the conflict from the last forty years:

- 1974 (November): The Palestine Liberation Organization (PLO) was granted observer status at the UN.[30]

- 1975 (November): The UN General Assembly passed a resolution attacking the legitimacy of the State of Israel by equating Zionism with racism.[31]

- 1976 (July): Palestinian and German terrorists hijacked an Air France flight that departed Tel Aviv with an intended destination of Paris, which was diverted by the terrorists to Entebbe, Uganda. All passengers were released except the Jews, who were held hostage as the hijackers demanded that Israel release fellow terrorists serving time for their crimes. This led to the remarkable Israeli commando raid that freed all but one of the hostages and returned them safely to Israel.[32] Notably, the only Israeli soldier killed during the operation was Jonathan Netanyahu, the brother of future prime minister Benjamin Netanyahu.

- 1977 (November): Egyptian president Anwar Sadat accepted Israeli prime minister Menachem Begin's offer to visit Jerusalem to address the Knesset. This began the process that ultimately led to the signing of a peace treaty between Egypt and Israel in 1979.[33]

- 1982 (June): Israel invaded Lebanon to expel PLO leaders from that country after a Palestinian assassination attempt maimed Israel's ambassador to London. The IDF then occupied the southern portion of Lebanon to halt attacks against Israel's northern settlements.[34]

- 1987 (December): The first Arab intifada began. "Intifada" literally translates as "shaking off" and is used to describe specific Palestinian uprisings with widespread Palestinian support against Israel in the West Bank and Gaza Strip.[35] And, as a result, the Muslim Brotherhood in the Gaza Strip formed Hamas.[36]

- 1988 (November): PLO leader Yasir Arafat declared Palestinian statehood while in exile in Tunisia. He did this despite the fact that the Palestinians did not control a single square inch of territory in Palestine.[37]

- 1991 (October): The United States and the Soviet Union sponsored the Madrid conference, which brought together representatives from Israel, Lebanon, Syria and Jordan, as well as Arab Palestinian officials, for the first time since 1949.[38]

- 1993 (September): Israeli prime minister Yitzhak Rabin and Yasir Arafat signed the Oslo Declaration.[39]

- 1994 (May): Pursuant to the terms of the Oslo Accords, Israel began withdrawing from most of the Gaza Strip and the area around Jericho to allow the Palestinian Authority to establish itself.[40]

- 1994 (October): Jordan and Israel signed a peace agreement.[41]

- 1995 (September): Israeli prime minister Yitzhak Rabin and PLO leader Arafat signed the Interim Agreement to transfer further responsibility to the Palestinian Authority.[42] The purpose of these agreements was to create a transitional period wherein the vast majority of Arab Palestinians in the

West Bank and Gaza Strip would be placed under the leadership of the autonomous Palestinian Authority. During this period, negotiations were intended to resolve agreed-upon final status issues between Israel and the Palestinians, including borders, settlements, refugees, Jerusalem, and security arrangements. The interim agreement formed the basis for the 1997 Hebron Protocol and the 1998 Wye River Memorandum.[43]

• 2000 (July): Talks broke down between Israelis and Palestinians as Arafat walked away from a generous deal.[44]

• 2001: Palestinian violence against Israel, including a spate of suicide bombings, flared up again.[45]

• 2002: Due to the increasing incidents of suicide bombings, the IDF conducted a massive military operation in the West Bank. Further, Israel began building a security barrier to stop suicide bombers from entering Israel proper.[46]

• 2003 (April): The international community sponsored the so-called road map for peace in an attempt to restart negotiations between Israelis and Palestinians.[47]

• 2008 (September): Israeli prime minister Ehud Olmert negotiated a generous agreement with Palestinian Authority president Mahmoud Abbas, but Abbas rejected the agreement at the last minute.[48]

Again, the point of this quick review of key moments from the past forty years is not to provide a full, detailed history but to give a basic chronology of events in the ongoing conflict. It was at this point—2009—that I became more personally involved in the courtroom battles.

THE INTERNATIONAL CRIMINAL COURT

In Chapter 9, I started the section on Israel's legal defense by talking about how the ACLJ and I presented our first case on Israel's behalf before the International Criminal Court (ICC). At this point in the chronology of the last forty years, it's worthwhile to revisit that case and see its impact in historical context. I was in Israel during this time, witnessing the conflict to get a firsthand look at the daily dangers facing Israel and its people.

In 2009, following Israeli offensive Operation Cast Lead and the withdrawal of Israel Defense Forces from the Gaza Strip, the Palestinians attempted to bring charges before the ICC against Israeli political and military leaders for alleged war crimes and crimes against humanity.[49] We at the ACLJ got involved and pulled together the world-class team of legal minds from the various countries we discussed earlier. We were prepared, polished, and professional. We quickly found out, however, that the ICC was not.

Before we presented our case, some members of our team and I sat in on a trial at The Hague that was unrelated to the case against Israel. We just wanted to see the court in action to get a better understanding of what we were up against. Needless to say, the proceedings were not what we expected. It was nothing at all like American courts, where certain rules of propriety require some degree of fundamental fairness and objectivity. Our entire team was surprised at how drastically different the proceedings were, and we discussed later how we would never want any Israeli or American soldier to be subjected to such procedures.

We returned to the ICC for a second meeting with the prosecutor in 2010 at his request. This was the meeting I discussed before, where four people from our team and four people from the Palestinian side met for what the prosecutor called a "roundtable." The issue at hand was whether or not the Palestinians could even bring a case before the ICC, given that they did not have state status (a requirement for ICC cases). Convening such a debate came as a huge surprise to us. The ICC is a criminal court, yet the prosecutor acted as if he were a law professor running a moot court competition, not a criminal prosecutor dealing with serious crimes.

The entire procedure was almost farcical and clearly one-sided. The movements of the pro-Israel side were closely monitored and controlled throughout our visit to the court's facilities, while the pro-

Palestinian side was allowed to roam freely throughout the building unmonitored. There was no attempt whatsoever to appear unbiased and objective between the two sides. Moreover, despite having been provided with the rules for the roundtable in advance, at the very outset of the proceedings, just as I was about to begin speaking, I was informed that the rules had been revised. Having traveled three thousand miles to make the case, I wasn't going to take that sitting down and immediately challenged the changes.

Given my forceful response, the prosecutor quickly backed down and reinstated the original rules. What was especially telling during the debate was that each member of the pro-Israel side was focused and well prepared, and argued the law and facts correctly. The pro-Palestinian side, on the other hand, resorted to emotional arguments and personal attacks against Israel rather than relying on legal arguments. Although it was obvious to us that the prosecutor was looking for a way to permit the Palestinians to accede to ICC jurisdiction, the law was clearly on our side and he could not refute our legal and factual arguments. Moreover, he would have been seriously embarrassed had he nonetheless granted access to the Palestinians. The ICC prosecutor ultimately accepted our arguments and rejected the Palestinian attempt to accede to ICC jurisdiction on the basis that Palestine was, in fact, not a state. The prosecutor did suggest, however, that Palestine would likely be able to accede if the UN were to recognize Palestinian statehood.[50] The Palestinians then sought to obtain full admission to the UN via the UN Security Council, which rejected its request.

In response to the UN Security Council's rejection, the Palestinians turned to the UN General Assembly, which agreed to change Palestine's status from "Entity" with observer status to "nonmember State" with observer status.[51] With this change, the Palestinians then sought to accede to the ICC once again. This time they succeeded. Later, in 2016, the Palestinians sought help from the UN Security Council to condemn Israeli settlements in the so-called occupied Palestinian territories. Because of the Obama administration's decision to abstain on the vote, Security Council Resolution 2334—which calls Israeli settlements in the West Bank and east Jerusalem illegal and wholly disregards Israel's legitimate claims to the territories—was passed.[52]

THE TWO-STATE SOLUTION

After considering all of this legal, political, and military history, it is reasonable to ask: What is the solution to the seemingly irreconcilable, ongoing Israeli-Palestinian impasse? As noted earlier, successive Israeli governments have stated that they sympathize with Arab Palestinians' aspirations for statehood and self-rule.[53] Although a people's right to self-determination yields to *uti possidetis juris* when conflicts arise between the two, Israel has nonetheless agreed *in principle* to negotiate bilaterally with Palestinian leaders in an attempt to reach an agreement.

> After considering all of this legal, political, and military history, it is reasonable to ask: What is the solution to the seemingly irreconcilable, ongoing Israeli-Palestinian impasse?

However, such an agreement would need to permit Israelis to remain safe and secure in the Jewish State of Israel while Arab Palestinians govern themselves in their own state. To date, Palestinian intransigence has prevented such a resolution to the conflict.

Even though, pursuant to *uti possidetis juris*, the State of Israel can claim sovereignty over the entirety of the territory of the Mandate for Palestine within the borders as they existed on May 15, 1948, there is nothing in international law to preclude a state from deciding freely and intentionally to divest itself of territory it otherwise lawfully possesses. This has happened on several notable occasions in the not-too-distant past, including the breakup of Yugoslavia, the Soviet Union, and Czechoslovakia. Hence, should Israelis and Palestinians enter into serious negotiations without preconditions, there should be no reason why an Arab Palestinian state could not someday come into existence.

The major impediment to establishing an Arab Palestinian state is Palestinian reluctance to make the difficult concessions and compromises that such negotiations will undoubtedly require. Further, in order to achieve what they claim they desire—*a viable, independent Arab Palestinian state living in peace with Israel*—Palestinian leaders will have to engage in direct negotiations with Israel rather than indirectly appealing to the UN and other organizations and states. Until the Palestinians are prepared to negotiate seriously via good-faith bilateral negotiations with Israel and acknowledge Israel's right to exist as a Jewish state, their desire for a state will remain unrealized.

> **Until the Palestinians are prepared to negotiate seriously via good-faith bilateral negotiations with Israel and acknowledge Israel's right to exist as a Jewish state, their desire for a state will remain unrealized.**

THE LAW IS CLEAR

Throughout the previous three chapters, we have reviewed the legal underpinnings for Israel's declaration of independence and established that Israel has a clear legal right to exist. We've also reviewed the arguments for Israel's right to the territories to which it lays claim. In conclusion, without rehashing every detail, it is important to hit the three main legal defenses one last time:

1. *Uti possidetis juris* ("as you possess under law"): As the only state to emerge from the Mandate for Palestine upon the departure of all British forces in May 1948, the then-nascent Jewish State of Israel gained absolute title to all territory within the previous administrative boundaries of the mandate (which, in turn, pursuant to *uti possidetis juris*, became the legal boundaries of the State of Israel).[54] Accordingly, Israel also gained sovereignty over all such territories, even those that were under belligerent foreign military occupation for eighteen years (the West Bank and Gaza Strip).[55]

2. **The continuing applicability of the Mandate for Palestine:** As mandatory, Britain defined the Jewish State's

boundaries as the territory west of the Jordan Rift Valley, which included the area now known as the West Bank and the Gaza Strip. The mandate's definition of Israel's boundaries did not dissolve upon Great Britain's departure in 1948 or upon Israel's membership into the United Nations.[56] These mandate provisions are still considered binding and the UN is still required to enforce them, thereby permitting continuing settlement by Jews in the West Bank (including east Jerusalem) and the Gaza Strip.

3. Capture of the West Bank and Gaza Strip as self-defense: Even if Israel did not physically control these territories prior to 1967, it would still have a valid legal claim to them after the Six-Day War of 1967. Because Israel acted and took control of the territories in self-defense against serial aggressors, they are not obligated to return control of them to the aggressor states. That would be a violation of the legal principle *ex injuria jus non oritur* ("illegal acts cannot create law"), designed to penalize aggressors and prevent future attacks.

Despite its clear legal sovereignty over these areas, as we have seen, Israel continues to encourage peace in the region by entering into and inviting negotiations with its Arab neighbors. If such a peaceful resolution is to occur, however, it will require Israel's enemies to finally engage in well-intentioned, meaningful bilateral talks— a step, I'm afraid, most of Israel's enemies have been unwilling to take.

KEY TAKEAWAYS

1. Israel gained control of the West Bank (including east Jerusalem), the Gaza Strip, the Sinai Peninsula, and the Golan Heights during the Six-Day War of 1967, in which Israel defeated Egyptian, Syrian, and Jordanian aggressors.

2. Consistent with the terms of UN Security Council Resolution 242 of 1967, Israel has repeatedly stated that it is ready to negotiate in good faith with its Arab neighbors. Israel has demonstrated that it is prepared to make the difficult decisions peace requires by entering into peace treaties with Egypt (which required the complete return of the Sinai Peninsula to Egyptian control) and with Jordan.

3.   Israel has also repeatedly agreed in principle to negotiate bilaterally with Palestinian leaders to resolve the seemingly irreconcilable conflict. Such a solution would need to permit Israelis to remain safe and secure in the Jewish State of Israel while Arab Palestinians govern themselves in their own state. To date, Palestinians have rejected such efforts.

SECTION V

JERUSALEM, THE ETERNAL CAPITAL OF ISRAEL

From the establishment of the Provisional Government we made the peace, the security and the economic consolidation of Jerusalem our principal care. In the stress of war, when Jerusalem was under siege, we were compelled to establish the seat of Government in Tel Aviv. But for the State of Israel there has always been and always will be one capital only—Jerusalem the Eternal. Thus it was 3,000 years ago—and thus it will be, we believe, until the end of time.[1]

—PRIME MINISTER DAVID BEN-GURION, DECEMBER 13, 1949

12

JERUSALEM'S SPIRITUAL AND HISTORICAL SIGNIFICANCE

If I forget you, Jerusalem, may my right hand forget its skill. May my tongue cling to the roof of my mouth if I do not remember you, if I do not consider Jerusalem my highest joy.

—*PSALM 137:5–6*

Jerusalem is always in the news. Obviously, this is true in modern times. You can hardly watch cable news or read a newspaper without seeing some report about Jerusalem. But Jerusalem's impact and renown isn't new; this has been the case for thousands of years. In the New Testament book of Luke, in fact, two first-century travelers were walking down the road toward a village called Emmaus, which was about seven miles outside of Jerusalem. As they walked, a stranger (whom the Bible says was the resurrected Jesus) came up to them and asked what they were talking about. Their response was the same as what you might hear today if you were to ask someone in the Israeli airport what they were talking about: "Are you the only one visiting Jerusalem who does not know the things that have happened there in these days?" (Luke 24:13–18). Jerusalem, it seems, has always been the center of news, faith, history, politics, conflict, and suspense. It is also the center of hope for the Jewish people. And it's no wonder why.

Jerusalem has a rich religious and spiritual history, second to no other city in the world. The three major monotheistic faiths of the world claim Jerusalem either as their religious center or as having special significance. Beyond that, Jewish and Arab nations have long laid claim to the city of Jerusalem as their capital. In fact, both Israel and the Palestinians currently claim Jerusalem as their capital, making this the most sought-after and contested piece of real estate in the world. And yet, despite the conflicting views, legal arguments, and debates, let me be absolutely clear on this point: Jerusalem is the capital—the *eternal* capital—of the Jewish State of Israel. I know this is a bold statement in today's political climate, but I

> **Despite the conflicting views, legal arguments, and debates, let me be absolutely clear on this point: Jerusalem is the capital—the *eternal* capital—of the Jewish State of Israel.**

can back it up. In this chapter and the next, we are going to zero in on Jerusalem and discuss why it is deemed so significant to Jews, Christians, and Muslims; why world nations have debated about the location of their embassies; and how history and international law support my assertions here. This is a contentious argument on the world stage, so let's understand what this struggle is all about.

THE SIGNIFICANCE OF JERUSALEM

The significance of Jerusalem predates modern history. Any combination of the administrative, economic, educational, and cultural grounds we'll discuss might be enough for the nations of the world to recognize Jerusalem as Israel's capital. However, the religious division—particularly the precarious coexistence of three great religions in and around Jerusalem's Old City and the Temple Mount—has been the primary obstacle to a final resolution. Politically, both Israelis and Palestinians claim Jerusalem as their capital—the Israelis in the practical and real sense as their current seat of government, and the Palestinians in terms of an aspirational future in which Jerusalem might return to its control. Even the religious denominations within a single tradition face conflict over Jerusalem. The Church of the Holy Sepulcher only just began renovations in 2016 over damage from an earthquake in 1927, simply because the different Christian officials could not agree over the specifics.[2] The Church of the Holy Sepulcher is ruled by six distinct branches of Christianity, each vying to maintain its own stake over the space. The dysfunction is so great that the same wooden ladder has been resting outside a window since the 1750s because no one dares touch the ladder or claim responsibility for its existence.[3] Further, to maintain peace, the keys to the church have been entrusted to the same Muslim family for generations.

With these conflicts in mind, we have to ask the key question: *What makes Jerusalem so special?*

JERUSALEM AS THE POLITICAL CAPITAL

Jerusalem has been the site of all three branches of Israeli government—executive, legislative, and judicial—since Israel's first prime minister, David Ben-Gurion, described it as the "eternal capital" of Israel during his December 5, 1949 message.[4] The Basic Law of Israel, the bedrock of modern Israeli law, proclaims, "Jerusalem, complete and united, is the capital of Israel" and "the seat of the President of the State, the Knesset, the Government and the Supreme Court."[5] These statements, while seemingly simple, have proven to be some of the most contentious in the modern era.

> **"Jerusalem, complete and united, is the capital of Israel" and "the seat of the President of the State, the Knesset, the Government and the Supreme Court."**

In addition to being the base of the three main branches of the Israeli government, Jerusalem has become home to many leading financial, media, educational, and cultural institutions. These include the Bank of Israel (the central bank of the State of Israel), the Israel Broadcasting Authority (along with other national and international television and radio broadcasting media), and leading national print media, such as the *Jerusalem Post* and the *Times of Israel*. Jerusalem is the location of three of Israel's leading colleges and universities: Hebrew University (ranked among the top one hundred universities in the world), Al-Quds University (Israel's leading Arab and Palestinian University), and the Jerusalem College of Technology. Leading cultural institutions based in Jerusalem include the Israel Museum, Israel's national cemetery at Mount Herzl, the Yad Vashem national Holocaust memorial, the Jewish National and University Library, and many more.

You may have assumed by watching the news that Tel Aviv is the capital of Israel, but that's not the case. Tel Aviv is certainly a major, influential Israeli city, but it is not the seat of government. While significant functions of Israel's financial, technological, and defense sectors are based in Tel Aviv, and although Tel Aviv is currently the home of many national embassies, Jerusalem is the administrative capital of the country.

JERUSALEM AS THE RELIGIOUS CENTER

In *From Empire to Empire: Jerusalem Between Ottoman and British Rule*, Abigail Jacobson writes:

> [Jerusalem] is mentioned in the Bible by name seven hundred times, and by the name *Zion* (indicating first the Temple Mount, then Jerusalem as the capital city, and later Palestine as a whole) some 150 times. It served as the capital of the country three times; it received its special political status from King David and King Solomon, the latter built the temple on the site that was purchased earlier by King David and was called the Temple Mount (Har ha-Bayit in Hebrew). This is also the site the Bible refers to as the site in which Abraham was willing to sacrifice his son Isaac.[6]

While the overwhelming 850 references in the Bible clearly demonstrate the city's religious centrality, those mentions only begin to tell the story of Jerusalem's spiritual significance.

As we've seen, Jerusalem is a center of the three great Abrahamic religions. As such, many sites in Israel, particularly in Jerusalem, have religious significance to Jews, Christians, and Muslims. On this point, the Basic Law provides:

> The Holy Places shall be protected from desecration and any other violation and from anything likely to violate the freedom of access of the members of the different religions to the places sacred to them or their feelings towards those places.[7]

That is, protecting the sites and granting access to adherents of all three faith groups is a key provision of fundamental Israeli law.

Enforcing that law isn't always easy, as the international community views Israel as lawfully controlling only the western half of Jerusalem—a view the Israeli government vehemently rejects. And yet, today the world continues to view Jerusalem as divided between west Jerusalem—which was acquired by Israel in the 1948–1949 Arab-Israeli War—and east Jerusalem (including the Old City), which was acquired by Israel in the 1967 Six-Day War following eighteen years of unlawful Jordanian military occupation and which has since been incorporated as part of Israel's undivided capital. The international community has rejected Israel's presence in east Jerusalem and considers it to be part of "Palestinian territory" that is "illegally occupied" by Israel—a claim we have already thoroughly discredited in previous chapters. Complicating the matter is the fact that the Old City in east Jerusalem is also the location of the Temple Mount, which is both the holiest and most disputed site in Jerusalem and therefore all of Israel. This dispute is one of many that bring truth to the words of the prophet Zechariah,

"On that day, when all the nations of the earth are gathered against her, I will make Jerusalem an immovable rock for all the nations. All who try to move it will injure themselves."

"On that day, when all the nations of the earth are gathered against her, I will make Jerusalem an immovable rock for all the nations. All who try to move it will injure themselves" (Zech. 12:3).

There will always be an inherent inseparability in Jerusalem between religion and politics. As a study of sacred space where God and people meet, each of the three great monotheistic religions seeks a physical link to Jerusalem, which is why it is extremely important to recognize and understand why the city is so significant to each.

SIGNIFICANCE OF JERUSALEM TO JUDAISM

Jerusalem exists as both a political and religious focal point for the Jewish people, as it is the seat of Israel's secular government and the site of countless religious places, including the Kotel, the remaining retaining wall of the Temple Mount, also known as the Western Wall. Within the Jewish tradition, the city is associated with where the Messiah will eventually come, where the Third Temple will be built, and where a reestablished monarchy will usher in a great era of peace.[8] Notably, Israeli social, legal, and political conflicts related to religious issues in Jerusalem are uniquely rooted in the history of Israel and the Jewish people.[9] These conflicts are not isolated examples to be considered in a vacuum but part of the grander narrative of how these religious traditions coexist together.

The Temple Mount is of paramount importance to Judaism. Located in the Old City, the Temple Mount is on the site Jews have historically associated with the biblical Mount Moriah. This is hallowed ground to Jews, believed to have been a holy site long before the existence of the Temple. In fact, Jewish tradition teaches that this site was the starting point for the Creation of the world, the place from which the whole earth expanded. As the Midrash, the ancient Bible commentary, explains:

> The Almighty created the world in the same manner as a child is formed in its mother's womb. Just as a child begins to grow from its navel and then develops into its full form, so the world began from its central point and then developed in all directions. The navel of the world is Jerusalem, and its core is the great altar in the Holy Temple.[10]

When God drew the dust to form Adam (Gen. 2:7), he drew it from the peak of Mount Moriah.[11] When Abraham bound Isaac as a sacrifice (Gen. 22:2), he did so on the very spot where the Jewish Temple would one day stand. When Jacob dreamed of angels (Gen. 28:10–18), his head was resting on Mount Moriah's rock. When the Holy Temple was finally built, the Shechina (the Divine Presence) settled there forever (2 Chron. 5:2–14).

> The land of Jerusalem is unquestionably tied to the Jewish faith in a unique way, and, as such, the Jewish people will never turn their back on it.

The land of Jerusalem is unquestionably tied to the Jewish faith in a unique way, and, as such, the Jewish people will never turn their back on it.

SIGNIFICANCE OF JERUSALEM TO CHRISTIANITY

In Christianity, Jerusalem is significant as the location of much of Jesus's ministry, as well as the location of His death, burial, resurrection, and ascension. Because of those events, Jerusalem is considered the center of the Christian religion. Sites like the Mount of Olives, the Garden of Gethsemane, the Way of the Cross, the Garden Tomb, and the Church of the Holy Sepulcher continue to attract Christian pilgrims from around the globe.[12]

In an attempt to preserve and control the Christian holy sites of Jerusalem, Christians entered Jerusalem in the fourth century under the rule of Constantine.[13] Christian powers remained in Jerusalem until the Arab conquest in A.D. 632, then returned again at the end of the eleventh century with the advent of the Crusades.[14]

The New Testament clearly explains that "Jerusalem symbolizes the new people of God redeemed by the Messiah, Jesus Christ."[15] Christians believe that Jerusalem is the location where a victorious Christ will one day return through the Eastern (or Golden) Gate, walking from the Mount of Olives. This triumphant return is a key part of the Christian faith, as Christians look expectantly toward the One who will judge the world of sin and reign and rule for one thousand years.[16]

Jerusalem is also important for Judaism's sake to the growing number of Christians who consider themselves to be "Christian Zionists." While different Christian denominations have varying opinions regarding Israel's place in prophetic history, Christian Zionists view the establishment of the modern State of Israel as the fulfillment of Ezekiel's "dry bones" prophecy, which we discussed in Chapter 4. As such, this particular Christian community is committed to supporting Israel's rights as a nation, including their rights in and to Jerusalem.

Significance of Jerusalem to Islam

Historically, Jerusalem was under Muslim rule for nearly thirteen centuries, beginning in the first half of the seventh century A.D., when the Muslims occupied Jerusalem during the reign of the second Muslim caliph, 'Umar ibn al-Khattab (A.D. 636).[17] Named Aelia, "the City of the Temple," early Islam recognized Jerusalem as a significant location because the Prophet Mohammad visited the tomb of the Prophet Ibrahim (Abraham) in Hebron (al-Khalil) and the Church of the Nativity in Bethlehem, where the Prophet Jesus ('Isa) was born.[18] Since Islam respects all the prophets before the time of Mohammad, the holiness of Jerusalem is important to the Islamic faith.

Jerusalem is considered the third-holiest city in Islam after Mecca and Medina, and it has historically served as a pilgrimage site for Muslims for prayer, study, and residence.[19] The Al Aqsa Mosque, built on the Temple Mount, marks the place in the Islamic tradition where the events of the Isra and Mi'raj took place. The tradition is that Muhammad traveled on the steed Buraq to the "farthest mosque" and prayed there before visiting heaven and speaking with God. Upon returning to earth, Muhammad brought with him new rules regarding prayer that Islam adopted and uses to this day.

> **Jerusalem is considered the third-holiest city in Islam after Mecca and Medina.**

THE HISTORY OF JERUSALEM

We have already spent a lot of time in this book reviewing the history of Israel, detailing its entire four-thousand-year journey. That

history is important to any student of Israel, and it is especially relevant now, with the Balfour Declaration of 1917 having just celebrated
its one-hundredth anniversary and the Six-Day War of 1967 having
just hit the fifty-year mark. Now, as we turn our focus to Jerusalem,
it's important to take a quick look at what impact all of those events
throughout history have had on Israel's capital city.

ANCIENT JERUSALEM

Jerusalem is rather unique in the world. I can't think of another city
that can trace their roots back over three millennia, but Jerusalem
can. A fifteen-month celebration kicked off on September 4, 1995,
to commemorate the three-thousandth anniversary of Jerusalem as
Israel's capital. A portion of Jerusalem actually dates back a thousand
years further. The area known as the City of David, near the Old
City, has been inhabited since the fourth millennium B.C. As described in 2 Samuel 5, Jerusalem's roots go back to King David, who
conquered the city from the Jebusite people and united the kingdoms
of Judah and Israel to form the Kingdom of Israel.[20]

King David moved his capital from the Judean capital of Hebron
to Jerusalem in 1006 B.C.[21] His son and successor, King Solomon,
constructed the First Temple at Jerusalem in 957 B.C. As we've discussed already in this book, the biblical nation of Israel was divided
under King Rehoboam, splitting the region into two kingdoms, Israel and Judah. The kingdom of Judah would continue to exist as
a separate state, with Jerusalem as its capital, until 586 B.C., when
it was conquered by the Babylonian Empire. A small community of
Jewish people remained in their homeland, but the majority of the
nation was exiled. In 538 B.C., Cyrus the Great of Persia allowed the
Jews held captive in Babylon to return to Judah in order to rebuild
the Temple, and that Second Temple was completed in 516 B.C.[22]
Jerusalem was besieged and conquered once again sometime after
485 B.C. and rebuilt around 445 B.C. At this point it again served as
the capital of Judah and a center of Jewish worship.

Alexander the Great, the Ptolemaic dynasty of Egypt, and the

Hellenistic Seleucid Empire subsequently conquered Jerusalem. Following the Maccabean Revolt of 168 B.C., Jerusalem became the capital of the Hasmonean Empire in 152 B.C.[23] The Romans began their efforts to gain control over Judah, including Jerusalem, in 68 B.C., sparring with Hasmoneans, Parthians, and eventually the Edomite leader Herod. Herod was installed by the Romans as a client king and embarked on a number of building projects in Jerusalem, including the expansion of the Temple Mount area.

ROMAN, ARAB, AND CRUSADER RULE

The Jewish people rose up against their Roman rulers in the First Jewish-Roman War from A.D. 66–73, and the Second Temple was subsequently destroyed in the Roman siege of Jerusalem in A.D. 70.[24] Following the Bar Kokhba revolt of A.D. 132–135, the Romans combined the province of Iudaea (Judea) with surrounding territory, renaming it as the province of Syria Palaestina. The city of Jerusalem was renamed Aeolia Capitolina and rebuilt in a Roman style. Jews were prohibited from entering Jerusalem during this period with only one exception. They were allowed into the city on the holiday of Tisha B'Av, known as the saddest day of the Jewish calendar and intended to commemorate disasters of Jewish history, including the destructions of the two Temples.

These prohibitions were also applied to Christians and essentially "secularized" the city until the seventh century. Beginning in the fourth century, however, the Romans allowed the Christians to construct religious sites, most notably the Church of the Holy Sepulcher on the reputed site of the crucifixion and burial of Jesus Christ. Archaeological evidence suggests that the city's population was primarily Christian at the time.

PRE-OTTOMAN MUSLIM RULE IN JERUSALEM

In the fifth century A.D., Jerusalem passed from Roman, to Byzantine, to Persian, and then back to Roman-Byzantine rule before ultimately landing in Muslim hands for an extended period. This series of transitions can best be seen in a simple chronology:

- A.D. 629: The Persians lost Jerusalem to the Byzantines.

- A.D. 638: Jerusalem was conquered by Arab Muslims. This kicked off a period of Islamization of Jerusalem as Arab powers vied for control of Jerusalem for roughly four hundred years.

- 1073: The Seljuk Turks captured the city.

- 1098: The North Africa–based Fatimid Caliphate recaptured Jerusalem.

- 1099: The Fatimids expelled the Christians from Jerusalem. This sparked the Crusades, during which the Christian victors massacred the city's Jewish and Muslim populations and set up the Kingdom of Jerusalem.[25] Eastern Christians who had been displaced from the city began to return and repopulate.

- 1187: Saladin, the Muslim sultan of Egypt and Syria, regained control and allowed Jews, Muslims, and Eastern Christians to remain in the city.

- 1229: Jerusalem returned to Christian control following a general decline of the city throughout the thirteenth century.

- 1244: Jerusalem was sacked and fell under the control of Persian Tatars, who destroyed Christian communities and drove out most of the Jews.

- 1260–1517: Jerusalem was ruled by the Egyptian Mamluks. Jews and Christians were afforded various rights during this period, and Christian pilgrimage to Jerusalem was common.

This frequent turnover of the city ended in 1517, when the Ottoman Turks conquered Jerusalem and began a four-hundred-year reign.

JERUSALEM UNDER OTTOMAN RULE

The Ottoman leader Suleiman the Magnificent (1494–1566) resurrected the city from relative obscurity and embarked on many construction projects, including building the walls surrounding the Old City, which remain to this day. He also laid the foundations of the millet system, which regulated relations between the city's different religious communities. As we've discussed in previous chapters, this period was generally one of prosperity, peace, and modernization. Despite its lack of any economic, military, or political significance to the Ottoman Empire, they considered Jerusalem to be of great *religious* importance, as it was regarded as the third-holiest site in Islam after Mecca and Medina.[26]

In the early nineteenth century, foreign missions and consulates began to appear in the city.[27] Despite the Islamic law that provided certain rights and protections to *dhimmi*s (non-Muslims), Christians and Jews were occasionally the targets of attacks and general religious discord. By the mid-1800s, international powers, through their consulates, began pushing for protection of religious minorities in Palestine, as the territory was then still known, and the volume of Christian pilgrimages to the region began to increase.[28] It was also in the nineteenth century that the four quarters of the city (Jewish, Muslim, Christian, and Armenian) were given their modern designations and boundaries, although these had been recognized since the medieval period.

By this point Jerusalem and the region of Palestine had returned to the stage of international politics with Napoleon's 1798 invasion of Egypt. This revived European interest in the region and its holy places. Napoleon desired not simply to conquer Egypt but to transfer "contemporary French civilization to the historic cradle of civilization."[29] The Crimean War (1854–1856) further cemented Jerusalem's international importance and served as the pretext for war between a Franco-Ottoman alliance and Russia over control of the Holy Land. This war, while fought far away from the city, impoverished Jerusalem's citizens and led to rising tensions and violence between Muslims and Orthodox Christians, whom they accused of supporting fellow Orthodox Russia.[30]

JERUSALEM DURING THE WORLD WAR I ERA

The period immediately before, during, and after World War I (roughly 1912–1920) were "formative years in the [modern] history of the city and its residents," in which the "future relations between Jews and Arabs were negotiated" amid foreign "assistance," "meddling," and "intervention."[31] It is hard to estimate Jerusalem's population before the war, but it appears to have been roughly 75,000 in 1910, including 12,000 Muslims, 13,000 Christians, and 45,000 Jews. During this same period, the population of Palestine was roughly between 689,000 and 800,000 people.[32]

By 1914, the city of Jerusalem was a patchwork of religious, social, and cultural activities shared by Jews, Christians, and Muslims. The Jewish community included Sephardic Jews from Spain, Eastern European Jews, and Jews from the Orient.[33] The Christian community was divided along denominational lines, including Roman Catholic, Greek Orthodox, Armenian Catholic, Greek Catholic, Armenian Orthodox, Coptic Orthodox, Ethiopian Orthodox, Syrian Orthodox, Anglican, and other Protestant denominations. In contrast to the coastal towns of Jaffa and Haifa, which were far more concerned with commercial interests, Jerusalem sat as the political, cultural, and religious center of the region before the war.[34]

Abigail Jacobson notes that the vibrancy of Jerusalem prior to the war was due in part to Jewish entrepreneurial efforts in the mid-nineteenth century to begin building homes and neighborhoods outside the city walls of the historic, cramped, and segmented Old City. These neighborhoods became the New City of Jerusalem and were notably ethnically diverse, including Arabs, Greeks, and Armenians. Along with this growing diversity and entrepreneurial spirit, the city's population and tourism began booming, resulting in proposals to modernize the city with new trams and electricity.[35] This period of prosperity and progress ended with the start of World War I in 1914, which saw poverty, starvation, and forced migrations of Jerusalem's population as the Ottomans prepared to defend Jerusalem against the British.[36]

Jerusalem's Transition to British Control

The British captured Jerusalem on December 9, 1917. Two days later, British officials entered the city and ended four hundred years of Ottoman rule over Palestine. However, after several hours, no officer wanted to be the one to accept the keys to the city and thereby take responsibility for this dramatic moment: the formal surrender of Jerusalem.[37] The British forces promised to preserve all holy sites and maintain the status quo under British military rule, and they were greeted warmly by the city's communities and faiths. As Abigail Jacobson points out, "In Palestinian historiography, this moment clearly signaled the end of one period, that of 'Ottoman Palestine,' and the beginning of a new era, that of 'Mandatory Palestine.'"[38]

When Jerusalem changed hands from the Ottoman Empire to the British Empire, Jerusalem became an "inter-imperial city," or one that shifts between two empires. This moment of transition marked the end of a difficult period of war and crisis and the beginning of a long, complicated, ambivalent, and sensitive period in the city's storied history.

The preparation for the transition began long before British forces took the city. Although the Crusades were eight centuries in the distant past, Britain was concerned about what Jerusalem's inhabitants would think of a Christian force ousting an entrenched Muslim elite. The British were also acutely aware of the tensions that would arise in Christendom over Jerusalem's occupation by Britain, rather than France or Italy. The British made concessions, placing the French and Italians in Ramlah and Lydda while leaving the administration of Jerusalem to Britain. In order to keep the peace among the local religious communities and prevent the city's inhabitants from viewing the British presence as a "religious occupation," the British authorities also limited the presence of foreign clergymen.[39]

Once the occupation began, the British eagerly adopted the concept of the "Status Quo in the Holy Places," adopting the method used by the Ottoman authorities since 1852. The British adopted this policy to regulate who should control and access the Christian holy places in Jerusalem and Palestine. This policy and other early agreements were enshrined in Articles 13 and 14 of the Charter of the British Mandate in 1920, making the mandatory government responsible for "preserving the existing rights and securing free access to the Holy Places, religious buildings, and sites, and the free exercise of worship, while ensuring the requirements of public order and decorum."[40] The British methodically discharged this duty and tried to satisfy all parties and communities who had an interest in those holy sites.[41]

Britain was not only concerned with Jerusalem's holy sites; it was also focused on the general improvement to life in the city. When the British first encountered Jerusalem, they found a series of problems and a growing list of issues to address. The city was in disrepair and dirty. Refugees were pouring in. The economy was a wreck, with major housing and food shortages. The financial crisis was so bad, in fact, that they discovered children selling alcohol to British soldiers and young girls selling themselves into prostitution to support their families.[42]

Despite Britain's best efforts, the city's inhabitants were increasingly unhappy with the new administration. This discontentment, combined with the growing influence of the Zionist Commission for Palestine, greatly increased tensions between the Jewish and Arab Palestinian populations, further fueling criticism of the British military administration.

After several years of investments in the region, Britain was formally charged by the League of Nations with the administration of the Mandate for Palestine in 1922. It is important for us to note that Jerusalem—not Tel Aviv or any other Israeli city—served as the administrative capital of Mandatory Palestine, which included present-day Israel, the Gaza Strip, the so-called West Bank, and the present-day Hashemite Kingdom of Jordan. The population of Jerusalem roughly tripled during the mandate, composed of two-thirds Jews and one-third Arabs of both Muslim and Christian faiths.

> **It is important for us to note that Jerusalem—not Tel Aviv or any other Israeli city—served as the administrative capital of Mandatory Palestine, which included present-day Israel, the Gaza Strip, the so-called West Bank, and the present-day Hashemite Kingdom of Jordan.**

THE BEGINNING OF THE MODERN JEWISH STATE

As we've seen earlier in this book, Britain's economy could no longer support its duties under the Mandate for Palestine after World War II, and they ultimately announced their departure from the region in 1948. At that point, the UN General Assembly adopted a partition plan that recommended, in addition to creating separate Jewish and Arab states, "the creation of a special international regime in the City of Jerusalem, constituting it as a *Corpus separatum* under the administration of the UN."[43] The partition was to remain in effect for a period of ten years, after which time Jerusalem residents were to hold a referendum to decide the future regime of their city.

The partition plan collapsed when the Arabs rejected its terms. Following the Arab rejection of the UN partition plan, the British withdrew their forces, Israel declared its independence as a state, and the 1948–1949 Arab-Israeli War erupted. We have discussed what these events meant generally for Israel in previous chapters, but we cannot miss the particular significance these events had on the city of Jerusalem. At the time of the 1949 armistice agreements, Israel controlled territory that included west Jerusalem, and Jordan occupied the West Bank, made up of east Jerusalem, Judea, and Samaria. Jews were expelled from the Jewish Quarter of the Old City, and Arabs were expelled from many of their residential neighborhoods. The 1949 armistice divided the city, and barbed wire and concrete barriers were erected to mark those boundaries.

In the fall of 1949, the United Nations began debating how to turn Jerusalem into a separate international entity under its control. On the eve of the debate, the Israeli prime minister, David Ben-Gurion, announced in a Knesset session that the city of Jerusalem is "an organic and inseparable part of the State of Israel" and must remain independent of UN auspices.[44] This announcement was met largely with indifference from UN member states, which went on to vote (by a large majority) to "internationalize Jerusalem."[45] In response, Ben-Gurion remained defiant, requesting that the Knesset be reconvened in Jerusalem after Hanukkah—and subsequently leading the Israeli government in moving its offices into the city emblematic of the new capital of

Israel.[46] A few months later Jordan annexed the West Bank—including east Jerusalem—proclaiming it to be a "second capital" of Jordan under Jordanian law and dividing the city of Jerusalem.[47]

This created an unusual situation in that Jerusalem was claimed as a capital by two separate nations. However, Jordan's claim to sovereignty over Jerusalem was illegitimate under international law because Jordan's occupation—their only claim to the land—occurred pursuant to an act of aggression.[48] Even during the formation of the Mandate for Palestine decades earlier, Jordan had no claim whatsoever to the land in question, as they had been given their own kingdom on the other side of the Jordan River. It was only through their military aggression that any control existed at all, which made their claims to Jerusalem wholly illegitimate.

During the period of Jordanian control from 1948 to 1967, Jews were denied all access to their holy sites in the city, many of which were destroyed or converted to other uses. Christians were given only limited access to their holy sites, even as Muslim sites underwent renovation and expansion. The Western Wall, for example, was converted into an exclusively Muslim holy site. The renovations and restricted access to holy sites were clear violations of the 1949 Israel-Jordan Armistice Agreement, but they were violations that the international community largely ignored.[49]

Also during this period (1949–1967), the international community rejected west Jerusalem as Israel's capital based on UN General Assembly Resolution 147, the resolution designed to make Jerusalem an international city. This was in spite of the fact that west Jerusalem did, in fact, serve as the nation of Israel's seat of government.

Upon the outbreak of the 1967 Arab-Israeli war, Israel informed Jordan that if it refrained from attacking Israel, Jordanian-occupied territory would not be attacked by Israeli forces.[50] Nevertheless, on the second day of the Six-Day War, Jordan attacked the Israeli-held west Jerusalem area. Following the Jordanian attack, Israel counterattacked into the West Bank and defeated the Jordanian forces, thereby gaining control of the entire West Bank and reunifying the previously divided city of Jerusalem. Following the Six-Day War, Arab residents of Jerusalem were given permanent residency status with the option to apply for formal Israeli citizenship. Within Jerusalem itself, the population grew nearly 200 percent overall, with the Arab Palestinian population outpacing the Jewish population by a ratio of 6 to 5. The result has been an ever-growing population where housing is a luxury. This problem is compounded by Israel's inability to engage in any meaningful building projects in Jerusalem. Due to political pressures, any Israeli construction in Jerusalem has been met with international outrage, leaving all those in the city in a difficult situation. East Jerusalem, in particular, remains a flashpoint for clashing Palestinian Muslim and Israeli Jewish populations.

THE SPIRITUAL AND HISTORICAL CENTER

The history of Jerusalem cannot be separated from the history of Israel. Every invader, conqueror, and empire that came into Palestine impacted life in Jerusalem in one way or another, and many of those forces specifically set their sights on Jerusalem. This has truly been the world's most sought-after and hotly debated piece of real estate throughout history—and that remains true today.

> **This has truly been the world's most sought-after and hotly debated piece of real estate throughout history—and that remains true today.**

What is significant for us to see at this point is that Jerusalem is unquestionably the center of the Jewish faith, not only as the source of their most holy sites, but in their view that Creation itself sprang out of the Temple Mount. Furthermore, since the time of King David, Jerusalem has always been the Jewish people's political capital whenever the government was within their control.

> **Jewish life, governance, and faith are intimately tied to and inextricably intertwined with the city of Jerusalem in a historical and spiritual bond that cannot be broken.**

Jewish life, governance, and faith are intimately tied to and inextricably intertwined with the city of Jerusalem in a historical and spiritual bond that cannot be broken; any casual observer of history can see that. Why, then, can't the international community come to this obvious conclusion? That's what we'll examine next.

KEY TAKEAWAYS

1. Jerusalem has been the capital of Israel throughout history.

2. The Basic Law of Israel declares united Jerusalem to be the capital of Israel and the seat of government.

3. Jordan illegally occupied east Jerusalem from 1948 to 1967. Israel regained control of east Jerusalem in 1967 and unified the city. The international community has wrongly rejected Israel's claim to the area ever since.

4. Jerusalem is home to many holy sites for all three great monotheistic religions, and Israel's Basic Law ensures protection of access to these sites by adherents of all three faith groups. In contrast, free access to religious sites was severely restricted during Jordanian rule of the City.

13

THE LEGAL BASIS FOR JERUSALEM AS ISRAEL'S CAPITAL

We see it our duty to declare that Jewish Jerusalem is an organic and inseparable part of the State of Israel, as it is an inseparable part of the history and religion of Israel and of the soul of our people. Jerusalem is the very heart of the State of Israel. We feel pride in that Jerusalem is sanctified—also in the eyes of adherents of other faiths, and we freely and willingly are ready to make all the necessary arrangements to enable the adherents of the other faiths to enjoy their religious needs in Jerusalem.[1]
—DAVID BEN-GURION, DECEMBER 5, 1949

June 2017 marked a significant anniversary for the State of Israel, and Israelis were set on having a massive celebration to mark the occasion. The nation was celebrating the fiftieth anniversary of the unified Jerusalem, commemorating a half century since Israel regained the parts of Jerusalem that had been illegally occupied by the nation of Jordan for the previous eighteen years. We discussed in the previous chapter how Israel reclaimed the entire West Bank, including the Jordanian-occupied portion of Jerusalem, in 1967 following what became known as the Six-Day War. Although this was a perfectly legal action and, as we have seen, Israel's legal claim to Jerusalem dated all the way back to the mandate and certainly to its founding in 1948, the international community has spent the last fifty years refuting, rebutting, denying, and protesting Israel's right to Jerusalem.

Despite the international pressures surrounding the Jerusalem issue, Israel secured a location for their 2017 celebration: the United Nations. As a full member state to the UN, Israel had a right to use the facilities; their opponents at the UN couldn't keep them out. However, the UN seemed to go out of their way to make the one thousand invited guests feel extremely unwelcome. My son Jordan was asked to be one of the keynote speakers at the event, and he was taken aback by what he saw. Jordan noted that the United Nations had rescheduled the event—which had originally been scheduled during the busy midday—for a time later in the evening when the UN was shut down, meaning there was no other activity in or around the Jerusalem celebration. No stranger to the UN building, Jordan was surprised to see that none of the flags were flying at the UN. It seemed like a subtle way to say that none of Israel's world neighbors supported their celebration of a unified Jerusalem. The UN Police were openly hostile to the guests and routinely commented on how there were too many people there, although the room could have held hundreds more. The guests were bottlenecked through insufficiently staffed security checkpoints and ushered down dark hallways. It appeared to Jordan that the United Nations had gone out of its way to hide the celebratory event from the public's view while making sure that everyone in attendance knew they were unwanted and unwelcome. Jordan told me later that it felt like "an event with no allies."

I'd love to say I was surprised to hear these details about his experience, but I wasn't. Israel's enemies, the United Nations, and much of the entire international community have a fifty-year history of rejecting Israel's claim to a unified Jerusalem. The issue has appeared in what feels like an endless stream of UN resolutions, debates about international embassy locations, and even in our own presidential election campaigns here in the United States. Jerusalem has always been and still remains a hot topic on the world stage, and it is important to understand all the reasons why. That's what we'll do in this chapter.

ISRAELI LAW ON JERUSALEM AS ISRAEL'S CAPITAL

When Israel declared its independence, the declaration stated that a formal constitution would be drafted by October 1, 1948. However, this goal was interrupted by the Arab-Israel War of 1948–1949. When the war was over, the Constituent Assembly convened but was unable to reach an agreement. Despite the lack of a constitution, the Transition Law of 1949 created the Knesset as Israel's legislative body, and the Knesset ultimately tasked a committee to draft the Basic Laws of Israel—essentially their constitutional law—piecemeal over time. The first Basic Law was drafted in 1958 and outlined the functions of the Knesset. From that starting point, all future constitutional laws of the nation were passed over the next several decades.[2]

THE JERUSALEM LAW

More than twenty years after the first Basic Law was drafted, the Knesset passed the Basic Law: Jerusalem, Capital of Israel (known as the Jerusalem Law), on July 30, 1980. In addition to designating Jerusalem as the nation's capital, the law also secured the integrity and unity of Jerusalem, addressed issues dealing with the status of the holy sites, guaranteed basic rights to members of all religions, and granted special preferences regarding development of Israel's eternal capital.

The Jerusalem Law began as a private member's bill introduced in the Knesset by Geulah Cohen, a member of the ultranationalist Tehiya Party. The original text of the law stated that "the integrity and unity of greater Jerusalem in its boundaries after the Six-Day War shall not be violated."[3] This clause was rejected by the Knesset, which declined to specify boundaries or to make any pronouncements that would amount to annexation or sovereignty. The law elicited protest around the world, and UN Security Council Resolution 478 condemned the law as "null and void," calling for its rescission because of its assertion of Jerusalem's "integrity and unity," even without the overt language of annexation and sovereignty.[4] The UN resolution called upon member states to withdraw their diplomatic missions from Jerusalem.

Resolution 478 was adopted on August 20, 1980. Two decades later, on November 27, 2000, the Knesset passed an amendment to the Jerusalem Law that finally specified Jerusalem's jurisdiction based on the 1967 boundaries—including, most controversially, the territory of east Jerusalem.[5] The amendment further stated that authority over Jerusalem could not be "transferred either permanently or for an allotted period of time to a foreign body, whether political, governmental or to any other similar type of foreign body."[6] In its final provision, the amendment stated that its terms could only be overturned by a Basic Law passed by a majority of the members of the Knesset.[7]

TALKS OF DIVISION

In 2000 a team of experts assembled by then Israeli prime minister Ehud Barak concluded that the city must be divided, as Israel had failed to achieve any of its national aims there. This proposal was considered in preparation for the 2000 Camp David Summit, an effort to end the Israeli-Palestinian conflict that included U.S. president Bill Clinton, Israeli prime minister Ehud Barak, and Palestinian Authority chairman Yasir Arafat. The division proposal became public just after the meeting.

THE 2000 CAMP DAVID SUMMIT

During the summit, the Palestinians demanded complete sovereignty over east Jerusalem, including the holy sites. They also called for the dismantling of Jewish neighborhoods that had been established since 1967. Regarding the Western Wall and Jewish Quarter, the Palestinians proposed that Israel retain authority but not sovereignty over these areas.

In response, Israel proposed granting the Palestinian Authority "custodianship"—but not authority—over the Temple Mount, except for the Western Wall, which would remain in Israeli Jewish control. They further proposed that Palestine be given administrative authority, but not sovereignty, over the Muslim and Christian quarters. This included Palestinian administration of Muslim and Christian holy sites therein, with the Jewish and Armenian quarters remaining in Israeli hands. There was even talk of having an independent authority administer the holy sites of Jerusalem. Other provisions of the Israeli proposal would have allowed Israel to retain control over Jewish settlements in parts of Jerusalem and the West Bank.

The Palestinians objected to the lack of sovereignty and the retention of Israeli control over Jewish settlements in east Jerusalem. Further, the status of Jerusalem and the Temple Mount became a central point of dispute at the Camp David summit. These issues led to the suspension of the Israeli-Palestinian talks before any agreement had been made.

2010 KNESSET LEGISLATION

In 2010, ten years after the failed Camp David Summit, the Knesset passed legislation that gave Jerusalem the highest national priority status in Israel. In practical terms, the law prioritized construction throughout the city, offering grants and tax benefits for housing, infrastructure, education, employment, business, tourism, and cultural events. Communications minister Moshe Kahlon said that the bill sent "a clear, unequivocal political message that Jerusalem will not be divided" and that "all those within the Palestinian and international community who expect the current Israeli government to accept any demands regarding Israel's sovereignty over its capital are mistaken and misleading."[8]

Even so, disputes continue to this day over not just Jerusalem's priority but also its unity and integrity. These disagreements go all the way up to the prime ministers, as then prime minister Ehud Barak concluded in 2000 that Jerusalem had to be divided, whereas Prime Minister Benjamin Netanyahu said in 2014 that "Jerusalem will never be divided."[9] Moreover, a June 2013 poll found that while 74 percent of Israeli Jews reject the idea of a Palestinian capital in Jerusalem, 72 percent still regard Jerusalem as a divided city.[10]

THE PALESTINIAN VIEW

Palestinian laws on Jerusalem practically mirror the Israeli position. The Palestine Liberation Organization's 1988 Palestinian Declaration of Independence declared Jerusalem as the capital of the State of Palestine. In 1997, the Palestinian Legislative Council passed the Palestinian Basic Law, again designating Jerusalem as its capital. Palestinian president Mahmoud Abbas has made it clear that any agreement with Israel that does not include east Jerusalem as the capital of Palestine would be unacceptable. As such, the status of Jerusalem as a capital continues to be enshrined in both Israeli and Palestinian law as a matter of national legality and national identity.

> **The status of Jerusalem as a capital continues to be enshrined in both Israeli and Palestinian law as a matter of national legality and national identity.**

INTERNATIONAL LAW ON JERUSALEM

Discussing international law's view on Jerusalem as Israel's capital is an unusual matter. As Professor Eugene Kontorovich, international law expert from Northwestern University, explains, "Nothing in international law gives other countries a say in where a country's capital is."[11] This points to a fundamental principle of international law that anything not covered by international agreements is considered a domestic matter, to be decided by the laws of the individual country. So, because Israel determined that Jerusalem is its capital, then Jerusalem is its capital; it is as simple as that. And yet, as we've seen, Jerusalem's status as Israel's capital has been outright disputed by some and deemed ambiguous by others ever since the country's inception. To better understand what this

> **"Nothing in international law gives other countries a say in where a country's capital is."**

international disagreement is all about, let's examine some of the key declarations, laws, and legal concepts related to Jerusalem's status in international law.

THE 1993 OSLO ACCORDS

In the decade before the failed Camp David Summit of 2000, leaders from Israel and the PLO conducted months of secret negotiations that ultimately led to the signing of the 1993 Oslo Accords in Washington, DC, on September 13, 1993.[12] The Oslo Accords were a pivotal milestone in Israeli-Palestinian relations, aimed at propelling the peace process forward and providing for the expansion of Palestinian self-rule throughout most of the West Bank.

The agreement included the Declaration of Principles (DOP) and Letters of Mutual Recognition whereby the PLO recognized the existence of the State of Israel, and Israel recognized the PLO as the legitimate representative of the Palestinian people. Under the DOP, Israel committed itself to withdrawing from parts of the Gaza Strip and the West Bank and acknowledged the Palestinian right to self-government in those territories under a Palestinian Authority (PA). The DOP went into force one month after it was signed, and two months later Israel and the PLO agreed on Israeli withdrawal from the Gaza Strip and Jericho (excluding Israeli settlements).[13]

Pursuant to the 1993 Oslo Accords, Israel turned over administrative but not military control over large portions of the West Bank and Gaza Strip to the newly established Palestinian Authority. In August 2005, Israel withdrew from the entire Gaza Strip, turning it over to the PA. However, the PA was expelled from the Gaza Strip just two years later when Hamas, a militant Islamic Palestinian political party, took control of the Gaza Strip in a coup d'état in June 2007.[14]

UNITED NATIONS RESOLUTIONS ON JERUSALEM

In contrast to Israel's understanding of Jerusalem as its capital, the United Nations, a variety of countries throughout Europe and Asia, and the entire Arab world do not recognize Jerusalem as the capital of Israel. Indeed, Jerusalem is the only example in the world of other nations refusing to recognize a sovereign nation's capital. In the international arena, UN resolutions have been the key venue for declarations pertaining to Jerusalem. These include nonbinding resolutions by both the UN Security Council and the General Assembly, statements that are completely political in nature but are often confused with and misunderstood as being statements of international law. To better understand the UN's view of Jerusalem, we need to examine the relevant resolutions from the past seventy years.

> **Jerusalem is the only example in the world of other nations refusing to recognize a sovereign nation's capital.**

UN GENERAL ASSEMBLY RESOLUTION 194

UN General Assembly Resolution 194 was adopted on December 11, 1948, near the end of the 1948–1949 Arab-Israeli War.[15] The resolution defined principles for reaching a final settlement and returning Palestinian refugees to their homes. It also called for the establishment of the United Nations Conciliation Commission to facilitate peace between Israel and Arab states. Of the fifty-eight member states of the UN at that time, the resolution was adopted by a 35-vote majority, with 15 votes against and 8 abstentions.[16] All six Arab League countries then represented at the UN—Egypt, Iraq, Lebanon, Saudi Arabia, Syria, and Yemen, all of which were parties to the conflict in question—voted against the resolution. A number of Communist bloc members also voted against the resolution—including the Belorussian SSR, Czechoslovakia, Poland, the Ukrainian SSR, the USSR, and Yugoslavia—despite the fact that they had all recognized Israel as a legal state. Though not a member of the United Nations at the time, Israel objected to many of the resolution's articles. The Palestinians were not directly consulted.

Resolution 194 has frequently been invoked by Palestinians in claims of a right of return to their communities of origin, but those claims have been rejected by the Israeli government. Several articles of the declaration addressed the demilitarization of Jerusalem and its surroundings, as well as the creation of an international zone or jurisdiction around Jerusalem, including protection of and free access to the holy sites.[17] Many of the resolution's provisions were never fulfilled because they were opposed by Israel, rejected by the Arab states, or were overshadowed by the 1948 war.

UN General Assembly Resolution 273

UN General Assembly Resolution 273, which admitted the State of Israel to the UN as a full-fledged member state, was adopted on May 11, 1949.[18] Resolution 273 notably declared that "Israel is a peace-loving State and is able and willing to carry out the obligations contained in the [UN] Charter."[19] It also noted Israel's own declaration that it "unreservedly accepts the obligations of the United Nations Charter and undertakes to honour them from the day when it becomes a member of the United Nations."[20] There are no references to or provisions dealing with Jerusalem, but the passage of the resolution was a signal event for Israel's emergence on the international political stage.

UN Security Council Resolution 242

UN Security Council Resolution 242 was adopted unanimously by the members of Security Council on November 22, 1967, in the aftermath of the Six-Day War.[21] Its preamble, which is nonbinding, referenced the "inadmissibility of the acquisition of territory by war and the need to work for a just and lasting peace in the Middle East in which every State in the area can live in security."[22] The first paragraph conditioned peace in the Middle East on:

> (i) Withdrawal of Israeli armed forces from territories occupied in the recent conflict,

> (ii) Termination of all claims or states of belligerency and respect for and acknowledgment of the sovereignty, territorial integrity and political independence of every State in the area and their right to live in peace within secure and recognized boundaries free from threats or acts of force . . . [23]

Egypt, Jordan, Israel, and Lebanon participated in UN consultations on how to implement this declaration. Israel indicated its acceptance on May 1, 1968. After their initial denunciation, Syria accepted the resolution four years later, in 1972. In September 1993, the PLO agreed that Resolution 242, among other resolutions, should be the basis for negotiations with Israel in signing the Declaration of Principles of the Oslo Accords.[24] Resolution 242 is one of the most widely affirmed resolutions on the Arab-Israeli conflict, and it has formed the basis for many later negotiations between the party nations.

Despite its lasting influence and widespread affirmation, Resolution 242 was a sticking point in the negotiations at the time and in subsequent negotiations since. There was some failed discussion among the negotiators that Jordan should have some sort of special administrative authority in the Old City, while also getting much of the West Bank.[25] U.S. diplomats and the Israeli ambassador at the time, Avraham Harman, held out the possibility of some negotiable role for Jordan in Jerusalem, apparently up to and including "sovereignty."[26] Although the U.S. agreed with neither the Israeli nor the Jordanian positions on Jerusalem, it was prepared to advocate for some role for Jordan.[27] Even so, U.S. and British diplomats began to use the controversial terms "annexation" and "occupation" to describe Israeli control of Jerusalem post-1967.[28] The U.S. secretary of state at the time, Dean Rusk, observed afterward that the status of Jerusalem, especially the Old City, had been left open for subsequent consideration and that there was no grant of territory made to Israel after the Six-Day War.[29]

In later decades the U.S., unlike many other nations, moved closer to the pro-Israeli position on Jerusalem. President Ronald Reagan would later state, with specific reference to Resolution 242, "We remain convinced that Jerusalem must remain undivided, but its final status should be decided through negotiations."[30] The British diplomat Lord Caradon observed in later commentary on Resolution 242:

> So important is the future of Jerusalem that it might be argued that we should have specifically dealt with that issue in the 1967 Resolution. It is easy to say that now, but I am quite

sure that if we had attempted to raise or settle the question of Jerusalem as a separate issue at that time our task in attempting to find a unanimous decision would have been far greater if not impossible.[31]

The agreement, notably, did not mention the Palestinians, as the West Bank was recognized by the United Kingdom to be part of Transjordan.

Still later, in discussing an entirely separate resolution of the UN Commission on the Status of Women, Secretary of State Madeleine Albright told the UN Security Council:

> We simply do not support the description of the territories occupied by Israel in 1967 as "Occupied Palestinian Territory." In the view of my Government, this language could be taken to indicate sovereignty, a matter which both Israel and the PLO have agreed must be decided in negotiations on the final status of the territories. Had this language appeared in the operative paragraphs of the resolution, let me be clear: we would have exercised our veto. In fact, we are today voting against a resolution . . . precisely because it implies that Jerusalem is "occupied Palestinian territory."[32]

This statement, offered in a context that had nothing to do with the issue of Jerusalem, demonstrates how Resolution 242's lack of clarity over Israel's capital has continued to serve as a contentious point of discussion within international diplomacy.

UN Security Council Resolution 476

UN Security Council Resolution 476 was adopted on June 30, 1980. Resolution 476 declared that "all legislative and administrative measures and actions taken by Israel, the occupying Power, which purport to alter the character and status of the Holy City of Jerusalem have no legal validity and constitute a flagrant violation of the Fourth Geneva Convention . . ."[33] Resolution 476 was adopted by a vote of 14 to 0, with the United States abstaining.

UN SECURITY COUNCIL RESOLUTION 478

Two months later, on August 20, 1980, UN Security Council Resolution 478 was adopted in condemnation of Israel's attempted annexation of east Jerusalem. The resolution was directed specifically at Israel's noncompliance with the earlier Resolution 476. Resolution 478 particularly condemned as a violation of international law Israel's passage of the Jerusalem Law provisions of the Basic Law that declared Jerusalem to be the "complete and united" capital. Resolution 478, like Resolution 476 before it, was also passed by a vote of 14 to 0, with the U.S. abstaining. Israel rejected the resolution, in response to which its foreign ministry stated, "[Resolution 478] will not undermine the status of Jerusalem as the capital of a sovereign Israel and as a united city which will never again be torn apart." [34]

Then U.S. secretary of state Edmund Muskie initially repeated the standard post–Resolution 242 position in stating, "The question of Jerusalem must be addressed in the context of negotiations for a comprehensive, just and lasting Middle East peace." [35] This statement seemed to reaffirm the openness and negotiability that the Resolution 242 talks had left in place thirteen years prior regarding the status of Israel, along with the idea that Israelis and Palestinians should determine the issue between themselves.

Secretary Muskie further observed that:

> the draft resolution before us today is illustrative of a preoccupation which has produced this series of unbalanced and unrealistic texts on Middle East issues. It fails to serve the goal of all faiths that look upon Jerusalem as holy. We must share a common vision of that ancient city's future—an undivided Jerusalem, with free access to the Holy Places for people of all faiths. [36]

The notion of an "undivided" Jerusalem at least nominally played to the Israeli understanding, as did further remarks Secretary Muskie made concerning the issue of embassy location. Indeed, Muskie described portions of the draft resolution relating to the transfer of embassies away from Jerusalem as "fundamentally flawed," noting further that the U.S. considered the instruction that states remove their diplomatic missions from Jerusalem to be "not binding" and "without force," as well as a "disruptive attempt to dictate to other nations."[37] In the view of some Israeli observers, Muskie refused to use the problematic description of Jerusalem as an "occupied territory" in his remarks, but he also did not openly deny the claims. Further, his comments did not explicitly support the Israeli declaration of Jerusalem as capital. So the U.S. position on Jerusalem remained somewhat ambiguous.[38]

In 2004 a nonbinding advisory opinion of the International Court of Justice expressed the view that all states are obliged to reject the illegal situation in and around east Jerusalem.[39] This further demonstrates the specter of illegality that continues to swirl around Jerusalem's control of east Jerusalem as a result of Resolution 478. This particular resolution and the subsequent advisory opinion have had a significant impact on Israel's foreign relations, as most nations have since relocated their embassies to Tel Aviv, Ramat Gan, or Herzliya. Since the withdrawals of Costa Rica and El Salvador in 2006, there have been no foreign embassies located in Jerusalem, with many nations, including the United States, keeping their embassies in Tel Aviv. The embassy issue is a major point of discussion on the world stage, and we will explore it in more detail later in this chapter.

UN General Assembly Resolution 58/292

UN General Assembly Resolution 58/292, titled "Status of the Occupied Palestinian Territory, including East Jerusalem," was passed on May 6, 2004, just before the last embassies pulled out of Jerusalem. The resolution affirmed that the post-1967 status of the Palestinian territory, including east Jerusalem, remains one of two military occupations. As such, Israel's duties and obligations for the protection of civilian persons are those of an occupying power under the Geneva Convention and the Hague Convention. Resolution 58/292 further affirmed that the Palestinian people have rights of self-determination and sovereignty over their territory. The General Assembly expressed determination to secure the rights of the Palestinians and the view that a peace settlement should result in two sovereign and independent states based on the pre-1967 borders. The preamble also referred to the inadmissibility of the territory acquired by force and the need to enable Palestinian sovereignty and independence. The resolution was adopted with 140 votes in favor and 11 abstentions. Israel, the U.S., and four Pacific Island nations were the only six nations that voted against the resolution.[40]

UN Security Council Resolution 2334

UN Security Council Resolution 2334, adopted on December 23, 2016, is the most recent resolution on Israel as of this writing. The title of the resolution is "Palestinian territories occupied since 1967, including East Jerusalem," and it concerns Israeli settlements in the Palestinian territories. The resolution passed with a vote of 14 to 0 and was supported by four Security Council member nations—China, France, Russia, and the United Kingdom—with the United States abstaining. The resolution declared the Israeli settlements to be a "flagrant violation" of international law with "no legal validity."[41] It called upon Israel to cease settlement activity in the Palestinian territory and to fulfill its obligations as an occupying power under the Fourth Geneva Convention. The resolution was contentious for its pronouncements regarding illegality and occupation, and it was also controversial for U.S. ambassador Samantha Power's abstention.

The U.S. abstention was ordered by outgoing President Barack Obama, despite then president-elect Donald Trump's expressed desire to pursue closer relations with Israel. Let me be clear here: The Obama administration outright betrayed Israel by deciding to abstain from this vote. The United States allowed this resolution to pass by not using its veto power. Even though it was only a political statement and not binding, this resolution empowers the terrorists, empowers international legal attacks against Israel and the United States, and undercuts global peace and stability. The Obama administration's decision was a dark day for U.S.-Israeli relations. Although the resolution deals with an Israeli settlement policy being pursued throughout the Palestinian territories—not just east Jerusalem—the specific references to east Jerusalem and the 1967 borders in the resolution's title make it the latest manifestation of ongoing disputes about the status and integrity of Jerusalem.

The UNESCO Resolution of 2016

The UN Security Council and the UN General Assembly, while the main bodies of the United Nations, are not the only UN bodies to pass resolutions pertaining to Israel and, specifically, to Jerusalem. On October 13, 2016, UNESCO, the UN's body on education, science, and culture, passed a resolution declaring the Western Wall to be part of the Al Aqsa Mosque and Temple Mount complex. The vote was 24 in favor of the resolution, 26 abstaining, and only 6 voting against. While the text of the UNESCO resolution contained text acknowledging the importance of the Old City to Judaism, Christianity, and Islam, the term "Western Wall" was used only twice and in quotation marks, and the plaza containing the wall was elsewhere in the resolution referenced with the Muslim name of Buraq Plaza. This was widely viewed in Israel as a denial of Jewish religious, spiritual, and historical links to the Western Wall and Temple Mount that form the heart of Israel's Old City.[42]

The UNESCO resolution drew a sharp international response. On October 20, 2016, nineteen parliamentarians from seventeen countries signed the first international declaration calling for recognition of Jerusalem as the eternal capital of Israel. This stood as a statement against UNESCO's resolution, which ignored the Jewish connection to Jerusalem.[43] Incidentally, the parliamentarians were in Jerusalem at the time to attend a conference celebrating the fiftieth anniversary of the reunification of Jerusalem as Israel's capital.

AMERICAN FOREIGN
POLICY RESPONSES

Jerusalem's political standing has long been, and remains, one of the most sensitive issues in American foreign policy, and indeed it is one of the most delicate issues in current international affairs. The debate in the United States over Jerusalem's status as Israel's capital isn't just a political issue; it has spilled over into the American legal arena as well. Questions about the constitutional powers given to the president, Congress, and our courts have driven this debate for decades. These legal debates matter because they cut to the core of our discussion here, identifying which players on the world's stage acknowledge Israel's right to determine its own eternal capital as Jerusalem.

> **Jerusalem's political standing has long been, and remains, one of the most sensitive issues in American foreign policy, and indeed it is one of the most delicate issues in current international affairs.**

THE POWER OF RECOGNITION

In 1948, President Truman—over the U.S. State Department's objections—recognized Israel's statehood in a signed statement of "recognition," but that statement did not acknowledge Israeli sovereignty over Jerusalem.[44] Recognition is a "formal acknowledgement" that a particular "entity possesses the qualifications for statehood" or "that a particular regime is the effective government of a state."[45] This acknowledgment could also extend to the determination of a state's territorial bounds.[46] Recognition doesn't have to be an overt statement, either; it could be implied—for example, by concluding a bilateral treaty or by sending or receiving diplomatic agents.[47]

Legal consequences follow formal recognition. Recognized sovereigns may sue in United States courts and can benefit from sovereign immunity when they are sued.[48] The actions of a recognized sovereign committed within its own territory also receive deference in domestic courts under the Act of State Doctrine.[49] Recognition at international law, furthermore, is a precondition for regular diplomatic relations.[50] For all these reasons and more, recognition is useful and necessary to the existence of a state.[51]

Despite the importance of the recognition power in foreign relations, however, the Constitution does not use the term "recognition." The secretary of state asserts that the president exercises the recognition power based on the Reception Clause, which asserts that the president "shall receive Ambassadors and other public Ministers."[52] At the time of the founding, however, prominent international scholars suggested that receiving an ambassador was tantamount to recognizing the sovereignty of the state that sent him. So, if the president alone has the power to receive ambassadors, and if the founders saw receiving ambassadors as a recognition of their state's sovereignty, we can logically infer that the Reception Clause gives the president the power to recognize other nations.[53]

The inference that the president exercises the recognition power is further supported by his additional Article II powers. It is for the president, "by and with the Advice and Consent of the Senate," to "make Treaties, provided two thirds of the Senators present concur."[54] In addition, "he shall nominate, and by and with the Advice and Consent of the Senate, shall appoint Ambassadors" as well as "other public Ministers and Consuls."[55]

No single precedent resolves the question of whether the president has exclusive recognition authority and, if so, how far that power extends. This is largely due to the fact that the branches of government have historically agreed on questions of recognition. When such questions have come up, the president and Congress have come to a mutual decision. We've seen this several times throughout history, such as President Lincoln's desire to recognize Liberia and Haiti, which he took to Congress for mutual consent. More recently, President Carter's refusal to recognize China's claim that Taiwan was part of China was accepted by Congress as a complete and lawful act. Where there *has* been recognition disagreement—such as the New York State courts' refusal to fully execute President Roosevelt's decision to recognize the Soviet government of Russia—those disagreements existed between the federal government and the states or between the courts and the political branches, *not* between the president and Congress.[56]

BACKDOOR RECOGNITION: THE 2002 FOREIGN RELATIONS AUTHORIZATION ACT

There has been one case in recent history wherein Congress has tried to circumvent the president's right to recognition. In 2002, Congress passed the Foreign Relations Authorization Act, Fiscal Year 2003.[57] Section 214 of the Act is titled "United States Policy with Respect to Jerusalem as the Capital of Israel," and subsection 214(d) addresses passports.[58] That subsection seeks to override existing precedence by allowing citizens born in Jerusalem to list their place of birth as Israel. Subsection 214(d) states, "For purposes of the registration of birth, certification of nationality, or issuance of a passport of a United States citizen born in the city of Jerusalem, the Secretary shall, upon the request of the citizen or the citizen's legal guardian, record the place of birth as Israel."[59]

When the act was signed into law by President George W. Bush, he issued a statement declaring his position that Section 214 would, "if construed as mandatory rather than advisory, impermissibly interfere with the President's constitutional authority to formulate the position of the United States, speak for the Nation in international affairs, and determine the terms on which recognition is given to foreign states."[60] The president concluded, "U.S. policy regarding Jerusalem has not changed."[61]

As a matter of policy, the United States acknowledges neither Israel nor any other country as having sovereignty over Jerusalem. In this way, Section 214(d) "directly contradicts" the "carefully calibrated and long-standing Executive branch policy of neutrality toward Jerusalem."[62] In 2015, the United States Supreme Court heard arguments on this issue.[63]

In the case *Zivotofsky v. Kerry*, the Supreme Court asserted that the purpose of Section 214(d) was to infringe on the recognition power— a power the Court held is the sole prerogative of the president.[64] The House Conference Report proclaimed that Section 214 "contains four provisions related to the recognition of Jerusalem as Israel's capital."[65] The Court stated that, from the face of Section 214, from the legislative history, and from its reception, it is clear that Congress wanted to express its displeasure with the president's policy by commanding the executive to contradict his own, earlier-stated position on Jerusalem. This, the Court declared, Congress may not do.[66]

Recognition is an act with immediate and powerful significance for international relations, so the president's position must be clear: There is no precedent to support Congress's ability to *require* the president to contradict his own statement regarding a determination of formal recognition.[67] And although recognition is an important issue in foreign affairs, none of this changes the fact that sovereign governments—like Israel—have complete authority to declare a nation's capital. That power resides within that country itself.

THE JERUSALEM EMBASSY ACT OF 1995

Since the establishment of the State of Israel in 1948, the United States has had an embassy located in Tel Aviv. Embassy location has been a point of contention internationally, as the U.S. and other nations do not formally recognize Jerusalem as Israel's capital. However, on October 24, 1995, Congress overwhelmingly passed the Jerusalem Embassy Act (JEA) with a vote of 93 to 5 in the Senate and 374 to 37 in the House of Representatives.[68] The primary aim of JEA was to call for the relocation of the United States embassy in Israel from Tel Aviv to Jerusalem by May 31, 1999.[69] The act also called for Jerusalem to remain an undivided city and to be recognized as the Israeli capital. Despite the wide bipartisan support, President Clinton did not sign the bill into law. Instead, the bill became public law without his signature, pursuant to Article 1, Section 7, of the U.S. Constitution.[70]

The JEA was the result of three primary congressional findings: First, under international law and custom, Israel, as a sovereign state, is free to determine its own capital, and for many decades Israel has considered its capital to be Jerusalem. Second, Congress found that Jerusalem is not only the spiritual center for Judaism and other faiths, but that "the city of Jerusalem is the seat of Israel's President, Parliament, and Supreme Court, and the site of numerous government ministries and social and cultural institutions." Third, when part of Jerusalem was under Jordanian control from 1948 to 1967, Israelis of all faiths were denied access to the holy sites in that part of Jerusalem. However, since Israel has been in control of Jerusalem, all religious faiths have been granted full access to the holy sites.[71]

Despite the JEA becoming law, Presidents Clinton, Bush, and Obama all declined to move the American embassy. They exercised their right to file the "Suspension of Limitations Under the Jerusalem Embassy Act" notice, which allows the president to defer relocating the embassy every six months for national security reasons."[72] Congress attempted to press the matter again with the passage of the Foreign Relations Authorization Act, Fiscal Year 2003 (discussed above), which provided that "the Congress maintains its commitment to relocating the United States Embassy in Israel to Jerusalem and urges the President, pursuant to the Jerusalem Embassy Act of 1995 (Public Law 104–45; 109 Stat. 398), to immediately begin the process of relocating the United States Embassy in Israel to Jerusalem."[73]

As we've already seen, President Bush signed the act, but he specifically called out those sections that were found to overreach into the powers of the executive branch. In the Supreme Court's ruling on this matter in *Zivotofsky*, specifically pertaining to the president's power to recognize foreign nations and governments, the Court found that

> the President's exclusive recognition power encompasses the authority to acknowledge, in a formal sense, the legitimacy of other states and governments, including their territorial bounds. Albeit limited, *the exclusive recognition power is essential to the conduct of Presidential duties.* The formal act of recognition is an executive power that Congress may not qualify. If the President is to be effective in negotiations over a formal recognition determination, it must be evident to his counterparts abroad that he speaks for the Nation on that precise question.[74]

This is consistent with the doctrine that there can only be one voice speaking for the United States on the world stage at any given point in time, and that naturally that one voice is the sitting president. Given this clarification of executive recognition powers, and with the inauguration of President Trump—who has expressed his support for an American embassy in Jerusalem—there has been renewed interest in the relocation debate.[75] Further, if President Trump were to recognize Jerusalem as Israel's capital, based on what we've seen regarding recognition, this would settle the issue, at least for domestic purposes.

> **If President Trump were to recognize Jerusalem as Israel's capital, based on what we've seen regarding recognition, this would settle the issue, at least for domestic purposes.**

CONCERNS ABOUT THE EMBASSY RELOCATION

The prospect of relocating the embassy has prompted fears of instigating a conflict that could potentially involve much of the Middle East.[76] In 2017, I met with members of the United States Senate who had just left a meeting with King Abdullah of Jordan. Israel and Jordan have been at peace for nearly three decades, and there is good cooperation among Jordanian and Israeli security forces. The king of Jordan has expressed concerns that moving the American embassy to Jerusalem goes to the core of his kingdom's stability. The key worry is that this would further incite radical groups like ISIS that are already operating in the region.

This is certainly a legitimate concern. While there is renewed sentiment in the United States concerning embassy relocation and recognizing Jerusalem as the Israeli capital, this is tempered by the precarious situation of the Middle East. Factors include the ongoing civil war in Syria and the rise of ISIS in Syria and Iraq.[77]

> **While there is renewed sentiment in the United States concerning embassy relocation and recognizing Jerusalem as the Israeli capital, this is tempered by the precarious situation of the Middle East.**

Most directly and ominously, the Palestinian Authority has vowed to revoke all previously signed agreements with Israel, including its 1993 recognition of the Israeli State, if the U.S. moves its embassy to Jerusalem—prompting concerns about the larger fate of peace in the region.[78] The Israeli government is fully aware of the political dynamics of a potential move of the embassy, with the U.S. taking into account any and all security implications of such a decision.

The proposal to move the U.S. embassy to Jerusalem has recently gained traction in light of President Trump's expressed desire to improve relations with Israel after a perceived distancing from Israel under the Obama administration. To that end, President Trump selected as his ambassador to Israel David M. Friedman, an American bankruptcy lawyer and campaign adviser who has supported the embassy move and affirmed his own recognition of Jerusalem as the Israeli capital.[79] In spite of the renewed interest, as of the time of this writing, it remains to be seen what the ultimate outcome (and subsequent fallout) will be. And yet, whether or not the U.S. or any other nation moves their embassy to Jerusalem, the fact remains that Israel—and Israel alone—has the authority and responsibility of declaring its own capital city. No foreign embassy, UN resolution, outside pressure, or U.S. Supreme Court decision will change that.

> **Whether or not the U.S. or any other nation moves their embassy to Jerusalem, the fact remains that Israel—and Israel alone—has the authority and responsibility of declaring its own capital city.**

THE BOTTOM LINE

Over these previous two chapters, we have seen the long and dynamic history and significance of Jerusalem—a city with no equal on earth. History has shown us Jerusalem's uncanny ability to adapt and persevere, regardless of the obstacle at hand. As we move forward into an era of renewed interest and debate over Jerusalem's status as the Israeli capital, the eyes of the world are once again upon this incredible city. As the nations of the world weigh in on the issue, four general solutions are most often promoted or suggested. These are Jerusalem's transition into:

- a *united* capital, under the sovereignty of one state

- a *former* capital, in which both parties relinquish their claims to the city as their capital

- an *international* capital, in which Jerusalem serves as a capital for neither claimant but instead functions as a religious capital for all Jews, Christians, and Muslims of the world, or possibly as a federal capital of a potential union in the eastern Mediterranean comprised of at least Israel, Palestine, and Jordan; or

- a *shared or joint* capital, in which the city functions as the capital of two states.[80]

However, these debates—as exciting, interesting, and explosive as they may be—should not negate this fundamental principle and truth of law: Israel as a sovereign state chooses its own capital. And as they have chosen and we have seen, Jerusalem was, is, and always will be the eternal capital of Israel.

KEY TAKEAWAYS

1. As a sovereign state, Israel has every right to declare its own capital within its borders regardless of international pressure. Hence, because Israel has declared Jerusalem to be the capital, Jerusalem is its capital.

2. Jerusalem is the only example in the world of other nations refusing to recognize a sovereign nation's capital.

3. In 1995 the U.S. Congress passed the Jerusalem Embassy Act, which called for the relocation of the American embassy in Israel from Tel Aviv to Jerusalem for all of the legal reasons enumerated in this chapter. However, Presidents Bill Clinton, George W. Bush, and Barack Obama all declined to move the embassy.

ISRAEL AND THE LAW: ANCIENT PRINCIPLES AND MODERN LAWFARE

Israel can either be Jewish or democratic—it cannot be both . . . [1]
—SECRETARY OF STATE JOHN KERRY, DECEMBER 28, 2016

14

LOVING YOUR NEIGHBOR AS A MODEL FOR GOVERNANCE

By these will the State be judged, by the moral character it imparts to its citizens, by the human values determining its inner and outward relations, and by its fidelity, in thought and act, to the supreme behest: "and thou shalt love thy neighbor as thyself."[2]
—DAVID BEN-GURION, FIRST PRIME MINISTER OF ISRAEL

Many Americans are not defenders of Israel even if they don't have all the facts. These supporters may be intelligent and well-intentioned, but they are simply ignorant of the realities Israel faces every day. They just don't know what exactly is happening in the Middle East, they don't understand the nuances of what they hear in the news and in pro-BDS propaganda, and they don't see the implications these things have on global stability, U.S. sovereignty, and our own national security. Putting religious reasons aside, they may ask why Americans should care so much about a small nation halfway around the world. These good-hearted Americans truly care about human rights, diversity, and freedom for all people groups and find it hard to reconcile that with the collateral damage of war that so often ravages that part of the world.

Whenever I meet these people or talk to them on my radio show, I tell them exactly what I'm telling you now: If you care about human rights, diversity, and religious freedom, you *must* support Israel. No other nation in the region is such a staunch defender of these things as Israel is. That no doubt comes as a complete shock to anyone who has bought into the bigotry, hate speech, confusion, and apartheid nonsense that are splashed across our headlines every week. And yet it's right there at the heart of Israel's legal system.

When Israel's enemies attack the Jewish State on the world's stage, they are also attacking Israel's biggest supporter, the United States. If Israel's right to defend itself against terror is weakened, so is America's. The United States and Israel have always been and must always remain steadfast allies, because we are the cities on the hill standing for freedom for everyone in the face of terrorism. Our two nations are unique in the world, built upon ideologies and ideas that go to the very heart of what it means to be human, to be made in the image of God and worthy of dignity regardless of where you're from or what you believe. It is this love of humanity—of *all* peoples—that permeates Israeli law.

THE LAW AND NATIONAL VALUES

Israel's independence in 1948 presented Jewish tradition with all-new challenges and unprecedented opportunities. Having wandered in exile and at the mercy of conquering nations since their crushing defeat by the Romans, it had been almost two thousand years since the Jewish people had a state to call their own. Amid the euphoria of their biblical homecoming and against the backdrop of war, the Jewish people set out to create a system of government that ideally melded their faith-based values with the law. Unlike many secular systems, Jewish law does not stop at merely determining what is legal or illegal; Jewish law also aims to regulate what is ethical.[3] One big challenge for the new nation, then, was to *honor* ancient Jewish law, such as the Talmud, while still *translating it for modern times* through an ongoing process of deliberation, debate, and development.[4]

Israeli lawmakers quickly realized that this would not be an easy task. While some of the classic works of Jewish law—most notably the Talmud and the legal works of Maimonides (1135–1204)—do include some scattered references and a few brief guidelines about how to run a country, it became abundantly clear that Jewish law had never fully developed its own laws of state. And so, when the 1948 Israeli Declaration of Independence affirmed that the state and its laws would "be based on freedom, justice and peace as envisaged by the prophets of Israel,"[5] there was room to wonder what exactly that lofty ideal would mean when translated into practice.

NATIONALIZING AN INDIVIDUAL PRINCIPLE

It's only natural for Israel, in its quest to find and revive a corpus of *traditional* Jewish national values, to begin by returning to safer hallowed grounds. The lawmakers believed that advancing the ideal of the Jewish legal spirit could be as simple as translating and extending Judaism's highly developed moral code. In terms of living, dealing, and relating with each other, the Jews had long followed the biblical principle of Leviticus 19:18, "Love your neighbor as yourself." So, when seeking a guiding principle for their burgeoning legal system, they sought to expand the Jewish principle of loving your neighbor onto a national and even international scale.

In the waning days of the Obama administration, then secretary of state John Kerry thought this to be an impossible task. He said in 2016, "Israel can either be Jewish or democratic—it cannot be both . . ."[6] I already told you at the start of this book that I vehemently disagree with that sentiment. More important, so does the nation of Israel. The truth is, Israel has already shown that it *is* possible to be both democratic and Jewish at the same time. It is what they have done for the last seventy years, and what they continue to do today.

In order to show that the doctrine of loving your neighbor is at the core of the Jewish state, we need to prove two things:

1. Love your neighbor is at the center of Jewish law, and

2. Love your neighbor is reflected as such in Israeli law.

We can answer these assertions on two fronts: the religious level and the secular level.

THE RELIGIOUS JUSTIFICATION

First, on the religious level, there are those who have argued that human rights themselves are inherently religious in nature, since the idea of the human person as *sacred*—foundational to human-rights thinking—is itself inescapable based on religion.[7] The worth and dignity of the human being is fundamental to the Jewish tradition and many other monotheistic traditions. This cornerstone belief shows up in hundreds of ways, such as the assertions that human beings are made in the image of God and endowed with rationality, choice, a capacity to pray, a capacity to love, and a moral consciousness. When asked to formulate the main principle behind all of Judaic law, Rabbi Akiba famously said: "Love (and respect) your neighbor as you do yourself."[8] Both Christianity and Islam also assert this principle: Christians with the "Golden Rule" and Muslims with the edict to "hurt no one so that none may hurt you." In all three faiths, the assumption is that human beings are endowed with a set of natural and reciprocal rights, and those rights deserve to be respected and protected.

> When asked to formulate the main principle behind all of Judaic law, Rabbi Akiba famously said: "Love (and respect) your neighbor as you do yourself."

Challenged to sum up all of Jewish law in just one sentence, Hillel the Elder confidently replied: "That which is hateful to you, do not do to your fellow. That is the whole of Jewish law, the rest is explanation."[9] As Justice Menachem Elon of the Israeli Supreme Court put it:

> The very foundation in the religious world is the idea that every person is created in the image of God (Genesis 1:27).

Thus begins the Jewish Bible, and from it Jewish law derives the basic principles with regard to the value of the human being—each person as he is—his equality and his love.[10]

From the religious perspective then, the law of loving neighbors is in fact *the* meta-legal operating principle behind the entire body of Jewish religious law. So, when the Declaration declared that the law would "be based on freedom, justice and peace *as envisaged by the prophets of Israel*," this must be what it was referring to.[11]

THE SECULAR JUSTIFICATION

On the second, secular level, David Ben-Gurion, the first prime minister of Israel and the reader and first signatory on the Declaration, positively confirmed that the concept of loving your neighbor stands as the essence and heart of all Israel. In *Rebirth and Destiny of Israel*, a collection of essays and addresses that were delivered or written by Ben-Gurion from 1915 to 1952, he addressed his personal and public philosophy of the State of Israel. To our point, he said:

> By these will the State be judged, by the moral character it imparts to its citizens, by the human values determining its inner and outward relations, and by its fidelity, in thought and act, to the supreme behest: "and thou shalt love thy neighbor as thyself." Here is crystallized the eternal law of Judaism, and all the written ethics in the world can say no more. *The State will be worthy of its name only if its systems, social and economic, political and legal, are based upon these imperishable words.* They are more than a formal precept which can be construed as passive or negative: not to deprive, not to rob, not to oppress, not to hurt.[12]

This discussion of the law of "love thy neighbor" is more than just a theoretical notion of what the Fathers of the country might have meant. What we are really seeing is the essence and the backbone of what we now think of as Israeli law.

Historically, the love your neighbor doctrine as a foundational principle of Israeli legislation has expressed itself primarily in three impressive ways:

1. internally, in Israeli national law

2. externally, in how Israel deals with and incorporates international law; and

3. how Israel deals with its enemies.

These expressions of the love your neighbor philosophy are critical to our understanding of Israel's legal system, so let's take a deep dive through each one.

INTERNAL ISRAELI LAW

Perhaps the most *accurate* translation of Leviticus 19:18 is to love *reiacha* (literally, "your friend" or "your fellow") like yourself. "Friend" or "fellow" denotes someone with shared values or culture, and so this understanding of the principle is most applicable when thinking about how Israel deals with its own citizens. In laying out the framework for the practical fulfillment of this commandment, the great medieval Jewish philosopher and codifier Maimonides says:

It is a commandment for each person to love everyone from Israel like himself, as it says "love your friend like yourself." Therefore he needs to praise others, and be concerned about their money just as he cares about his own money and his own dignity. And one who aggrandizes himself at the expense of his friend, he has no share in the World to Come.[13]

The State of Israel codified these notions in the adoption of two constitutional Basic Laws in 1992. To better understand this, let's break down how these came to be.

LEGISLATING HUMAN RIGHTS AND DIGNITY

Basic Law: Human Dignity and Liberty opens with the following statement: "The purpose of this Basic Law is to protect human dignity and liberty, in order to establish in a Basic Law *the values of the State of Israel as a Jewish and democratic state*."[14] The language here is extremely important. Constitutional scholars and legal thinkers, such as former Israeli chief justice Aharon Barak, have noted that the implications for Israel as both Jewish and democratic should extend far beyond *only* human rights issues.[15] It is inconceivable, they say, that the State of Israel is both Jewish and democratic when it comes to human rights, but not when it comes to other important matters of law.[16] The constitutional interpretation must be seen in the greater context of all Basic Laws. So, if the values of the State of Israel as both a Jewish and a democratic state are enshrined in the Basic Laws that refer to human rights, they must also apply to *all* of the provisions of the Israeli constitution and statutes.[17]

This understanding reflects, as Chief Justice Barak notes, the application of loving your neighbor as yourself that has been termed the essence of Israeli law:

> What are the values of the State of Israel as a Jewish state from the heritage aspect? We learn about these values from the "world of *Halacha*" (religious law). They include the values of the State of Israel as a Jewish state in various levels of abstraction; from a specific law on a certain issue to abstract values such as "*love your neighbor as yourself*" [Lev. 19:18, emphasis added] or "do that which is honest and good" [Deut. 6:18]. It contains particular and universal values; it contains values developed over generations throughout the history of the Jewish people.[18]

> **The idea of Israel as a Jewish and a democratic state reflects Israel's treatment of its own citizens and becomes the filter through which it views its own constitutional ideals.**

If the values are indeed universal, then they must apply universally. Therefore, the idea of Israel as a Jewish and a democratic state reflects Israel's treatment of its own citizens and becomes the filter through which it views its own constitutional ideals. And, as we'll see, this provides a framework for how Israel engages with international concerns, as well.

ISRAEL AMONG THE NATIONS

While above we interpreted Leviticus 19:18's mention of "neighbor" as referring to a friend, now let's take a more common view: A neighbor is someone who is not necessarily kin, but who lives nearby and shares a greater community. In his discussion of this commandment, the great medieval Jewish philosopher and legal arbiter Nachmanides notes that, in his opinion the phrase cannot truly be taken literally, "since man cannot be expected to love his neighbor as his own soul." Indeed, he further notes that "Rabbi Akiva himself ruled to the contrary, that 'your life takes precedence over your fellow man's.'"[19]

GIVING PARITY TO OTHERS

Nachmanides then suggests that the real commandment here is not to literally love the neighbor like oneself but rather to give parity and kindness to the other, to treat what is important to them as important to you. On this, Nachmanides says:

> The Torah here implied that we should wish our neighbor to enjoy the same well-being that we wish ourselves. Perhaps this is the reason for the dative instead of the accusative form of the verb phrase. It does not state, "Love your neighbor," but "Love /for (le) your neighbor/ as yourself." Love your fellow with all the qualities and modes of love with which you love yourself. . . . The text is concerned with love in its qualitative and not its quantitative sense."[20]

This understanding of the verse—one that promotes a sense of mutual respect, an acknowledgment of the good that the other has to offer, and a recognition of one's place in a larger societal context—is perhaps most applicable when considering Israel's position in the community of nations. After the establishment of the State of Israel in 1948, the young country experienced diplomatic isolation and Arab League boycotts. Today, after years of tireless work, Israel has diplomatic ties with 154 out of the other 191 member states of the United Nations, as well as with nonmember the Holy See. The development of Israeli constitutionalism has been to a large extent about facilitating the admission of the new nation into the community of civilized states.[21] The refusal of so many nations over so many years to recognize Israel has perhaps made the concept of national citizenship more important for Israelis than for any other country. Simply put, they have always wanted to have a place among the community of nations and have worked hard to that end, despite decades of war, persecution, and obstruction.

Israel's International Reputation

It is also important to briefly mention the status of Israel's reputation internationally, particularly on the civil rights and freedoms front. For quite some time, Israel has considered the international legal system as another battlefield where its legitimacy is constantly being challenged.[22] For years, Israel has had to contend with a plethora of anti-Israel resolutions passed in the United Nations General Assembly and its constituent organizations. The best-known example was Resolution 3379 of November 10, 1975, which concluded with the statement "Zionism is a form of racism and racial discrimination."[23] The resolution also condemned Zionism "as a threat to world peace and security" and called "upon all countries to oppose this racist and imperialist ideology."[24] With the majority of the United Nation members automatically siding with the Arab nations, Israel has been left with little or no room to maneuver, making them dependent on America's veto power in the UN Security Council.

Perhaps due in part to its location and its unique security concerns, Israel's movements are scrutinized and criticized more so than those of almost any other country. It's no wonder, then, that Israel has made a point to include the international legal tradition of protecting human rights as part of their constitutional efforts. Explicitly making this point, Chief Justice Barak, in his treatise on legal interpretation, stated that "the international conventions on human rights to which Israel is a party should be given a special interpretive status, because they reflect the consensus of the international community to which Israel aspires to belong on an equal standing."[25] This is why Israel has increasingly accepted international law in order to gain international acceptance.

> Perhaps due in part to its location and its unique security concerns, Israel's movements are scrutinized and criticized more so than those of almost any other country.

Also to the issue of human rights on the international field is Israel's ongoing, intentional efforts to maintain religious diversity. It can never be overstated how unique Israel is among its neighboring Arab countries in its religious diversity and practice. This includes Jews, Christians, Muslims, Bahá'ís, and others. This wonderful religious diversity is unique among Middle East countries. Israel's neighboring Arab states certainly cannot list religious diversity and openness among their human rights successes. In fact, as Israel loves its diverse neighbors, that love is not mutual in the least. From its inception as a Jewish state, these same neighbors have done nothing but constantly attack Israel through war and terror while also levying lawfare and other forms of attacks against Israel's legitimacy on the world's stage.

> It can never be overstated how unique Israel is among its neighboring Arab countries in its religious diversity and practice.

JOINING THE COMMUNITY OF CIVILIZED STATES

Incorporating facets of international law has been incredibly important to Israel's judicial development.[26] The Israeli Supreme Court has even cited provisions of international law that have never been incorporated into domestic legislation anywhere else. In return for the gifts that international law has contributed to its constitutional corpus, the court has handed down precedent-setting decisions in areas such as detainee rights and targeted killings.[27] These decisions have dealt with some of the day's toughest questions about individual rights and collective security, and they have paved the way for future thought and international development.[28] The court—and Israel as its sponsor—has participated in the complex processes of adherence, dialogue, and inspiration within the international community of judges and jurists. Further, they have helped set standards for the protection of human rights in both Israel and the world. This, of course, has led to Israel being recognized as one of the *enlightened*— or civilized—nations at the table, at least in the area of human rights jurisprudence.

Israel's history of incorporating international norms and rights into its own legal system and the subsequent impact that practice has had on its foreign policy have gone a long way toward facilitating Israel's admission into the community of civilized states. The Jewish State has not only established and enshrined greater protections for its own human rights issues, it has also contributed to the international conversation.

> **It is clear that Israel's unique talents, expertise, and jurisprudence have made the state a real contributing member in the community of nations.**

As such, it is clear that Israel's unique talents, expertise, and jurisprudence have made the state a real contributing member in the community of nations.

ISRAEL AND ITS ENEMIES

The commandment to "love thy neighbor" is discussed a total of ten times in the entire corpus of the Babylonian Talmud.[29] Interestingly, of these ten times, six of the instances appear in the context of administering the death penalty and to the obligation to carry out the executions in a humane and sympathetic manner.[30] Of course, the

Hebrew word *reiacha* here no longer connotes any *sameness* or *nearness* as we've seen above; there is a radical *otherness* that necessarily separates the executioner and the executed.

Judaism believes that man is both created in the image of God and commanded to act like Him. Of this commandment, Maimonides writes: "Just as He is called gracious, so should you be gracious; just as He is merciful, so too should you be Merciful."[31] So, at the heart of the commandment to love thy neighbor is a palpable ethos of mercy, even in the face of *radical otherness*—someone who is so far gone and disconnected that you are obligated to kill them. This insight into the love your neighbor doctrine is perhaps most applicable in the context of how Israel deals with and treats its enemies. Even in these dark times, the words of Maimonides, quoting Rabbi Yose ben Chanina, ring true: "One who glorifies himself with the denigration of his fellow has no share in the World to Come."[32]

> At the heart of the commandment to love thy neighbor is a palpable ethos of mercy, even in the face of radical otherness—someone who is so far gone and disconnected that you are obligated to kill them.

SEEK PEACE BEFORE WAR

From a religious and ethical perspective, nearly all the preliminary rabbinic requirements for fighting a permissible war are designed to *limit* such wars and to remove noncombatants, civilians, and others who do not wish to fight from the battlefield. The halakhic three-party requirement of agreement between the king, Sanhedrin (the High Court), and *Urim veTumim*, for instance, renders warfare genuinely difficult to start under Jewish law.[33] Moreover, according to Jewish law, war cannot be the first option. Deuteronomy 20:10–12 says:

> When you march up to attack a city, make its people an offer of peace. If they accept and open their gates, all the people in it shall be subject to forced labor and shall work for you. If

they refuse to make peace and they engage you in battle, lay siege to that city.

So, as we see, the Bible clearly sets out the obligation to seek peace as a prelude to any military activity.

This procedural requirement is quite significant. It prevents the immediate escalation of hostilities and allows both sides to rationally plan the cost of war and the virtues of peace, to genuinely seek peace without requiring them to compromise their goals in order to achieve it.

> **The Bible clearly sets out the obligation to seek peace as a prelude to any military activity.**

This obligation to seek peace applies specifically before battle between armies, where no civilian population is involved or threatened at all. Jewish law requires an additional series of overtures for peace and surrender in situations where the military activity involves attacking populated cities. Maimonides states that

Joshua, before he entered the land of Israel sent three letters to its inhabitants. The first one said that those who wish to flee should flee. The second one said that those that wish to make peace should make peace. The third letter said that those that want to fight a war should prepare to fight a war.[34]

This warning to the population ensured that Israel's armies had done everything possible to prevent civilian casualties before fighting ever began.

This requirement to warn civilians wasn't enough to fulfill the moral obligation, however. Maimonides outlines a number of other specific rules of military ethics based on Talmudic sources culled from biblical texts. When the army surrounds a city to lay siege to it, for instance, it is prohibited to surround it from all four sides; they must leave an escape path open for those who wish to flee for their lives during the battle. Nachmanides elaborates:

God commanded us that when we lay siege to a city that we leave one of the sides without a siege so as to give them a place to flee to. It is from this commandment that we learn to deal with compassion even with our enemies even at time of war; in addition by giving our enemies a place to flee to, they will not charge at us with as much force.[35]

Nachmanides believes that this obligation is so basic that it is to be counted as one of the 613 basic biblical commandments in Jewish law.

COMPASSION IN WARTIME

It is clear that Jewish tradition is very much in favor of compassion and humanitarian assistance, even in wartime. Scripture states that, after losing a battle, Hadad, king of Syria, sought refuge with the victor, Ahab, king of Israel; his advisers had counseled him that the Israelite kings were *malkhei hesed*—"merciful kings" (1 Kings 20:31). As one medieval rabbi put it, "It is fitting for us, the holy seed, to act [with compassion] in all matters, even towards our idolatrous enemies."[36]

That mercy is not only reserved for people; it applies to the land as well. While many of Israel's enemies have employed a scorched-earth approach, seeking to lay waste to enemy territory as part of their conquest, the Bible sets forth a much different ethic. Deuteronomy 20:19 commands:

When you lay siege to a city for a long time, fighting against it to capture it, do not destroy its trees by putting an ax to them, because you can eat their fruit. Do not cut them down. Are the trees people, that you should besiege them?

Rabbi Norman Solomon points out that "in its biblical context this is a counsel of prudence rather than a principle of conservation . . ."[37] The tradition, however, saw it as much more.

Philo of Alexandria, a first-century Jewish philosopher, extended the prohibition against axing fruit-bearing trees to include vandalizing the environs of a besieged city. He wrote, "Indeed, so great a love for justice does the law instill in those who live under its constitution that it does not even permit the fertile soil of a hostile city to be outraged by devastation or by cutting down trees to destroy the fruits."[38] Josephus similarly expands this to include a prohibition against incinerating the enemy's country and killing their animals employed in labor if there is no direct military advantage to be gained.[39]

Nachmanides writes that removing all trees is permissible if needed for building fortifications; it is only forbidden when it is done specifically to induce suffering.[40] Maimonides, in his *Book of Commandments*, also explicitly links this prohibition to the deliberate intent of exposing the enemy to undue suffering.[41] He then takes the next step in extending the prohibition to categorically forbid *all* wanton destruction: "Also, one who smashes household goods, tears clothes, demolishes a building, stops up a spring, or destroys articles of food with destructive intent, transgresses the command 'You shall not destroy.'"[42]

According to *Sefer HaKhinukh*, a thirteenth-century work discussing the commandments of the Torah, the prohibition was meant "to teach us to love the good and the purposeful and to cleave to it so that the good will cleave to us and we will distance ourselves from anything evil and destructive."[43] Although the purpose of an army at war is to win, the rabbinic tradition rejected the claim of military necessity as an excuse for military excess. Simply put, everything needs to be in proportion.

> Although the purpose of an army at war is to win, the rabbinic tradition rejected the claim of military necessity as an excuse for military excess. Simply put, everything needs to be in proportion.

ISRAEL'S ETHICAL CODE

How does all the above play out in the modern-day context of Jewish war? Let's look at some specific, practical examples. During Operation Peace for the Galilee, a military campaign into Lebanon in 1982, the Israel Defense Forces sent a message to the soldiers regarding how they should conduct themselves during the war. The message included the following excerpts:

- It is forbidden to fire unless fired upon.

- It is forbidden, without any exception, to take booty from any source.

- Do not harm, do not disturb, the peaceful civilian population.

- Treat women with respect; they are not to be molested.

- You are not to disturb any cultural center, any antiquities, museums, art galleries, churches, mosques or sacred places.

- Despite these perfectly natural emotions and sentiments, you must remember that you are a human being.

- Though you are fighting a vicious enemy that has resorted to terror against innocent people . . . you are not to engage in any vengeful act against your enemy if you take him prisoner.

- Whatever you do will reflect upon the people of Israel. Any act of desecration, taking of booty or desecration of holy places, mistreating your enemy, will reflect badly upon the army.

- Above all, you must remember to value the Jewish tradition that, even in times of war, you remember that man to man—*k'adam l'adam hu*—you are a human being.[44]

It is a safe assumption that most of Israel's enemies do not put such restrictions on their soldiers during times of war and conflict.

The Spirit of the IDF, the latest incarnation of the ethical code of the Israel Defense Forces, draws its values and basic principles from four sources:

1. the tradition of the IDF and its military heritage as the Israel Defense Forces

2. the tradition of the State of Israel, its democratic principles, laws, and institutions

3. the tradition of the Jewish people throughout their history; and

4. universal moral values based on the value and dignity of human life.[45]

Explicit here are the values of human dignity: "The IDF and its soldiers are obligated to protect human dignity. Every human being is of value regardless of his or her origin, religion, nationality, gender, status or position."[46] Perhaps most notable regarding human dignity is the IDF "Purity of Arms" doctrine:

> Explicit here are the values of human dignity: "The IDF and its soldiers are obligated to protect human dignity. Every human being is of value regardless of his or her origin, religion, nationality, gender, status or position."

> The IDF servicemen and women will use their weapons and force only for the purpose of their mission, only to the necessary extent and will maintain their humanity even during combat. IDF soldiers will not use their weapons and force to harm human beings who are not combatants or prisoners of war, and will do all in their power to avoid causing harm to their lives, bodies, dignity and property.[47]

In a policy that is a direct descendant of Joshua's military letters of warning, the IDF also makes public announcements, private phone calls, and public radio transmissions, as well as distributes thousands of leaflets, all in an effort to protect the citizens of the nations it is at war with. Through these means, Israel warns the populations of impending attacks and of areas to avoid for their own safety. And, echoing the tradition of exercising personal restraint and forbidding the destruction of trees, Israel's *Manual on the Laws of War in the Battlefield* outlines guidelines for taking prisoners' personal effects and prohibits attacking targets that are essential to the continued survival of the civilian population.[48]

> The army's code of conduct, as well as the standards and expectations of their soldiers during wartime, reflect religious thought and ethical consideration that both rabbis and generals can be proud of.

In these efforts, even in their darkest moments, Israel's commitment to following the love your neighbor principle shines through. The army's code of conduct, as well as the standards and expectations of their soldiers during wartime, reflect religious thought and ethical consideration that both rabbis and generals can be proud of.

BOTH JEWISH AND DEMOCRATIC

All of Jewish law can be seen as a study in the balance of competing values that often exist in tension. One value, however, *always* remains constant, whether the question involves a friend, a neighbor, or an enemy. That is the value of loving the other—even when it is difficult, even where it might incur loss, even when there is a difference in faith and morals, even when there are political or doctrinal differences, and even if the enemy is using innocent, vulnerable populations as shields for its own terror.

> Only one country in the Middle East fosters religious freedom and tolerance, and that is Israel, which protects religious freedom for all and officially recognizes fifteen different religions.

In terms of legislation, Israel does not discriminate in any way against non-Jews, the LGBT community, or any other class of persons. Only one country in the Middle East fosters religious freedom and tolerance, and that is Israel, which protects religious freedom for all and officially recognizes fifteen different religions.

Arabic is an official language and on equal footing with Hebrew. Israel holds free and fair elections, with legal opposition parties and full minority participation. Israel protects women's rights and civil rights for all, including the rights to free speech and assembly; fair and open trials; free, uncensored media; free artistic and academic expression; and free entry of foreign arts, books, and press. Israel, in short, protects *the other* by minimizing otherness and by opposing "othering" behaviors or policies.[49]

Those who claim that the idea of a Jewish state is incompatible with democracy for all severely undervalue the prevailing policy of love your neighbor. While it is obvious that individual laws and policies may need updating at any time, the spirit of Jewish law, which pervades and underlies Israel, is one of democratic, noble neighborliness. This ideal can be found on both the national and international levels, and both the founders and the most important judicial thinkers in the land have acknowledged its influential presence.

> While it is obvious that individual laws and policies may need updating at any time, the spirit of Jewish law, which pervades and underlies Israel, is one of democratic, noble neighborliness.

With their faith standing behind their incredible ethic and driving their deeply rooted sense of human dignity, I can say without hesitation that Israel is, in fact, both a Jewish and a democratic state. John Kerry was wrong.

KEY TAKEAWAYS

1. Israel's legal spirit is an effort in part to translate and extend Judaism's highly developed moral code, best summed up as "Love your neighbor as yourself" (Lev. 19:18).

2. Israel's commitment to govern by the "Love your neighbor" principle is evident in how it governs its own citizens,

how it interacts with other nations, and how it treats its enemies.

3. Israel is unique in the Middle East for its commitment to religious freedom and tolerance, as well as its non-discriminatory stance toward all classes of people.

15

HOW WE ARE DEFEATING THE BDS MOVEMENT

Either smarter people have abandoned Zionism or the average IQ of Zionists has gone down, but they're really not thinking straight. Because they haven't come up with one smart tactic to fight BDS . . . since 2005. We're not being cocky about that . . . we're not facing serious challenges there. It's becoming an open door."[1]

—OMAR BARGHOUTI, COFOUNDER OF THE BOYCOTT, DIVESTMENT, AND SANCTIONS MOVEMENT

Challenge accepted.

—JAY SEKULOW

At the beginning of this book, we took some time to understand the changing landscape of modern lawfare, and we saw how those legal tactics are being used against Israel. We also explored the beginnings of the Boycott, Divestment, and Sanctions movement and discussed how BDS has tried to discredit, delegitimize, and ultimately destroy the Jewish State. And, of course, we spent a lot of time digging into the biblical history, archaeological and extra-biblical evidence, and the legal history supporting Israel's right to exist as a Jewish state. Now, as we near the end of this book, I want to return to the current struggle—the challenges that modern-day Israelis and Jewish people across the globe are facing every day. While so many of Israel's battles, go back four thousand years, we can't forget that the war is still raging. The story of Israel is not *just* ancient history written on scrolls and stone tablets. It is a modern war that is still being waged today in courtrooms and classrooms around the world.

The BDS movement has toxic and terrifying roots, and we've seen that their goal is to deprive Israel of its fundamental right to exist. So, how do we battle such a nefarious foe? I'm proud to say that the ACLJ has partnered with several other organizations to take on the fight against the BDS movement anywhere it crops up, defending innocent Jewish college students and allies of Israel wherever they are attacked. Now that we've come to understand the history and the opposition, let's take a close look at some real-world, modern-day case studies of how Israel's right to exist is being attacked all around us and how the ACLJ and others are fighting back.

> **The story of Israel is not *just* ancient history written on scrolls and stone tablets. It is a modern war that is still being waged today in courtrooms and classrooms around the world.**

ENTER THE AMERICAN CENTER FOR LAW AND JUSTICE

Our firm focuses on constitutional and human rights law worldwide. We have been described by *Bloomberg Businessweek* as the "leading advocacy group for religious freedom" and recognized by *Time* magazine for our significant impact on constitutional law.[2] We enjoy close working relationships with members of Congress on both domestic and international issues; we handle cases in state, federal, and international courts; and our numerous major wins, including multiple Supreme Court victories, have given us a reputation for innovative legal strategy with far-reaching implications.[3]

We have affiliates around the world, including the European Center for Law and Justice, a nongovernmental organization (NGO) with consultative status before the United Nations. This is a special status provided to certain NGOs that enables them to formally participate and advise the global community at the United Nations.

The ACLJ also has long-standing relationships in several nations, including, of course, the State of Israel, where we opened a permanent Jerusalem office in 2009. Since then, we have engaged in litigation and advocacy on behalf of Israel's interests, including at The Hague, where I had the opportunity to deliver oral arguments before the Office of the Prosecutor of the International Criminal Court on Israel's behalf. We won that case, just as we will win against the anti-Israel BDS movement.

OUR STRATEGY FOR FIGHTING BDS

Throughout this chapter, I want to detail the ACLJ's basic strategy for fighting BDS. It is a strategy we've developed over the past few years through our tireless work in this important yet often overlooked field. Our strategy has four prongs:

- First, expose the true nature of BDS for what it is: a long-term project created by anti-Israel activists and designed to delegitimize the State of Israel and the Jewish people by any means possible.

- Second, identify and quash BDS manifestations, including subtle ones that violate existing law and policy.

- Third, enshrine into law additional protections for Jewish citizens and Israeli interests in the hope of improving these and other legal protections for people of all races, cultures, and ethnicities.

- Fourth, change the international conversation about Israel, clearing away the anti-Semitic lies and other distortions perpetrated through the narrative of the BDS movement and its allies.

To illustrate these strategies in action, I'm also going to share several highlights from some of our cases where we've implemented our strategy on a national scale. I could fill a whole book, in fact, with examples of cases we've fought, discussions we've had, and battles we've won. However, because so many of these things are privileged conversations or ongoing cases, I'm limited in what I'm able to share in a book. The examples in this chapter, though, should be sufficient to give you a clear picture of the various ways Israel is being attacked every day and the legal, political, and advocacy tools the ACLJ is using to successfully defend Israel and its allies from anti-Semitic attacks.

The examples in this chapter should be sufficient to give you a clear picture of the various ways Israel is being attacked every day and the legal, political, and advocacy tools the ACLJ is using to successfully defend Israel and its allies from anti-Semitic attacks.

THE ACLJ'S REACH

Through advocacy, educating the public about the true nature of BDS, and revealing the untruths in the public BDS narratives, the ACLJ's reach is almost unprecedented. We have a constant presence through our own outlets as well as other national media. We are reaching millions of people each week through our weekly television show *ACLJ This Week*, the daily live radio show *Jay Sekulow Live!*, and a dynamic website, ACLJ.org. Plus, our attorneys frequently appear as guests on FOX News, ABC, NBC, CNN, CNBC, MSNBC, and PBS, and our advocacy efforts are covered regularly by *USA Today*, the *New York Times*, the *Los Angeles Times*, the *Washington Post*, and the *Washington Times*.

We've entered the publishing and film arenas in recent years as well. Our books *The Rise of ISIS* (2014) and *Unholy Alliance* (2016), which focus on global geopolitical threats from jihadists and authoritarians, both landed on national bestsellers lists, extending the ACLJ's reach even further. Our production company, ACLJ Films, which produces documentaries chronicling the significant legal and advocacy issues of our time, has released two films shot on location in Israel, *The Export* and *Unshaken*.

Additionally, the ACLJ has:

- a team of experts with government affairs experience, tactics, and tools

- a sophisticated mix of high-profile activists, grassroots participants, and third-party coalition development partners

- a proprietary database of more than four million faith-and-values, citizen-activist households nationwide

- partnerships with sixty organizations that have a combined membership of three million; and

- a communications database of more than thirteen million subscribers.

Finally, in our effort to write into law additional protections for Jewish citizens and Israeli interests, the ACLJ has worked alongside legislators and legal professionals to review and advise on ongoing legislative initiatives. In fact, the ACLJ has also drafted its own innovative model anti-BDS legislation, the PEACE of Israel Act, which we'll discuss below.

Let me be clear here: I am not saying all of this just to brag about our hard work or our successes. The point of this summary is to show that the ACLJ is uniquely qualified to lead the charge in the fight for Israel's right to exist. We've been honored to work with several other partner organizations and individuals in this campaign, and we'll work with many more before we're done. We've spent so much time in this book talking about Israel's opposition that I just wanted you to have some perspective on the forces rallied against them. I've said many times that this is a fight we must win, and I know we can't win it alone.

FIGHTING BDS HEAD-ON

As we've said before, the unambiguous goal of the international BDS movement is the elimination of the State of Israel. To that end, the movement operates as a coordinated, sophisticated effort to disrupt

Israel's economic and financial stability. They accomplish this by targeting and causing direct harm to the economic interests of people who conduct business in and with the State of Israel.

BDS claims responsibility for doing significant damage to Israeli business interests. Their proponents have threatened and carried out acts of violence directed at the State of Israel and those who support it economically. They threaten to withdraw financial support as a way of coercing companies to stop doing business or refuse to do business in or with Israel, its nationals, its residents, and others around the world who are Jewish or who do business with the Jewish people. The result of these strategies is anti-Semitism and animosity where there should be discussion, learning, and collaboration. In a free society, this kind of hate cannot be allowed to exist.

> To put it bluntly, BDS constitutes nothing less than political and economic terrorism. This is not exaggeration: It's their stated purpose for existing. And they must be defeated.

To put it bluntly, BDS constitutes nothing less than political and economic terrorism. This is not exaggeration: It's their stated purpose for existing. And they must be defeated.

THE PEACE OF ISRAEL AND EXPORT ADMINISTRATION ACTS

The ACLJ has been on the front lines of drafting new, innovative legislation to fight the anti-Israel BDS movement. The Protection and Enforcement Against the Commercial Exclusion (PEACE) of Israel Act, which we modeled in part after the Export Administration Act (EAA), seeks to prevent American citizens, and the businesses that drive the free market economy of the nation, from becoming embroiled in foreign conflicts through coercion.[4] The "foreign conflicts" referenced here certainly include the Palestinian-Israeli conflict, and the "coercion" definitely includes the threat of economic loss or ruin that the BDS movement espouses. These things, we believe, are repugnant to American values and traditions.

The purpose of the PEACE Act is to protect the free market, as well as the economic interests of the United States, by legally prohibiting specified conduct in or affecting interstate or foreign commerce when it is undertaken with the intent to further any boycott movement initiated and/or directed by a foreign organization, however constituted (other than a foreign country), and against a country that is friendly to the United States. The act also serves to protect the economic interests of the United States, which are detrimentally impacted by efforts to disrupt the economic stability of Israel.

The PEACE of Israel Act is similar, in purpose and language, to provisions of both the EAA and antitrust law, with a few significant differences.[5] First, because of potential First Amendment concerns regarding anti-boycott laws, the bill is focused exclusively on the prohibition of *secondary* boycott activities rather than primary boycott activities, which are directed specifically toward countries friendly to the United States. You'll remember from Chapter 2 that the BDS movement practices secondary boycotts, in which one party pressures a second party not to do business with a third party. These secondary boycotts are not protected in the same way by the First Amendment. Second, the bill's nondiscrimination provisions are limited to the categories of race, ethnicity, and national origin—the three classifications targeted by the BDS movement. And third, unlike the EAA (but like the antitrust laws), the bill creates a private right of action for persons injured by violations of the law.

In addition to the efforts already mentioned, the ACLJ is working with legal groups, policy makers, and state and federal representatives on current anti-BDS resolutions and other legislative initiatives. We are a member of the Federalism and International Relations Task Force of the American Legislative Exchange Council (ALEC), a national organization of state legislators from all fifty states. Our attorneys have presented information about BDS (and anti-BDS initiatives) to create model legislation. We have taken the lead with a unique and aggressive approach, similar to our PEACE of Israel Act. To our knowledge, ours is the first proposed legislation to make certain BDS-related activities unlawful and to create a private right of action for those injured by them. Our anti-BDS language was lauded as innovative, thoughtful, and sophisticated by many, including the founder of a congressional staff working group established to study and propose further federal anti-BDS legislation.

FIGHTING DISCRIMINATION

In the fight to defeat any BDS maneuvers that target Israel and its allies, we successfully use existing legal structures to make sure that the civil and human rights of the Jewish and pro-Israel communities are protected and enforced. One fundamental piece of legislation we rely on is the Civil Rights Act of 1964. Title VI of that Act "prohibits discrimination in federally assisted programs and activities on the basis of race, color, or national origin."[6] A violation of Title VI may be found if discrimination is encouraged, tolerated, not adequately addressed, or ignored by the administration of a college or university.[7] If an organization violates Title VI, the victims of discrimination can file a complaint in the U.S. Department of Education's Office for Civil Rights or in a federal district court. As it pertains to this discussion, Jewish people earned protected status in 2004.[8] Although Title VI of the Civil Rights Act does not specifically list "religion" as a protected class, Jewish students are protected from discrimination based on their perceived ethnic, racial, or ancestral background.

And yet, as we've said before, activities and events meant to intimidate and marginalize Jewish citizens have seen a marked upswing on college campuses around the United States over the past fifteen years. That makes sense when you understand that the BDS movement calls for, among other things, academic institutions and individual scholars to boycott activities and programs sponsored by Israeli universities.

> **Activities and events meant to intimidate and marginalize Jewish citizens have seen a marked upswing on college campuses around the United States over the past fifteen years.**

This effort is "sold" to students and academics as a way to protest and change Israeli policies by equating them with oppressive or apartheid regimes. However, it doesn't take much to see that BDS has no interest in *changing* Israeli policies; they want to *eliminate* Israel altogether. As one leading BDS activist has explained, "The real aim of BDS is to bring down the state of Israel. . . . There should not be any equivocation on the subject. Justice and freedom for Palestinians are incompatible with the

> It doesn't take much to see that BDS has no interest in *changing* Israeli policies; they want to *eliminate* Israel altogether.

existence of the state of Israel."[9] Or, in the words of another BDS leader, "BDS does mean the end of the Jewish state. . . . BDS is not another step on the way to the final showdown; BDS is *the* final showdown."[10] Despite their claims for peace, the BDS movement's call for the complete elimination of a specific national identity certainly seems like discrimination to me.

Free Speech vs. Harassment and Anti-Semitism

As a nonprofit organization dedicated to protecting constitutional liberties—especially the right to free speech and religious expression—the ACLJ has had years of experience negotiating the legal line between right and wrong. We firmly believe that freedom of speech, even speech some may find offensive, should be cherished and respected in both public and private institutions as part of what makes our democracy so great. Nothing else is so meaningful in allowing the exchange of ideas, opinions, and beliefs among citizens and groups. But as the U.S. Department of Education's Office of Civil Rights has made clear, there are times when speech crosses the line into harassment and discrimination. Harassment can be verbal if, for example, it is severe, persistent, or pervasive enough to limit or deny a student's ability to participate in or benefit from an educational program.[11]

The ACLJ firmly believes in every individual's fundamental freedoms. But we also believe in upholding the law and ensuring no one country or people are singled out for attack. While some may argue that these principles—freedom and law—are in tension, they are actually complementary. It is a well-established tenet of basic political and legal philosophy that without the rule of law, the very nature of freedom itself would be in danger. Freedom cannot exist in an anarchic environment where might makes right. A world with no law would breed chaos, where the freedom of the majority to impose its will on the minority would erode freedom for everyone.

When you know what to look for, it becomes painfully easy to see where free speech crosses the line into discrimination or, as it pertains to this discussion, anti-Semitism. The U.S. Department of State defines "anti-Semitism" this way:

> Anti-Semitism is a certain perception of Jews, which may be expressed as hatred toward Jews. Rhetorical and physical manifestations of anti-Semitism are directed toward Jewish or non-Jewish individuals and/or their property, toward Jewish community institutions and religious facilities.[12]

The State Department definition goes on to note that "such manifestations could also target the state of Israel, conceived as a Jewish collectivity."[13]

According to the European Parliament Working Group on Antisemitism, anti-Semitic thought frequently charges Jews with conspiring to harm humanity, and it is often used to blame Jews for "why things go wrong."[14] It is expressed in speech, writing, visual forms, and action, and it employs sinister stereotypes and negative character traits.[15] The State Department and the European Parliament Working Group on Antisemitism list several examples of what would constitute problematic anti-Semitic speech, particularly as it relates to the State of Israel, including, but not limited to:

- denying the Jewish people their right to self-determination;

- accusing Jewish citizens of being more loyal to Israel, or to the alleged priorities of Jews worldwide, than to the interest of their own nations;

- applying double standards by requiring of Israel a behavior not expected or demanded of any other democratic nation;

- multilateral organizations focusing exclusively on Israel for peace or human rights investigations; and

- holding Jews collectively responsible for actions of the state of Israel.[16]

Organizations must be vigilant in ensuring that free and protected speech in any forums for which they are responsible does not cross the line into hate speech or remarks—the kind that singles out one group of people for disparate treatment and may limit their ability to participate. The BDS movement, however, actively engages in and/or encourages every one of the problematic behaviors listed above.

Despite their bluster, the BDS movement lacks any real direction or policy beyond promoting discrimination and anti-Semitic conduct. The result is that, although BDS claims to be actively working toward peace in Israel through nonviolent activism measures, it does substantial harm to individuals, regardless of their affiliation with Israel. In fact, victims of BDS are often Jews—or even people perceived to be Jews—

> **Despite their bluster, the BDS movement lacks any real direction or policy beyond promoting discrimination and anti-Semitic conduct.**

who may have no connection at all to the State of Israel.[17] The terrible outcome is that protests and speech claiming to be focused on Israel are nothing more than thinly veiled hate crimes perpetrated against people of all walks of life, both Jew and Gentile alike.

DEFENDING JEWISH STUDENTS AND ACADEMICS

A recent study confirmed that anti-Semitic discrimination is especially prevalent on American college campuses. A report published by the pro-Israel AMCHA Initiative detailed that there were more than 300 incidents of anti-Semitism on 113 campuses in 2015 alone. Significantly, nearly every institution with an active anti-Israel organization experienced at least one anti-Semitic incident during the year. It appears that the rise of the BDS movement is directly linked and correlated to the rise in anti-Semitism on college campuses. Importantly, the study found that pro-BDS activity "is the strongest predictor of anti-Jewish hostility on campus."[18] The ACLJ has been involved in many of these discrimination cases, and because some of these cases are now closed, I can actually discuss certain victories, how we accomplished them, and what they mean moving forward in our battle against the BDS movement.

> It appears that the rise of the BDS movement is directly linked and correlated to the rise in anti-Semitism on college campuses.

THE ASA'S ANTI-ISRAEL BOYCOTT

On December 4, 2013, the National Council of the American Studies Association (ASA) passed and then ratified the council resolution on Boycott of Israeli Academic Institutions, stating in relevant part "that the American Studies Association (ASA) endorses and will honor the call of Palestinian civil society for a boycott of Israeli academic institutions."[19] In its annual meeting, the ASA clarified its intention to deny participation to Israeli "institutions and representatives," which include all individual Israeli academics "serving as representatives or ambassadors of those institutions (such as deans, rectors, presidents and others), or of the Israeli government . . . [20] This resolution triggered condemnation from more than 250 universities and colleges, and at least 8 institutions terminated their relationship with the ASA as a result of the boycott. The Association of American Universities condemned the boycott as a violation of academic freedom and called upon scholars to oppose the boycott.

In response, the ACLJ conducted an information campaign to

ensure all organizations associating with the ASA were aware of their commitments and potential liability under U.S. anti-boycott laws, including the Export Administration Act (EAA) and various state civil rights acts. One specific ACLJ project included sending letters to all organizations associated with the ASA for business and other purposes. We sent a demand letter to the Westin Bonaventure Hotel in Los Angeles, the host site of the ASA's 2014 Annual Meeting, informing them of their obligations under state and federal nondiscrimination laws—including taking measures reasonably necessary to ensure that the ASA did not enforce its discriminatory boycott on the hotel's premises.[21] Due to our engagement with the hotel, the ASA backed down from its own boycott position and announced that all individuals, regardless of their affiliation with Israel, would be allowed to attend the event.

LOYOLA UNIVERSITY CHICAGO

In 2015, the ACLJ stepped in to help a student of the Loyola University Chicago who had been singled out and persecuted by other students and the school's administration. Our client, a young Jewish woman, had attended an event at which members of the school's Students for Justice in Palestine (SJP) chapter harassed her. Incredibly, although she was the victim in this incident, she was herself accused of violating the student code of conduct, due to fabricated allegations from the SJP that she had assaulted a photographer. It just so happens that the student was a board member of Hillel, an organization focused on the Jewish people and their traditions, and a visible Jewish leader on campus.

The student was denied a copy of the incident file, prevented from taking notes during her hearing, and subjected to a litany of other improper conduct and due process violations by the school administration. The ACLJ quickly took up the student's case. In our representation, the ACLJ pointed out that the university's conduct violated not only its own policies but federal discrimination and harassment laws as well. The student was very quickly cleared of all charges.

University of California

In 2014, the University of California Student-Workers Union (UAW 2865), a branch of the United Auto Workers (UAW), pushed for a membership vote in support of BDS. Over the objection of many of its members, UAW 2865 formally adopted a stance in support of BDS.[22] However, in a letter dated November 17, 2014, Gary Jones, director of UAW Region 5, stated that the United Auto Workers International Union (UAWIU) had, with the support of more than forty other national labor leaders, taken a stance *against* the BDS movement. As Mr. Jones made clear in his letter, "the International Union's previous position has not changed."[23] This actually put UAW 2865 in direct opposition to its parent organization.

In response to the UAW 2865 resolution, the ACLJ notified the local union, UAW national, and the University of California System (UC System) that the ACLJ intended to hold student workers fully responsible for complying with federal and state law, as well as university policies that bar—among other things—discrimination on the basis of national origin, race, and religion. Almost immediately the provost of the UC System responded and explicitly reminded all the university chancellors that the Policy on Course Content prohibits UAW 2865 graduate student instructors from promoting BDS and anti-Israel propaganda in the classroom. One year after the UAW 2865 vote, the UAWIU nullified it. In granting an appeal brought by other members of UAW 2865, the UAWIU stated that the local chapter had "overstepped its constitutional parameters," that the resolution "would harm UAW-represented workers and other union members," and that "the provisions of the [resolution] despite semantical claims to the contrary by the local union, can easily be construed as academic and cultural discrimination."[24]

University of Michigan

On December 4, 2015, the ACLJ joined a larger group of organizations in writing a letter to Mark Schlissel, the University of Michigan president, to address the free speech violations of a sophomore student of the University.[25] A Central Student Government (CSG) representative exercised his right to free speech and "objected to the timing, taste and appropriateness of the 'Students Allied for Freedom and Equality's (SAFE) anti-Israel display in the center of the campus on November 19, which was set up on the very day that two terrorist attacks occurred in Israel, killing five people.'"[26] In response, the members of SAFE initiated a crusade to remove the CSG representative from his student government position, simply for exercising his free speech.[27] Rather than recognizing the representative's First Amendment rights and outright denying SAFE's request to remove him from office, the CSG forced him to appear before its ethics committee to determine if his expression of pro-Israel sentiments and objections to SAFE's actions were grounds for punitive measures against him.

Specifically, the CSG representative voiced his objection to SAFE's public demonstration, which included two "massive walls" simulating the security fence Israel has constructed to protect its citizens from terrorist attacks. The display included the following message written across a map of Israel: "TO EXIST IS TO RESIST." Although video footage of the ethics committee hearing demonstrated no inappropriate behavior, the members of SAFE convinced the CSG to launch a full-scale ethics investigation against the CSG representative's allegedly "aggressive" and "hateful" behavior toward SAFE.

In the letter to President Schlissel, the ACLJ and other organizations demanded that this persecution be stopped immediately because (1) the ethics investigation by the CSG was causing enormous damage, pain, and suffering to the CSG representative himself; and (2) SAFE's actions sent a wrong and dangerous message of free speech suppression to other students at the university. The letter urged the university to terminate the unlawful CSG investigation and notify SAFE and CSG that the representative could not be punished for exercising his free speech rights. The letter also urged the university to require the CSG and SAFE to issue him an apology. The university was further urged to release a campus-wide statement explaining that the CSG representative had merely exercised his right to free speech and that the university would not permit students or student groups to obstruct another student's First Amendment rights. In the end, the CSG representative was "unanimously vindicated" of the charges against him.[28]

CITY UNIVERSITY OF NEW YORK

Anti-Semitism, often cloaked in BDS attire, continues to be a rampant problem in New York's public university system. City University of New York (CUNY) campuses throughout the state have been home to multiple disturbing incidents.

On April 15, 2016, the Doctoral Students' Council (DSC) at CUNY adopted a Resolution Endorsing the Boycott of Israeli Academic Institutions, commonly known as the BDS Resolution.[29] After a lengthy preface of inflammatory remarks against the State of Israel, the DSC resolved to "endorse the Palestinian call to boycott Israeli academic institutions for as long as the Israeli state continues to violate Palestinian rights under international law" and to "support . . . the efforts of Students for Justice in Palestine at CUNY and all others engaged in the struggle to end the occupation and colonization of Palestine."[30]

The DSC represents nearly four thousand members of the graduate school who are also students and faculty across many of the campuses within the CUNY system. Its affiliate, the Adjunct Project, a self-described resource center for Graduate Center student workers and CUNY adjuncts, has also endorsed the resolution. It has encouraged "all members of the CUNY community to raise awareness, through resources like those provided by Labor for Palestine, and to support or get involved with efforts on their campuses, including CUNY for Palestine and SJP chapters."[31]

In response to the BDS resolution, the ACLJ sent a letter to the university reminding the president and trustees that the school has an obligation to take sufficient action to return the CUNY campuses to a safe, non-harassing, non-discriminatory environment for students and employees alike. Additionally, the letter advised the university to take steps to protect itself from any potential liability based on the conduct of DSC members who are also employees of the university.

This information unequivocally put the CUNY administration on notice of its obligation to take all necessary steps to prevent hostile and discriminatory treatment of Jewish members of the campus community.

On May 10, 2016, Chancellor James B. Milliken responded to the ACLJ with a letter confirming the university's commitment to freedom of speech but acknowledged, as we pointed out, that this right has limitations, including in the context of hostile environment discrimination. Chancellor Milliken also informed us that, in light of the pervasive nature of recent campus anti-Semitism, a working group of administrators, faculty, and students had been assembled and was reviewing campus activities and practices. According to Chancellor Milliken, this group would "make recommendations for appropriate campus and University action."[32] Importantly, with regard to the DSC's BDS resolution, Chancellor Milliken asserted that the resolution actually had no teeth, as "the DSC has no authority to 'implement' its resolution . . . and CUNY has every intention to continue its long-standing practice of exchanges with international universities including those in Israel."[33]

Chancellor Milliken concluded by expressly agreeing with the ACLJ "that CUNY has an obligation to respond to unlawful discrimination by its employees or students and to take action to prevent the development of a hostile environment" on campus. He also committed to "see that [CUNY campuses] take appropriate action" concerning any complaints regarding such an anti-Semitic environment.[34]

The ACLJ continues to monitor the situation on the CUNY campuses to ensure that CUNY does, in fact, fulfill its obligation to provide a non-harassing, non-discriminatory environment for Jewish and other pro-Israel members of the campus community.

PARTNERING TOGETHER TO COMBAT THE BDS MOVEMENT

All of the examples above show that BDS-inspired anti-Israel hysteria is sweeping across America's colleges, but over and over again we have proven that the law is not on their side. The ACLJ has collaborated with many organizations to defend free speech rights on college campuses, especially as it pertains to the increasing anti-Israel activity in university settings. As part of our First Amendment campaign, we have issued letters to the administrators of major universities reminding them of a student's right to engage in pro-Israel speech and the student government body's right to refrain from speaking about Israel-Palestinian politics in an attempt to remain neutral as a governing body. Students should not fear retaliation or wrongful accusations for simply exercising their First Amendment right to speak out in defense of Israel. It is imperative that administrators successfully combat these oppressive tactics in order to safeguard an environment declared by the United States Supreme Court as "the marketplace of ideas."[35]

> **Students should not fear retaliation or wrongful accusations for simply exercising their First Amendment right to speak out in defense of Israel.**

In conjunction with our four-pronged approach outlined at the start of this chapter, we at the ACLJ are taking additional steps to combat the BDS movement. To see how you can join the fight with us, check out some of our initiatives and partner organizations below.

KNOW YOUR RIGHTS CAMPAIGN

The ACLJ has worked with some of our partner organizations to create a *Know Your Rights* pamphlet regarding the growing problem of anti-Semitism on college campuses. The document is for distribution to students, faculty, and administrators, and it lists the warning signs of anti-Semitic activity. It specifically explains how to respond and whom to contact regarding anti-Semitic discrimination on campus. Moreover, *Know Your Rights* provides contact information for the ACLJ, the Lawfare Project, the Louis D. Brandeis Center for Human Rights Under Law, and StandWithUs.

UNIwatch Initiative

In order to more efficiently combat the BDS movement, the ACLJ has spearheaded a collaborative effort with StandWithUs and the Louis D. Brandeis Center for Human Rights Under Law to review the governing documents of student body governments in every university where BDS abuses have occurred. The object is to identify provisions helpful in combating BDS resolutions, referenda, and actions. Known as the UNIwatch initiative, it provides easy access and clearly synthesized information to educate and mobilize students on campuses facing various manifestations of the BDS movement.

EndBDS.com

The ACLJ has also joined with other organizations in launching and maintaining EndBDS.com, a website that brings together partner organizations and pro bono lawyers throughout the pro-Israel community who are working to fight anti-Israel activity. EndBDS is meant as a one-stop destination for those fighting the BDS movement and the extremism and anti-Semitism that often accompany BDS, particularly on college campuses.

These things will help you join the fight against BDS on college campuses. We'll talk even more about how you can help in the struggle against the bigger issues in the next chapter.

REJECT THE NARRATIVE

We continue to urge college administrators to reject the false narratives spread by supporters of the BDS movement. To avoid the continued harassment, denigration, and marginalization of Israel supporters, we continue to stress the importance of colleges and universities denouncing anti-Semitism in all its forms and taking action against anti-Jewish discrimination on campus. In addition to all of this, the ACLJ has helped multiple Jewish students and professors who have been targeted by Palestinian/anti-Israel student organizations as in the cases discussed above, and our team of attorneys regularly travels the country, participating in conferences, meeting with administrators, and delivering lectures debating BDS ideology. We will never surrender in this fight.

If you are a student, faculty member, employee, or member of any organization who is threatened and harassed, the ACLJ is fighting to protect your freedoms. Let us know how we can help. And if you are the one singling out one nation and one people for discrimination and harassment, then consider this your official warning. We are on the case, and you will lose.

KEY TAKEAWAYS

1. In recent years, there has been a significant uptick in anti-Israel, pro-BDS activity on college campuses across the country.

2. The stated purpose of BDS constitutes nothing less than political and economic terrorism.

3. The American Center for Law and Justice has been on the front lines of the struggle, working with victimized college students and professors to fight back against BDS-driven attacks.

SECTION VII

CONCLUSION

16

CLOSING ARGUMENTS

Close powerfully. . . . Persuasive argument neither comes to an abrupt halt nor trails off in a grab-bag of minor points. [T]he conclusion of argument . . . is meant to move the listener to act on what the preceding argument has logically described.[1]
—ANTONIN SCALIA AND BRYAN A. GARNER

Whenever I argue a case—whether it's before a jury, the Supreme Court, or the prosecutor at The Hague—I always close the same way. Sure, every case is different and the facts and evidence involved are unique, but the framework for my closing argument remains consistent. No matter what the case is about, who I am representing, or who I'm presenting to, I always—*always*—close by pointing back to three themes that pull the whole case together. You see, throughout a trial, people can get distracted. They can lose sight of what you're presenting or why it even matters. Their minds wander. They may bring their own biases into the case that cause them to go off on rabbit trails or ask questions that have nothing to do with the case at hand. My job as an attorney is to keep them laser focused on the narrative I'm presenting. No matter where their minds are or where they try to take the discussion, I want to bring it back to the same three themes. So now, as we bring this book to a close, as I go into my closing argument in this case for Israel, it's time for me to point back to the key themes of this book to erase all reasonable doubt in your mind.

First, we have proven that the Jewish people have a clear and unquestioned right to the land today known as Israel. God gave this right to His chosen people, the Jews. This is confirmed not only in the Bible but also in the Quran. And this was not a temporary gift; the Bible clearly shows that God gave them the land *forever* in a one-sided, God-initiated, God-owned eternal covenant.

Second, we have proven that the Jewish people have *always* inhabited the land going back four millennia. We've seen this in biblical history. We've seen it in classical and modern history. We've seen it in archaeology, in linguistics, and in ancient letters. The Jews were present in the land during the time of Abraham and have had an unbroken presence there spanning multiple empires, conquests, and rulers up to the Ottoman Empire and into the modern era of the Jewish State. Despite periods of exile, the great Diaspora after the destruction of Jerusalem by the Romans in A.D. 70, and even the Holocaust of World War II, the land known as Israel has never been without a Jewish presence. While countless nations and empires have risen and fallen around them for thousands of years, the Jewish people continue to exist as a recognizable people.

Third, we have proven that the Jews have the right to the land under international law. Legal title to the land vests in the sovereign State of Israel. The United Nations itself has recognized Israel as a sovereign state. And while Israel's boundaries are the subject of many debates internationally, we've seen that the Israelis' legal title to the land goes back to the Mandate for Palestine—as Israel was the only state to emerge from the mandate when the British departed Palestine in 1948—and to their lawful acquisition of territories by defeating Arab aggressors in defensive battles.

These are the facts of the case. There are many other things we could say—and many other things we *have said*. However, the crux of the case rests on these three key arguments. We've discussed them all in detail throughout this book, but let's take one final look at the key elements one by one.

THE BIBLICAL EVIDENCE

As I've defended Israel both in and out of court, I've heard the counterargument "God is not in the real estate business." In the case of Israel, however, this claim is absolutely untrue. The Bible explicitly outlines the territory that God gave the Jewish people. God Himself set the land apart for His people. He initiated an everlasting covenant relationship with Abraham, taking full responsibility for carrying out that covenant. That covenant was then passed down to Isaac, to Jacob, and ultimately to the entire nation under Moses

As I've defended Israel both in and out of court, I've heard the counterargument "God is not in the real estate business." In the case of Israel, however, this claim is absolutely untrue.

at Mount Sinai. The Old Testament is a record of His faithfulness to the Jewish people in keeping His promise despite their rebelliousness. This is an incredible gift that God gave to Israel and no one else.

JUDAISM, CHRISTIANITY, AND ISLAM AGREE

It's no surprise that Christianity agrees with Judaism in recognizing God's gift of the land to the Jewish people, but you may have been surprised to see that the Quran supports this belief as well. Although the Arab people descended from Ishmael—who was explicitly left out of the covenant fulfilled through Abraham's other son, Isaac—the Muslim holy book affirms God's special relationship with the Jews and His gift of the land.

Even four hundred years of Egyptian slavery and captivity did not end the Israelites' claim to the Land of Promise. When God used Moses to lead the people out of bondage and back to their homeland, He had them stop at Mount Sinai, where God brought the entire nation of Israel into His covenant promise. The Quran itself mentions this covenant renewal at Mount Sinai and God's deliverance of the people to the land of Canaan. From the Muslim perspective, this formal covenant and settlement in Canaan ultimately fulfilled Allah's promise to Israel, acknowledged in the Quran, to settle the Jewish people in the Holy Land.

THE NATURE OF THE COVENANT

The story of this covenant does not stop there. As we discussed, it is critical to understand the nature of the covenant as well. The Bible presents passage after passage showing that God's covenant with Abraham and the Israelites was an *everlasting* covenant. No timetable was included. There were no conditions or clauses that, if triggered, would end the covenant. The covenant was and remains *eternal* and *forever*. These words were purposeful and deliberate. It is *not* mere hyperbole. "Forever" and "eternal" convey that this was not an ordinary agreement with ordinary terms, conditions, and time constraints. Because God Himself took sole responsibility for this covenant, neither party could break it. That means that there is absolutely no way for the covenant—or the Jews' exclusive right to ownership of the Holy Land—to ever cease. The Jews retain this exclusive and eternal right to this day.

> **Because God Himself took sole responsibility for this covenant, neither party could break it. That means that there is absolutely no way for the covenant—or the Jews' exclusive right to ownership of the Holy Land—to ever cease.**

The miraculous history of the Jews further demonstrates the everlasting nature of God's covenant with them. While other nations, people groups, and civilizations have risen, fallen, and in some cases totally disappeared, the Jewish people have persisted not only in their *existence* but, more important, in their *distinct identity as God's chosen people*. The Jews can trace their existence back almost four thousand years; no other group currently living in, or claiming a right to, the Holy Land comes even close to this. The ability of the Jews to defy the seemingly inevitable pattern of civilizations eventually dying out and disappearing speaks to the continuance of God's covenant with them.

OWNERSHIP VS. POSSESSION AND ENJOYMENT

We have also discussed at length the Jewish people's role in fulfilling the purpose of the covenant—and the consequences of failing to do so. God has called His people to be a blessing to the nations, an example to the world of a truly godly nation. Because obedience to God's law was critical to the covenant's purpose, God established harsh consequences for disobedience. If the Israelites failed to be God's holy nation, they would temporarily lose *possession and enjoyment*—but not their *ownership*—of the Holy Land.

The key thing for us to remember here, as we have discussed in detail, is that losing possession of the land for a time does not indicate the dissolution of the covenant. God said He would *never* break His covenant, and we can take Him at His word. The Bible makes it clear that God will always bring His people back to the land, even after times of disobedience. This is evidenced by the cyclical pattern throughout Israel's history. After Sinai, the Israelites angered God, and He subsequently prevented that generation from entering the Holy Land. After the offending generation had passed away, God allowed the next generation of Israelites to enter the land. Then, as we see in the Book of Judges, the Israelites again disobeyed God. Consequently, other nations and groups of people conquered the Israelites, and the Israelites lost possession and control but not ownership of the land. After they repented, God raised up judges to drive out the invaders and reestablish possession for the Israelites.

This sequence of events repeated itself many times throughout the record in the Book of Judges and beyond, well into Israel's kingdom era, when Israel's disobedience was met with repeated conquests by aggressor nations. Even during such a destructive time of dispossession and exile as the Babylonian Captivity, we can trace the outworking of God's covenant relationship and supernatural intervention in returning His people to the Land of Promise. This cycle of disobedience, dispossession, repentance, and repossession is repeated again and again throughout history.

Despite Israel's repeated disobedience and subsequent loss of the enjoyment of the land, passages like Ezekiel's dry bones prophecy confirm that the covenant *was not* and *has not been* broken. Just as the dry bones in the valley could be given new life, so also has Israel been given new life. It can keep possession of the land so long as its people obey God and keep God's commandments. But even when they stumble, they only lose the possession and enjoyment of the land: they never lose the title to it.

THE HISTORICAL AND ARCHAEOLOGICAL EVIDENCE

Even for those who do not give any credence to the religious significance of the Bible, we have also seen that the biblical claims are largely supported by extra-biblical historical accounts, archaeological evidence, and the post-biblical history of the last two thousand years. Like it or not, whether or not you find it religiously significant or not, the Jewish people have unquestionably been in the land of Israel for thousands of years. The way I see it, against all odds, God has not only enabled the Jewish people to endure as a people group without a recognized homeland for thousands of years, He has also brought them back to the land He promised them so long ago. Yet, regardless of whether you agree on a religious level, what is indisputably true is that the Jewish people—a tiny nation among giants and superpowers—have endured as the only rightful heirs to the covenant and to the Holy Land.

> **Against all odds, God has not only enabled the Jewish people to endure as a people group without a recognized homeland for thousands of years, He has also brought them back to the land He promised them so long ago.**

ALWAYS IN THE LAND

Throughout the long history of the Jewish people, we have seen that a remnant has always remained in the Holy Land. We've reviewed the overwhelming archaeological proof that conclusively establishes that, despite periods when their numbers were small, the Jews always had a presence in the land—including in Judea and Samaria, the so-called West Bank. We have archaeological evidence from as early as 1300 B.C. that mentions the Jews as a people in the Lower Levant, supporting the premise that the Jews have been there since ancient times. There is further evidence in the form of countless gravestones, letters, seals, stamps, inventories, and commemorations, many of which mention or show events that are described in the Bible. In addition to the ones that we mentioned above, *The Chronicle of Nebuchadnezzar*, a cuneiform table from 598/597 B.C., says Nebuchadnezzar "besieged the city of Judah" and took away its king. The Elephantine papyri indicate that there was a Jewish priesthood in operation in Judea, and coins minted in Aramaic and Hebrew without pagan symbols also indicate a Jewish presence. Additionally, there are letters of correspondence between the Diaspora communities and Jews living in the Holy Land.

Moving further along in history, when Alexander the Great conquered Palestine in 323 B.C., he was greeted by the Jewish high priest, who informed him that his coming to the Holy Land had been foretold in Holy Scriptures. Archaeologists have also found the remains of the Jewish Temple seen by Alexander, which dates back 2,300 years. Muhammad and the Islamic faith arrived *a thousand years after Alexander*. And, in 2016, archaeologists discovered the citadel built by the Greek Antiochus IV after he sacked Jerusalem. These archaeological artifacts, found under centuries of ruins, confirm what many today try to deny: a continuous Jewish presence in the Holy Land during ancient times, thousands of years before the Arabs even arrived.

LINGUISTIC EVIDENCE

Before Palestine, there was Judea. In fact, the word "Palestine" didn't even exist until the Roman occupation. This isn't advocacy at this point; this is the undisputed historical fact. After the failed Jewish rebellions against Rome, the Romans renamed the land—called Judea up until that point—to Palestine. This began an effort by Rome to rewrite history and erase the Jewish ties to the land. However, ancient inscriptions carved in stone cannot be so easily erased. The stones, with inscriptions in both Aramaic and Hebrew (the languages of the Jews), clearly call the land Judea.

After the time of the Arab conquest in the seventh century A.D., the Greek language brought by Alexander the Great disappeared, and Hebrew remained as a liturgical language only. The Islamic conquest of Palestine brought with it the Arabic language, which was scarcely found in Palestine prior to A.D. 630. What does this tell us about the Arabs and their relationship to the Holy Land? If their *language* did not arrive until the A.D. 630s, then the Arabic people *themselves* could not have been widely present in the Holy Land before then. Otherwise we would see evidence of their language in use. This again supports the historical account that the Arabs came to the Holy Land centuries *after* the Jews, and as we have clearly seen, the Jews were continuously present *after* the Arab conquest as well.

JEWISH POPULATION ALWAYS IN FLUX BUT NEVER ABSENT

The Jewish population has ebbed and flowed in the Holy Land throughout history—usually against their will—but it has never been completely absent. Even during Byzantine rule, when the Jews were forbidden to live in Jerusalem, they remained present outside the city in other parts of the Holy Land. After the Romans and Byzantines departed and the Abbasid Caliphate took control, the Jews returned to Jerusalem.

The Abbasid Caliphate was succeeded by the Fatimids and later by the Crusader armies. Evidence points to the Jewish population decreasing heavily during the Arab conquests and Crusader periods, and yet, despite this decrease, the Jewish presence never disappeared completely. On the contrary, evidence points to a continuous presence of Jewish communities. The Geniza documents, dated to the Fatimid period, have given us hundreds of letters between Jews living in Egypt and Jews living in Palestine, showing us that Jews continued to reside in the Holy Land throughout Fatimid rule. Accounts of the Crusader conquests and the massacre of the inhabitants of Jerusalem specifically mention a Jewish synagogue as well as a Jewish population. Crusader laws targeting Jews also indicate a Jewish presence in the newly occupied Crusader Levant.

After the Crusader kingdoms fell, the Mamluks rebuilt the synagogue in Jerusalem in 1287, which we can infer was for the city's Jewish inhabitants. The massacres of Jews by Arabs in Safed and Tiberias during the 1500s, as well as the persecutions of Ibn Barouk in the 1640s, show a Jewish presence during this time span. Ottoman censuses in the 1800s also clearly confirm a Jewish presence as well.

Those who fight against the legitimacy and existence of the Jewish State would have us believe that Jews are recent newcomers to Palestine. But the stones, inscriptions, coins, and letters do not lie. The Holy Land belongs to the Jewish people by all rights; its artifacts bear witness to a continuous Jewish presence extending almost four thousand years. In light of the historical and archaeological evidence, no one can reasonably doubt the Jewish people's continuous presence in and ties to the land of Israel throughout history.

> Those who fight against the legitimacy and existence of the Jewish State would have us believe that Jews are recent newcomers to Palestine. But the stones, inscriptions, coins, and letters do not lie.

THE LEGAL EVIDENCE

This brings us to my third and final argument. Not only have we established that the Jewish people have a historical and religious relationship with the land going back almost four thousand years, proving their special connection with the land that God gave them, we have also established that they have a legal right to the land under international law. We have proven this legal argument based on three key points:

1. *uti possidetis juris*

2. the continuing applicability of the Mandate for Palestine; and,

3. the capture of the West Bank and Gaza Strip in wars of self-defense.

As we round out this case for Israel, let's briefly refresh our understanding of these three legal points, which include Israel's right to a unified Jerusalem.

UTI POSSIDETIS JURIS

First, you'll remember that *uti possidetis juris* ("as you possess under law") is the customary international law principle for determining territorial sovereignty for "newly created states formed out of territories that previously lacked independence or sovereignty."[2] The principle "provides that states emerging from decolonization shall presumptively inherit the *colonial administrative borders* that they held at the time of independence."[3] The law treats decolonization and emerging from a mandate the same way.

Because one of the key purposes of this legal principle is to prevent the existence of a territory without a sovereign, the doctrine of *uti possidetis juris* requires that all territory pass to the new sovereign state at its birth. Hence, the external borders of the mandate *at the time of the British withdrawal on May 15, 1948*, became the borders of the state that emerged, i.e., the State of Israel. The borders of the mandate at that time were the present-day border with Lebanon, the borders with Syria and Jordan along the Jordan Rift Valley as they existed on May 15, 1948, and the present-day border with Egypt. Accordingly, Israel's lawful borders include the territories encompassing the present-day State of Israel, the so-called West Bank (i.e., Judea, Samaria, and east Jerusalem), and the Gaza Strip, thereby conveying to Israel sovereignty over all of them.

Contrary to this legal principle, Arab Palestinians and their allies label the West Bank (including east Jerusalem) and the Gaza Strip as "occupied Palestinian territories," by which they mean "Israeli-occupied *Arab Palestinian* territories." They claim that these lands will form an eventual Arab State of Palestine, yet such claims run counter to the customary international law that is binding on *all* nations and *all* peoples. Under *uti possidetis juris,* the legal outcome is clear: The Arab Palestinians' claims to sovereignty over the West Bank, east Jerusalem, and the Gaza Strip lack legal foundation in international law. Those territories became part of the sovereign State of Israel at its birth in 1948.

> **Under *uti possidetis juris,* the legal outcome is clear: The Arab Palestinians' claims to sovereignty over the West Bank, east Jerusalem, and the Gaza Strip lack legal foundation in international law.**

THE MANDATE FOR PALESTINE

Second, if *uti possidetis juris* either did not exist or did not apply in these circumstances, Israel still has valid, internationally recognized claims to the West Bank (including east Jerusalem) and the Gaza Strip pursuant to the terms of the Mandate for Palestine, an international legal document that still governs those territories. The Mandate for Palestine constituted a sacred trust assumed by the international community after the First World War on behalf of the people for whom the mandate was created. In the case of the Mandate for Palestine, that meant the Jewish people. The Mandatory for Palestine (Great Britain) was charged with implementing the Balfour Declaration to create a homeland for the Jewish people in Palestine. The terms of the mandate permitted—*even encouraged*—Jews to settle throughout the mandate, which, once again, includes the West Bank (including east Jerusalem) and the Gaza Strip. Hence, until the mandate's terms are either fulfilled as intended or the Jewish people release the trustees of their responsibility to do so, the terms of the mandate are still valid and binding over the West Bank, east Jerusalem, and the Gaza Strip.

It is important to note that the legality of the mandate issue is certainly not unique to Israel. In fact, other states—namely Syria and Lebanon—also emerged from the same group of mandates that created Israel. And yet, no one disputes their sovereignty or the legitimacy of their borders. Interestingly, Great Britain, the mandatory for Palestine, did create an Arab State of Jordan encompassing about 77 percent of the land originally designated for the Jewish State. No one disputes its legitimacy, either. Moreover, when Jordan achieved its independence in May 1946, its national borders were determined by *uti possidetis juris*. There is no principled reason why the same law that applied to Jordan in 1946 would not have applied to Israel in 1948.

The Jewish State of Israel emerged upon the departure of the British in 1948. Pursuant to the mandate, they took as their land the territory to the west of the Jordan Rift Valley that was designated for a Jewish national home. Accordingly, Jewish Palestinians (now called Israelis) have a continuing, valid, internationally sanctioned claim to the West Bank (including east Jerusalem) and the Gaza Strip. Any further partition of this land would have to be achieved via good-faith, bilateral negotiations between Israelis and Arab Palestinians. Until that occurs, Israel retains a valid claim to those territories, since there was no prior sovereign with greater claim to such territories than Jewish Palestinians themselves, especially since the Mandate for Palestine was intended to implement the terms of the Balfour Declaration.

LAND TAKEN IN DEFENSIVE WARS

Third, another basis for justifying Israeli control of the West Bank (including east Jerusalem) and the Gaza Strip is the fact that those territories were captured from foreign belligerent occupiers pursuant to a defensive war. Following the 1948–1949 Arab-Israeli War, the West Bank (including east Jerusalem) and the Gaza Strip were illegally occupied by Jordanian and Egyptian armed forces, respectively. No one has ever made a realistic claim that either Egypt or Jordan had the right to attack, invade, and occupy those lands. Both territories remained under foreign belligerent military occupation for eighteen years, until the 1967 Six-Day War. In 1967, surrounding Arab states once again openly prepared to attack Israel. Just prior to the Arab attack, Israel struck preemptively. In six days of war, Israel regained control of the West Bank (including east Jerusalem) from Jordan and the Gaza Strip from Egypt, as well as the Sinai Peninsula from Egypt and the Golan Heights from Syria.

Although aggressive war is outlawed by international law, all states have the right to engage in individual and collective self-defense—including the right to capture territory held by aggressors in order to ensure the victim state's security and to dissuade future aggression. If the victorious victim state were required to return the captured land to the invading nation, this would reduce the aggressor nation's consequences for waging an illegal war and thereby potentially encourage it to engage in further aggression. Further, requiring the return of such territory would reward the aggressor in violation of the customary international legal principle *ex injuria jus non oritur* ("illegal acts cannot create law"). Besides, if Israel *were* required to return the territory of the Mandate for Palestine it captured in the 1967 Six-Day War, to whom would Israel even return it? Neither Egypt nor Jordan had any lawful claim to the land under international law, since both countries had occupied it via aggressive war since 1948, and there was no recognized sovereign with a better claim to the title to the territory than Israel itself.

RECOGNIZED BY THE UNITED NATIONS

Further strengthening Israel's claim to the land is the fact that the UN recognizes Israel as a sovereign state and has admitted Israel as a full member to the United Nations. Israel declared its independence in May 1948 and was admitted to full membership in the UN one year later. Accordingly, Israel has the internationally recognized right to sovereignty over its own territory. Moreover, because the West Bank (including east Jerusalem) and the Gaza Strip were illegally occupied by foreign Arab armies between 1949 and 1967, no nation has a greater claim to sovereignty over those territories than Israel. This claim is bolstered by both *uti possidetis juris* and the continuing effect of the terms of the Mandate for Palestine over the areas illegally occupied by Egypt and Jordan. The U.S. Congress has also recognized these valid legal points.

JERUSALEM, ISRAEL'S ETERNAL CAPITAL

The city of Jerusalem has become a target for those seeking to delegitimize and destroy the modern Jewish State of Israel. United Jerusalem is the legally declared capital of Israel, and it has been that way on and off since King David captured the city from the Jebusites some three thousand years ago. Today, as a sovereign state, Israel has an absolute right to choose the location of its capital city. And yet, the international community has largely rejected Jerusalem as Israel's capital—something that, to my knowledge, has never happened to any other sovereign state in modern times.

> **United Jerusalem is the legally declared capital of Israel, and it has been that way on and off since King David captured the city from the Jebusites some three thousand years ago.**

Despite periods of exile and the great Diaspora, Jerusalem has remained central to the Jewish people, who have always esteemed the city above all others in the world. However, when the Holy Land was conquered and occupied by foreign powers, the invaders always considered and treated Jerusalem as a minor city of no special political value. In fact, no Muslim conqueror ever chose Jerusalem as his capital. Besides the Jews, only Crusaders and the British selected Jerusalem as their capital city. And yet, Palestinian Arabs today claim that Jerusalem should be the capital city of a future state of Palestine, and many in the world community have bought into this argument. Nonetheless, as we have seen, Jerusalem is part of the sovereign territory of the Jewish State of Israel.

Jerusalem has special meaning to the Jewish people. Jewish life has historically centered around Jerusalem, especially in light of the historical importance of the Temple rituals in Judaism and the fact that the Temple must be located on the Temple Mount. Further, Israel has shown itself to be the most respectful caretaker of Jerusalem for *all* faiths. It is Israel that allows religious freedom to flourish in Jerusalem. Prior to the unification of Jerusalem in 1967, Jordan had denied Jews the right to even visit the Western Wall for eighteen years, and Jordanian authorities either destroyed ancient synagogues in the Old City or converted them to profane uses without respecting their religious significance. Only Israel has protected the rights of all three great monotheistic religions whose holy places are present in Jerusalem.

> **Israel has acted responsibly and has earned the right to govern its capital without outside interference. It is Israel that has the right to designate its capital, and it is Israel that will determine what happens in and to Jerusalem.**

Israel has acted responsibly and has earned the right to govern its capital without outside interference. It is Israel that has the right to designate its capital, and it is Israel that will determine what happens in and to Jerusalem.

FACING TODAY'S ENEMIES

Finally, we have examined the modern issue of lawfare and have seen how the ongoing fight for Israel's right to exist has moved into the courtrooms of the world. We've pulled back the curtain on the BDS movement as one example of Palestinian lawfare attempts to delegitimize Israel and destroy its economy. I cannot be clearer in saying that, at its roots, the BDS movement is racist and anti-Semitic, and driven by hate. The ACLJ has joined with other like-minded organizations to expose the BDS movement's anti-Semitic motivation and to fight it tooth and nail when it seeks to bring such intolerance to the United States. We have also supported groups fighting BDS overseas. Our vigorous counterattacks have begun to throw the BDS movement off stride, and we have begun to turn the tide in Israel's favor. We will not cease until the BDS movement is fully exposed and its proponents fully discredited. We are well on our way to that end.

HOW YOU CAN HELP

Throughout this book, we have reviewed many ways in which the ACLJ and others have worked to help Israel, but there is still much to do—and you can join the fight. Your time, your money, and even your attention will go far toward putting an end to the hate speech and unfounded accusations directed at Israelis and Jews around the world.

Join with us in calling out the world's bigots by signing on to our ACLJ petitions in defense of Israel. These petitions identify and condemn the anti-Semitic tripe that all too often flows from the United Nations, UN agencies, the BDS movement, the Organization of Islamic Cooperation, and elsewhere. Stand and be counted with the hundreds of thousands of others who have signed our petitions! You can also help us respond on behalf of Israel in courts around the globe by contributing financially to our efforts. Find out more about our ongoing petition efforts and how you can get involved at www.aclj.org.

You can also support Israel with your purchasing decisions. When anti-Israel bigots seek to boycott Jewish businesses and Israeli products in your area, you can go out of your way to buy these Israeli products and shop at these stores. Boycotts fall apart without support, so be intentional about where you shop and what you buy. Together, we can make these hateful boycotts worthless and ineffective.

Many opponents will argue that Israel is guilty of war crimes or of continually violating the Law of Armed Conflict by endangering civilians with Israeli military actions in response to aggressor attacks against its own cities. When you hear that, take the accuser to task. Ask why nobody condemns the indiscriminate firing of hundreds of rockets and mortar rounds at Israeli civilians from Palestinian-controlled territories. Ask the accuser if he is aware that each indiscriminate firing constitutes a separate war crime by the Palestinians. Challenge the opponent of Israel to condemn the Palestinians for their own crimes against Israel. Ask how any country in the world would respond to such attacks.

When Palestinians and pro-BDS advocates seek to deceive the American people by misrepresenting what Israel is actually doing, dig into the details and find out all the facts. Do your research. Then write letters to the editors of your local papers to set the record straight. Write letters to your U.S. senators and congressional representative to let them know you support Israel—and that you expect *them* to support Israel on your behalf.

And finally, as the Psalmist says, "Pray for the peace of Jerusalem: 'May those who love you be secure . . . ' " (Psalm 122:6).

If people ask how they can find out the truth about what is happening in the region, suggest that they visit websites that expose what the Palestinians are doing. I suggest you check out the following sites to get started:

- the American Center for Law and Justice at www.aclj .org;

- Middle East Media Research Institute (MEMRI) at www.memri.org;

- Palestine Media Watch at www.palwatch.org; and

- NGO Monitor at www.ngo-monitor.org.

There's so much you can do, and we hope you'll join us in supporting Israel.

THE FIGHT CONTINUES

I would love to end this book by reporting that we have won, that the battle is over, that the world has finally and fully recognized Israel as a sovereign Jewish State in control of its own destiny. But I can't. Israel has won many battles in recent years, and we at the American Center for Law and Justice have been proud to stand with the Jewish people in the fight. However, even seventy years after the Holocaust, there is more hatred and bigotry against the Jews around every corner.

Still, today, vile anti-Israel rhetoric continues to flow out of the international community—including the United Nations itself. As recently as March 2017, a UN committee issued a report with the goal of completely delegitimizing Israel. The report, authored by 9/11 truther Richard A. Falk, was issued by the United Nations Committee for Western Asia, an area that includes Israel. In the report, Falk and his committee once again labeled Israel as an apartheid state in an attempt to seek international justification for ending Israel's existence as we know it—i.e., as a Jewish State.[4] Once it is determined that Israel is an apartheid state, the report asserts, "States have a collective duty (a) not to recognize an apartheid regime as lawful; (b) not to aid or assist a State in maintaining an apartheid regime; and (c) to cooperate with the United Nations and other States in bringing apartheid regimes to an end."[5]

Israel is not an apartheid state. This idea in and of itself should be inconceivable to anyone who understands that the very basis for Israel's legal system is, as we've seen, the principle of loving other people. What's frightening, though, is that the authors of the UN report—and many others around the world—believe that Israel has no right to exist. They actually buy into this madness and see Israel as an apartheid state. This goes beyond delegitimization; we are talking here about the very survival of the Jewish State.

U.S. ambassador to the United Nations Nikki Haley aptly called the report what it was: pure, unadulterated, "anti-Israel propaganda."[6] We at the ACLJ, along with others, raised this outrageous report to UN officials and demanded its retraction. I am happy to report that, not only has the report been pulled, but the chairman of the committee resigned. We won. But the damage this type of misrepresentation can cause if left unchecked is dangerous.

We're talking about Israel's survival against people who want to wipe it off the face of the earth. Israel's enemies have no plan B. They want the total destruction of the Jewish State. There is no second option in this argument. There are no appeals. No middle ground. No moral or symbolic victories. Israel will either win or lose. There either will be a Jewish State or there won't. And this isn't a far-off consequence. The next generation or the one after will decide the fate of Israel. This is why we fight. This is why we present facts and argue for justice—justice that demands the Jewish State of Israel be recognized for what it is: a free, fully legitimate, democratic, and sovereign Jewish state.

I rest my case.

NOTES

Introduction

1. Abbas Rips Into Trump: Palestinians Are Original Canaanites, Were in Jerusalem Before the Jews," by Jack Khoury. HAARETZ.com, January 17, 2018. (https://www.haaretz.com/middle-east-news/palestinians/abbas-palestinians-are-canaanites-were-in-jerusalem-before-jews-1.5743576). Accessed March 6, 2018.
2. "2013 'record year' for tourism, government says," by Yifa Yaakov. Times of Israel, January 10, 2014. (http://www.timesofisrael.com/2013-record-year-for-tourism-government-says). Accessed March 6, 2018.
3. "Statement by President Trump on Jerusalem." December 6, 2017. (https://www.whitehouse.gov/briefings-statements/statement-president-trump-jerusalem/). Accessed March 6, 2018.

Chapter 1: Opening Statement

1. Benjamin Disraeli, *Miriam Alroy: A Romance of the Twelfth Century*, 499 (2011).
2. June Glazer, *Gush Etzion Remembers Its Fallen*, Jewish Nat'l Fund, http://www.jnf.org/byachad/summer-2015-byachad-articles/feature_gush_etzion_summer_2015.pdf (visited July 6, 2017).
3. Ian Schwartz, "Kerry: Israel Can Either Be Jewish Or Democratic, It Cannot Be Both," RealClearPolitics (Dec. 28, 2016), http://www.realclearpolitics.com/video/2016/12/28/kerry_israel_can_either_be_jewish_or_democratic_it_cannot_be_both.html.

Chapter 2: The New Tools of Warfare

1. "Warfare," Merriam-Webster.com, https://www.merriam-webster.com/dictionary/warfare (visited July 13, 2017).
2. Charles J. Dunlap Jr., *Law and Military Interventions: Preserving Humanitarian Values in 21st Century Conflicts* (Kennedy School of Government, Harvard University, Working Paper, Nov. 29, 2001), 1–27.
3. Ibid., 2.
4. *Immigration to Israel: The Fifth Aliyah (1929–1939)*, Jewish Virtual Library, http://www.jewishvirtuallibrary.org/the-fifth-aliyah-1929-1939 (visited July 13, 2017).
5. Gil Feiler, "Arab Boycott," in *The Continuum Political Encyclopedia of the Middle East* (Avraham Sela ed., rev. ed., 2002), 54–57.
6. Mitchell Bard, *Arab League Boycott: Background and Overview*, Jewish Virtual

Library, http://www.jewishvirtuallibrary.org/background-and-overview-of
-the-arab-boycott-of-israel (last updated Feb. 2017).

7. Joyce Shems Sharon, *The Arab Boycott Against Israel and Its Unintended Impact on Arab Economic Welfare* (May 2003) (unpublished M.A. thesis, Tufts University).

8. Martin A. Weiss, *Arab League Boycott of Israel*, Congressional Research Service (June 10, 2015), https://fas.org/sgp/crs/mideast/RL33961.pdf.

9. Suhas Chakma, "The Issue of Compensation for Colonialism and Slavery at the World Conference Against Racism," in George Ulrich and Louise Krabbe Boserup, eds., 7 *Human Rights in Development: Yearbook 2001* (13th ed., 2003), 58–71.

10. Elihai Braun, "United Nations: UN World Conference Against Racism, Racial Discrimination, Xenophobia and Related Intolerance—Durban, South Africa," Jewish Virtual Library (Sept. 8, 2001), http://www.jewishvirtualli brary.org/durban-i-un-conference-against-racism-2001.

11. "U.S. Abandons Racism Summit," BBC News (Sept. 3, 2001, 5:41 p.m.), http://news.bbc.co.uk/2/hi/africa/1523600.stm.

12. "Mixed Emotions as Durban Winds Up," BBC News (Sept. 8, 2001, 7:17 p.m.), http://news.bbc.co.uk/2/hi/africa/1530976.stm.

13. Ibid.

14. "What Is BDS?," BDS Movement, https://bdsmovement.net/ (visited July 13, 2017) (hereafter BDS).

15. Alexander H. Joffe, "Why the Origins of the BDS Movement Matter," Middle East Forum (Aug. 13, 2016), http://www.meforum.org/6234/bds-origins.

16. Palestinian Civil Society, "Palestinian Civil Society Call for BDS," BDS Movement (July 9, 2005), https://bdsmovement.net/call.

17. Joffe.

18. Ibid.

19. BDS.

20. "BDS in the Churches," NGO Monitor, http://www.ngo-monitor.org/key -issues/bds-in-the-churches/background/ (visited July 13, 2017).

21. Ibid.

22. Globes, "Denmark to Label West Bank Settlement Products," *Jerusalem Post* (May 20, 2012, 1:23 p.m.), http://www.jpost.com/International/Denmark -to-label-West-Bank-settlement-products.

23. J. J. Goldberg, "How Matisyahu Ban Backfired on BDS Backers," Forward (Aug.21,2015), http://forward.com/opinion/319583/how-matisyahu-ban-back fired-on-bds-backers/.

24. Emily Harris, "When 500 Palestinians Lose Their Jobs at SodaStream Who's to Blame?," National Public Radio (March 27, 2016, 6:12 a.m.), http://www .npr.org/sections/parallels/2016/03/27/471885452/when-500-palestinians -lose-their-jobs-at-sodastream-whos-to-blame; see also "SodaStream Lays Off Last Palestinian Workers After Leaving West Bank," *Guardian* (Feb. 29,

2016, 10:12 p.m.), https://www.theguardian.com/world/2016/mar/01/soda
stream-lays-off-last-palestinian-workers-after-leaving-west-bank.

25. "Anti-Semitism: State Anti-BDS Legislation," *Jewish Virtual Library* (June 2017), http://www.jewishvirtuallibrary.org/anti-bds-legislation.

26. "Anti-BDS Legislation in the United States," Palestine Legal, http://pales tinelegal.org/legislation (visited July 13, 2017).

27. Tammi Rossman-Benjamin, "From Durban to Los Angeles: The BDS Movement's Long Trail of Anti-Semitism," *Jewish News Service* (March 12, 2015), http://www.jns.org/latest-articles/2015/3/12/from-durban-to-los-angeles -the-bds-movements-long-trail-of-anti-semitism.

28. K. C. Johnson, "Free Speech and CUNY Anti-Semitism," *Tablet* (Sept. 20, 2016, 10:00 p.m.), http://www.tabletmag.com/jewish-news-and-politics/213 844/free-speech-and-cuny-anti-semitism.

29. *NLRB v. Retail Store Employees Union*, 447 U.S. 607, 614–16, 617–18 (1980).

30. For a thorough discussion of Israel's chief enemies, see my books *Rise of ISIS* and *Unholy Alliance*.

Chapter 3: The Land of Promise

1. "Covenant," Merriam-Webster.com, https://www.merriam-webster.com /dictionary/covenant (visited July 6, 2017).

2. The New International Version (NIV) will be used exclusively throughout, unless noted otherwise.

3. Michael D. Coogan, "In the Beginning: The Earliest History," in Michael D. Coogan, ed., *The Oxford History of the Biblical World* (1998), 3, 10.

4. Ibid., 10.

5. 'Abdullah Yūsuf 'Alī, *The Meaning of the Holy Qur'an* (10th ed., reprinted 2001, 1999) (Introduction to Surah 2—Al Baqarah), 16.

6. Ken Spiro, *Crash Course in Jewish History: From Abraham to Modern Israel* (rev. ed. 2011), 13–14, 16.

7. Ibid., 16.

8. Philip Yancey and Tim Stafford, *The Student Bible: New International Version* (1996), 40, n.f5–g5 (explaining that "Abram means exalted father" and "Abraham means father of many").

9. Genesis 25:17; Psalm 83:5–6; see also Spiro, 24.

10. 'Abdullah Yūsuf 'Alī, 7:54.

11. Ibid., 3:189.

12. Ibid., 5:21 n.724.

13. Ibid., 28:5 n.3330.

14. Ilan Ben Zion, "Jerusalem Mufti: Temple Mount Never Housed Jewish Temple," *Times of Israel* (Oct. 25, 2015, 8:06 p.m.), http://www.timesofisrael.com /jerusalem-mufti-denies-temple-mount-ever-housed-jewish-shrine.

15. Yossi Aloni, "Arab Cleric: Israel Belongs to the *Jews*," *World Net Daily*

(Feb. 19, 2014, 9:03 p.m.), http://www.wnd.com/2014/02/arab-cleric-israel
-belongs-to-the-jews.

16. Ibid.

Chapter 5: The Nature of the Covenant

1. Ken Spiro, *Crash Course in Jewish History: From Abraham to Modern Israel* (rev. ed., 2011), 13.
2. Ibid.
3. Ibid., 12–13.
4. J. M. Roberts, *The History of the World* (3rd ed., 1995), 227, 283.
5. Spiro, 15, 19–20 (source for all summary statements in this paragraph).
6. Sandra Teplinsky, *Why Still Care About Israel?* (rev. ed., 2013), 44.
7. Ibid.
8. For example, Deuteronomy 7:6–8; Deuteronomy 14:2; Deuteronomy 26:17–19; Psalm 135:4; Isaiah 41:8.
9. 'Abdullah Yūsuf 'Alī, *The Meaning of the Holy Qur'an* (10th ed., reprinted. 2001, 1999) 4:46; 5:12–15 (discussing the replacement of Jews with Christians and then Muslims).
10. Matt Slick, "What Is Replacement Theology?," Christian Apologetics & Research Ministry, https://carm.org/questions-replacement-theology (lasted visited July 6, 2017).
11. Ibid.
12. See, e.g., Exodus 20:3; Exodus 21:3; Exodus 34:14; Leviticus 17:7; Deuteronomy 12:30–31; Deuteronomy 13:1–18; Deuteronomy 31:16; Jeremiah 10:2–5.
13. Spiro, 20–21.
14. Charles Aling, "Joseph in Egypt, Part I," Associates for Biblical Research, http://www.biblearchaeology.org/post/2010/02/18/Joseph-in-Egypt-Part-I .aspx (visited Mar. 22, 2017).
15. Exodus 1–14. Although it seems that, because the events were so humiliating, the Egyptians scrubbed much of the Exodus story from their records, some extra-biblical Egyptian evidence still exists. See Philippe Bohstrom, "Were Hebrews Ever Slaves in Ancient Egypt? Yes," *Haaretz* (April 14, 2016, 4:00 p.m.), http://www.haaretz.com/jewish/archaeology/1.713849.
16. Spiro, 112–27.
17. "Spain Virtual Jewish History Tour," Jewish Virtual Library, http://www .jewishvirtuallibrary.org/spain-virtual-jewish-history-tour (visited Mar. 22, 2017).
18. "The Jewish History of Amsterdam," Jewish History of Amsterdam, http:// jewishhistoryamsterdam.com/the-jewish-history-of-amsterdam (visited Mar. 21, 2017). The Edicto de Granada (the Edict of Granada, also known as the Alhambra Edict) was signed by the king and queen on March 1, 1492. The Jews had to leave the country by July of that year. *Edicto de Granada*, EcuRed.com, https://www.ecured.cu/Edicto_de_Granada (visited March 21, 2017).

19. "Spanish Armada Defeated," This Day in History, http://www.history.com /this-day-in-history/spanish-armada-defeated (visited Mar. 21, 2017) (retelling the defeat of the Spanish Armada on July 29, 1588); Mauricio Drelichman and Hans-Joachim Voth, "The Sustainable Debts of Philip II: A Reconstruction of Spain's Fiscal Position, 1560–1598," https://eml.berkeley .edu/~webfac/cromer/e211_f07/voth.pdf (visited July 6, 2017).

20. The Dutch Golden Age lasted from approximately 1580 to 1670. Donald J. Harreld, "The Dutch Economy in the Golden Age (16th–17th Centuries)," EH.net, https://eh.net/encyclopedia/the-dutch-economy-in-the-golden-age-16th -17th-centuries (visited March 21, 2017).

21. On Britain's rise to superpower: Ben Wilson, "The Rise of Britain as a World Power," *History Today* 7 (July 2013), 63, available at http://www.historytoday .com/blog/2013/07/rise-britain-world-power; and Tara Holmes, "Readmission of the Jews to Britain in 1656," BBC, http://www.bbc.co.uk/religion /religions/judaism/history/350.shtml (last updated June 24, 2011).

On Britain allowing Jews to return to their homeland: Victoria Honeyman, "Britain, Palestine, and the Creation of Israel; How Britain Failed to Protect its Protectorate," http://www.polis.leeds.ac.uk/assets/files/re search/working-papers/britain-palestine-and-the-creation-of-Israel.pdf (visited July 6, 2017).

On denying access to Israel at the onset of the Holocaust: "Immigration to Israel: British Restrictions on Jewish Immigration to Palestine (1919–1942)," Jewish Virtual Library, http://www.jewishvirtuallibrary.org/british-restric tions-on-jewish-immigration-to-palestine (visited July 6, 2017).

On Britain surviving the war with heavy damages: John Darwin, "Britain, the Commonwealth and End of Empire," BBC, http://www.bbc.co.uk/his tory/british/modern/endofempire_overview_01.shtml (last updated Mar. 3, 2011).

Section III: The Historical and Archaeological Evidence

1. "History," Merriam-Webster.com, https://www.merriam-webster.com/dic tionary/history (visited July 6, 2017).

2. "Archaeology," Ibid., https://www.merriam-webster.com/dictionary/archae ology (visited July 6, 2017).

Chapter 6: Supporting the Biblical History

3. Paul L. Maier, "Archaeology—Biblical Ally or Adversary?," *Bible and Spade* 17, no. 3 (Summer 2004), 83.

4. Adrian Curtis, *Oxford Bible Atlas* (4th ed., 2007), 15.

5. Barry J. Beitzel, ed., *The SPCK Bible Atlas* (2013), 55 (hereafter *Bible Atlas*).

6. Ibid.

7. Carl G. Rasmussen, *Zondervan Atlas of the Bible* (rev. ed., 2010), 96.

8. Kenton L. Sparks, *Ancient Texts for the Study of the Hebrew Bible* (2005), 463.

9. Rasmussen, 98; James B. Pritchard, ed., *Ancient Near Eastern Texts Relating to*

the Old Testament with Supplement (3rd ed., 1969), 482 (hereafter *Ancient Near Eastern Texts*).

10. *Ancient Near Eastern Texts*, 482.
11. Rasmussen, 98.
12. *Ancient Near Eastern Texts*, 483.
13. Sparks, 465.
14. Niels Peter Lemche, *The Israelites in History and Tradition* (1998), 35.
15. Ibid.
16. Ibid.
17. *Bible Atlas*, 97.
18. Ibid., 98.
19. Paul Lawrence (Richard Johnson, ed.), *The IVP Concise Atlas of Bible History* (2012), 56.
20. Ibid., 56–58.
21. Ibid., 68.
22. *Ancient Near Eastern Texts*, 483–90; Rasmussen, 244.
23. Curtis, 38–40.
24. Rasmussen, 124–25.
25. *Ancient Near Eastern Texts*, 490 n.26.
26. Rasmussen, 125.
27. Eliat Mazer, "Did I Find King David's Palace?" Bible History Daily (Jan. 8, 2017), http://www.biblicalarchaeology.org/daily/biblical-sites-places/jerusalem/did-i-find-king-davids-palace (visited July 17, 2017).
28. Hershel Shanks, " 'Oldest Hebrew Inscription' Discovered in Israelite Fort on Philistine Border," *Biblical Archaeology Review* (March/April 2010), 52.
29. See, e.g., "Archaeology," http://www.cityofdavid.org.il/en/archeology (visited July 8, 2017).
30. Lawrence J. Mykytiuk, *Identifying Biblical Persons in Northwest Semitic Inscriptions of 1200–539 BCE* (2004), 238; Lawrence J. Mykytiuk, "Sixteen Strong Identifications of Biblical Persons (Plus Nine Other Identifications) in Authentic Northwest Semitic Inscriptions from Before 539 B.C.E.," in Meir Lubetski and Edith Lubetski, eds., *New Inscriptions and Seals Relating to the Biblical World* (2012), 43; J. Andrew Dearman, *Studies in the Mesha Inscription and Moab* (1989) 97, 100–101; André Lemaire, " 'House of David' Restored in Moabite Inscription," *Biblical Archaeology Review* 2, no. 30 (1994), 20. David's name also appears in line 12 of the Mesha Inscription. Anson F. Rainey, "Mesha and Syntax," in J. Andrew Dearman & M. Patrick Graham, eds., *The Land That I Will Show You: Essays on the History and Archaeology of the Ancient Near East in Honor of J. Maxwell Miller* (2001), 287, 293; Mykytiuk, *Identifying Biblical Persons*, 265–77.
31. Lemaire, 30.
32. K. A. Kitchen, "A Possible Mention of David in the Late Tenth Century BCE, and Deity Dod as Dead as the Dodo?," *Journal for the Study of the Old Testament* 76 (1997), 39–41; Mykytiuk, *New Inscriptions and Seals Relating to*

the Biblical World, 43; Mykytiuk, *Identifying Biblical Persons in Northwest Semitic Inscriptions of 1200–539 BCE*, 214 n.3; see also Lawrence J. Mykytiuk, "Corrections and Updates to 'Identifying Biblical Persons in Northwest Semitic Inscriptions of 1200–539 B.C.E.,' " *Maarav* 16 (2009), 49, 119–21.

33. Lemche, 44.

34. Ibid., 46.

35. Niels Peter Lemche, *The Old Testament Between Theology and History: A Critical Survey* (2008), 147–48.

36. Ibid.

37. Ibid., 152; R. Campbell Thompson, *The Prisms of Esarhaddon and Ashurbanipal Found at Nineveh* (1931), 25; *Ancient Near Eastern Texts*, 291, 294.

38. "ABC 5 (Jerusalem Chronicle)," Livius.org, http://www.livius.org/sources /content/mesopotamian-chronicles-content/abc-5-jerusalem-chronicle/? (visited July 7, 2017).

39. W. D. Davies and Louis Finkelstein, eds., *The Cambridge History of Judaism*, *Vol. 1: Introduction; The Persian Period* (1984), 90 (hereafter *Cambridge History*). *See also* John Kessler, "Persia's Loyal Yahwists," in Oded Lipschitz and Manfred Oeming, eds., *Judah and the Judeans in the Persian Period* (2006), 93 (ebook).

40. Kessler, 93.

41. Simcha Gross, "Pearce and Wunsch, Documents of Judean Exiles and West Semites in Babylonia," AncientJewReview.com (Feb. 18, 2015), http://www .ancientjewreview.com/articles/2015/2/18/pearce-and-wunsch-documents -of-judean-exiles-and-west-semites-in-babylonia-1?rq=judahtown%5C; Kathleen Abraham, "The Reconstruction of Jewish Communities in the Persian Empire: The Al-Yahudu Clay Tablets," Academia.edu (2011), http:// www.academia.edu/1383485/The_Reconstruction_of_Jewish_Communi ties_in_the_Persian_Empire_The_%C4%80l-Yah%C5%ABdu_Clay _Tablets.

42. Ibid.

43. Ibid.

44. A. E. Cowley, ed., *Aramaic Papyri of the Fifth Century B.C.* (1923), 114.

45. Nadav Na'aman, "Text and Archaeology in a Period of Great Decline: The Contribution of the Amarna Letters to the Debate on the Historicity of Nehemiah's Wall," in Philip R. Davies and Diana V. Edelman, eds., *The Historian and the Bible: Essays in Honour of Lester L. Grabbe* (2010), 2, 20.

46. Israel Finkelstein, "Geographical Lists in Ezra and Nehemiah in the Light of Archaeology: Persian or Hellenistic," in Lester L. Grabbe and Oded Lipschits, eds., *Judah Between East and West: The Transition from Persian to Greek Rule (ca. 400–200 B.C.E.)* (2011), 111.

47. *Cambridge History*, 82–83, 111, 156.

48. Ibid., 85, 113.

49. Flavius Josephus, *The Works of Josephus Complete and Unabridged The Antiquities of the Jews*, trans. by William Whiston (1980), 306–307.

50. Ibid.

51. Ibid., 308.

52. "Syrian Wars," Alexander the Great, http://www.alexander-the-great .org/wars-of-the-diadochi/syrian-wars.php (visited July 5, 2017); Lawrence Schiffman, *From Text to Tradition: A History of Judaism in Second Temple and Rabbinic Times* (1991), 65.

53. Solomon Zeitlin, " 'The Tobias Family and the Hasmoneans': A Historical Study in the Political and Economic Life of the Jews in the Hellenistic Period," *Proceedings of the American Academy for Jewish Research*, vol. 4 (1932–1933), 169, 185.

54. Josephus, 323–24.

55. Andrew Lawler, "Jerusalem Dig Uncovers Ancient Greek Citadel," *National Geographic* (April 22, 2016), http://news.nationalgeographic .com/2016/04/160422-israel-jerusalem-hellenistic-archaeology-passover-ha nukkah.

56. Steven Weitzman, "Plotting Antiochus's Persecution," *Journal of Biblical Literature* 123, no. 2 (Summer 2004), 219–20.

57. Josephus, 325.

58. Ibid.

59. Robert Doran, "The Revolt of the Maccabees," *National Interest* 85 (Sept.–Oct. 2006), 99, 102.

60. Ibid., 102–103.

61. David A. Fiensy and Ralph K. Hawkins, eds., *The Galilean Economy in the Time of Jesus* (2013), 13–15.

62. Elon Gilad, "Meet the Hasmoneans: A Brief History of a Violent Epoch," *Haaretz* (Dec. 23, 2014, 11:19 a.m.), http://www.haaretz.com/jewish/features /1.633308.

63. E. P. Sanders, *Judaism: Practice and Belief 63 B.C.E.–66 C.E.* (1992), 46.

64. B. Kanael, "The Partition of Judea by Gabinius," *Israel Exploration Journal* 7, no. 2 (1957), 98, 99.

65. Sanders, 47.

66. Ibid., 49.

67. Hagith Sivan, *Palestine in Late Antiquity* (2008), 3.

68. W. Bowers, "Jewish Communities in Spain in the Time of Paul the Apostle," *Journal of Theological Studies* 26, no. 2 (1975), 395–99.

69. Birgit van der Lans, "The Politics of Exclusion: Expulsions of Jews and Others from Rome," in Michael Labahn and Outi Lehtipuu, eds., *People under Power: Early Jewish and Christian Responses to the Roman Power Empire* (2015), 33.

70. P. Bilde, "The Causes of the Jewish War According to Josephus," *Journal for the Study of Judaism: Persian, Hellenistic, Roman Period* 10, no. 2 (1979), 179, 182.

71. Josephus, 624. See also Martin Goodman, *The Ruling Class of Judaea* (1993), 152.

72. John R. Curran, "The Jewish War: Some Neglected Regional Factors," *Classical World* 101, no. 1 (207), 75, 83; Bilde, 190–91.

73. Curran, 80.

74. Aviva Bar-Am and Shmuel Bar-Am, "Masada, Tragic Fortress in the Sky," *Times of Israel* (April 13, 2013, 1:43 p.m.), http://www.timesofisrael.com/masada-tragic-fortress-in-the-sky.

75. Ehud Netzer, "The Last Days and Hours at Masada," *Biblical Archaeology Society Library* (1991), http://members.bib-arch.org/publication.asp?PubID=BSBA&Volume=17&Issue=6&ArticleID=13.

76. Bar-Am and Bar-Am.

77. "A.D. 70 Titus Destroys Jerusalem," *Christianity Today*, http://www.christianitytoday.com/history/issues/issue-28/ad-70-titus-destroys-jerusalem.html (last visited July 7, 2017).

Chapter 7: Life Under Muslim Rule

1. "Revolution," Merriam-Webster.com, https://www.merriam-webster.com/dictionary/revolution (visited July 7, 2017).

2. "Shimon Bar-Kokhba," Jewish Virtual Library, https://www.jewishvirtuallibrary.org/shimon-bar-kokhba (visited July 7, 2017).

3. Rendel Davis, "Hadrian's Decree of Expulsion of the Jews from Jerusalem," *Harvard Theological Review* 19, no. 2 (1926), 199.

4. Yigael Yadin, *Bar-Kokhba: The Rediscovery of the Legendary Hero of the Last Jewish Revolt against Imperial Rome* (1971), 244.

5. Eric M. Meyers and L. Michael White, "Jews and Christians in Roman World," *Archaeology* 42, no. 2 (1989), 26, 29.

6. Barbara Geller Nathanson, "Jews, Christians, and the Gallus Revolt in Fourth-Century Palestine," *Biblical Archaeologist* 49, no. 1 (1986), 26, 32.

7. Meyers and White, 30.

8. Zvi Uri Ma'oz, "Jews and Christians in the Ancient Golan Heights," *Israel Exploration Journal* 60, no. 1 (2010), 89, 90.

9. Katharina Galor and Hanswulf Bloedhorn, *The Archaeology of Jerusalem: From the Origins to the Ottomans* (2013), 128.

10. Jacob Mann, *The Jews in Egypt and in Palestine Under the Fatimid Caliphs: A Contribution to Their Political and Communal History Based Chiefly on Genizah Material Hitherto Unpublished*, vols. 1–2, (1920), 42.

11. S. D. Goitein, *Jews and Arabs: A Concise History of Their Social and Cultural Relations* (2005), 63.

12. Mann, 42.

13. Ibid., 43–45.

14. Ibid., 43.

15. "Tributary" status protected according to the rules of the pact of *dhimmi*, who, in return, were bound by various conditions: They were allowed freedom of worship provided that they paid the tribute known as *jizya* and ac-

cepted an inferior status. Dominique Sourdel and Janine Sourdel-Thomine, *A Glossary of Islam*, trans. by Caroline Higgitt (2007), 34–44.

16. Joan Peters, *From Time Immemorial: The Origins of the Arab-Jewish Conflict over Palestine* (1984), 34, 176.

17. Ibid., 176.

18. Sidney H. Griffith, "From Aramaic to Arabic: The Languages of the Monasteries of Palestine in the Byzantine and Early Islamic Periods," *Dumbarton Oaks Papers* 51 (1997), 23, 27.

19. "Islam: The Abassid Caliphate," Jewish Virtual Library, http://www.jewish virtuallibrary.org/the-abassid-caliphate-758-1258 (visited July 7, 2017).

20. Philip K. Hitti, *History of the Arabs* (rev. 10th ed., 2002), 284–86.

21. Bernard Lewis, *The Middle East: A Brief History of the Last 2,000 Years* (1997), 75, 288.

22. Hitti, 316.

23. Ibid., 356.

24. Lewis, at 56.

25. Quran 9:29.

26. Hitti, 356.

27. Ibid., 310, 354

28. Ibid.,356.

29. Steven M. Wasserstrom, *Between Muslim and Jew: The Problem of Symbiosis under Early Islam* (1995), 19.

30. Ibid., 20.

31. James Parkes, *Whose Land? A History of the Peoples of Palestine* (1970), 73.

32. Hitti, 353.

33. Parkes, 76.

34. Ibid.

35. Ibid.

36. Hitti, 617, 619.

37. S. D. Goitein, *A Mediterranean Society: The Jewish Communities of the Arab World as Portrayed in the Documents of the Cairo Geniza* (rev. ed. 1967), 29. See also Lewis, 83.

38. Hitti, 83, 620.

39. Parkes, 77.

40. Mann, 158–59.

41. Ibid., 42.

42. Ibid., 41–42, 159–63.

43. Ibid., 42.

44. Ibid., 47.

45. Ibid.

Chapter 8: Continued Battles and Conquests in the Holy Land

1. "Conquest," English Oxford Living Dictionaries, https://en.oxforddiction aries.com/definition/conquest (visited July 7, 2017).

2. Thomas F. Madden, "Crusaders and Historians," First Things (June 2005), https://www.firstthings.com/article/2005/06/crusaders-and-historians.
3. Philip K. Hitti, *History of the Arabs* (rev. 10th ed., 2002), 83, 639.
4. Steven Runciman, *A History of the Crusades*, vol. 2 (1951), 280.
5. Christopher Tyerman, *God's War: A New History of the Crusades* (2006), 155.
6. Hitti, 83, 639.
7. Ibid.
8. Runciman, 287.
9. Hitti, 83, 639 n.3.
10. "The Travels of Benjamin of Tudela," Internet Sacred Texts Archive, n.14, http://www.sacred-texts.com/jud/mhl/mhl20.htm (visited July 7, 2017).
11. Runciman, 304.
12. Ibid., 316.
13. James Parkes, *Whose Land? A History of the Peoples of Palestine* (1970), 97.
14. Ibid., 91, 93.
15. Ibid., 90.
16. Runciman, 4.
17. Ibid., 101.
18. Ibid.
19. Paul Johnson, *A History of the Jews* (1988), 199.
20. Ibid., 199–200 (the Genizah documents).
21. E. Ashtor-Strauss, "Saladin and the Jews," *Hebrew Union College Annual* 27 (1956), 305, 313.
22. Parkes, 98.
23. Johnson, 199.
24. Ibid., 201–202.
25. Ibid., 203.
26. Parkes, 101.
27. "Mamlūk,", http://www.britannica.com/topic/Mamluk (visited July 7, 2017).
28. Parkes, 101.
29. Hitti, 83, 671.
30. "Mamlūk," Encyclopædia Britannica; Hitti, 672.
31. "Mamlūk," Encyclopædia Britannica.
32. Ibid.; Hitti, 672.
33. Parkes, 100.
34. "Mamlūk," Encyclopædia Britannica.
35. Hitti, 487, 671, 679; C. E. Bosworth, "Christian and Jewish Religious Dignitaries in Mamluk Egypt and Syria: Qalqashandi's Information on Their Hierarchy, Titulature, and Appointment (II)," *International Journal Middle East Studies* 3, no. 2 (1972), 59, 60.
36. Hitti, 487, 671.
37. Parkes, 103.
38. Ibid., 104–105.
39. Hitti, 696; Parkes, 114.

40. Parkes, 111.
41. Ibid., 112.
42. Ibid., 111.
43. Sir Harry Charles Luke & Edward Keith-Roach, eds., *The Handbook of Palestine* (1922) (hereafter *Handbook of Palestine*), 50.
44. Ibid.
45. Parkes, 111–12.
46. *Handbook of Palestine*, 50.
47. Bosworth, 65.
48. Parkes, 112–113.
49. Hitti, 696.
50. Ibid.
51. Parkes, 108–10.
52. *Handbook of Palestine*, at 50–51.
53. Minna Rozen, *A History of the Jewish Community in Istanbul: The Formative Years, 1453–1566* (2010), 1.
54. Hitti, 727.
55. Ibid., 716; Parkes, 124.
56. Stanford J. Shaw, "The Editor's Desk," *International Journal of Middle East Studies* 5, no. 2 (1974), 121–23.
57. Parkes, 128.
58. Gudrun Kramer, *A History of Palestine: From the Ottoman Conquest to the Founding of the State of Israel*, trans. by Graham Harman and Gudrun Kramer (2008), 53–54.
59. Hitti, 727.
60. Parkes, 117.
61. Ibid.
62. Kramer, 54.
63. Hitti, 726.
64. Kramer, 57.
65. Ibid.
66. Joan Peters, *From Time Immemorial, The Origins of the Arab-Jewish Conflict over Palestine* (1984), 162 ("The Ottoman feudal system only exacerbated the conditions of corruption"); see also Bernard Lewis, *The Emergence of Modern Turkey* (3rd ed., 2001), 33.
67. Charles Issawi, *The Economic History of the Middle East, 1800–1914: A Book of Readings* (1975), 72.
68. Karl Sabbagh, *Palestine: A Personal History* (2008), 19.
69. Parkes, 115–16.
70. Hitti, 726.
71. Kramer, 54.
72. Ibid., 52.
73. Parkes, 129.
74. Peters, 178.

75. Marvin Heller, "Early Hebrew Printing from Lublin to Safed: The Journeys of Eliezer ben Isaac Ashkenazi," Academia.edu, http://www.academia.edu/4619862/Early_Hebrew_Printing_from_Lublin_to_Safed_The_Journeys_of_Eliezer_ben_Isaac_Ashkenazi (visited July 7, 2017).

76. Parkes, 131.

77. Peters, 178.

78. Ibid.

79. Parkes, 131.

80. Peters, 177.

81. Elli Kohen, *History of the Turkish Jews and Sephardim: Memories of a Past Golden Age* (2006), 97, 104; Peters, 177. Solomon ben Nathan Ashkenazi was also a rabbi and physician. He served as the Ottoman ambassador to Venice and a special counselor to the grand vizier.

82. Peters, 97.

83. Ibid., 178.

84. Ibid.

85. Ibid., 178 n.35. See also Jacob de Haas, *History of Palestine: The Last Two Thousand Years* (2007), 342.

86. Peters, 178–79.

87. Ibid.

88. Mark Twain, *The Innocents Abroad* (1984), 485–86.

89. Hitti, 728.

Chapter 9: World War I and the Dream of a Jewish Nation

1. "Texts Concerning Zionism: Excerpts from "The Jewish State" by Theodor Herzl (1896)," Jewish Virtual Library, http://www.jewishvirtuallibrary.org/excerpts-from-quot-the-jewish-state-quot (visited May, 30 2017).

2. *A Brief History of Anti-Semitism*, Anti-Defamation League (2013), 3, http://www.adl.org/assets/pdf/education-outreach/Brief-History-on-Anti-Semitism-A.pdf.

3. David Stevenson, *Europe before 1914*, British Library, https://www.bl.uk/world-war-one/articles/europe-before-1914 (visited Jan. 18, 2017).

4. "Revolutions of 1848," Encyclopædia Britannica, https://www.britannica.com/event/Revolutions-of-1848 (last updated June 8, 2010).

5. "Dreyfus Affair," Encyclopædia Britannica, https://www.britannica.com/event/Dreyfus-affair (last updated Nov. 12, 2014).

6. Jean-Denis Bredin, *The Affair: The Case of Alfred Dreyfus*, trans. Jeffrey Mehlman (1986) 170–78, 232, 237–42, 407–30.

7. Ibid., 3–8, 96–97, 124–33.

8. Leslie Derfler, *The Dreyfus Affair* (2002), 61.

9. Bredin, *The Affair: The Case of Alfred Dreyfus*, 232, 237–42, 407–30.

10. Ibid.

11. "Anti-Semitism: Alfred Dreyfus and 'The Affair,' " Jewish Virtual Library,

http://www.jewishvirtuallibrary.org/alfred-dreyfus-and-ldquo-the-affair-rdquo (visited May 30, 2017).

12. "Zionism," Encyclopædia Britannica, https://www.britannica.com/topic/Zionism (last updated June 9, 2015).

13. Theodor Herzl, *The Jewish State* (1896; Dover ed., 1988). "Zion" is a synonym for Jerusalem and refers to the name of a mountain (Mount Zion) upon which David built Jerusalem. The term is first mentioned in 2 Samuel 5:7.

14. "Zionist Congress: First Zionist Congress & Basel Program," Jewish Virtual Library, http://www.jewishvirtuallibrary.org/jsource/Zionism/First_Cong_&_Basel_Program.html (visited Jan. 11, 2017). "Eretz Israel" means "the land of Israel." "Eretz Israel," Dictionary.com, http://www.dictionary.com/browse/eretz-israel (visited Jan. 17, 2017).

15. Nahum Sokolov, *History of Zionism (1600–1918)*, vol. I, (1919, Elibron Classics Replica ed., 2005), 91–94.

16. Sokolov, vol. I, 99, 121–22 (discussing John Gill Anthony Ashley-Cooper's, 7th Earl of Shaftesbury, and Lord Lindsay's, 25th Earl of Crawford, support of the Zionist movement).

17. "Franz Ferdinand, Archduke of Austria-Este," Encyclopædia Britannica, https://www.britannica.com/biography/francis-ferdinand-archduke-of-austria-este (last updated Sept. 2, 2015). Note that the war formally began on July 28, 1914, when Austria declared war on Serbia. "Interactive WWI Timeline," National WWI Museum and Memorial, https://www.theworldwar.org/explore/interactive-wwi-timeline (visited Jan. 24, 2017).

18. "The Austro-Hungarian Ultimatum to Serbia" (English translation), WWI Document Archive, https://wwi.lib.byu.edu/index.php/The_Austro-Hungarian_Ultimatum_to_Serbia_(English_translation) (last updated May 29, 2009).

19. *The Serbian Blue Book*, no. 37, WWI Document Archive, https://wwi.lib.byu.edu/index.php/The_Serbian_Blue_Book (last updated May, 28, 2009).

20. Ken Porter and Stephen Wynn, *Laindon in the Great War* (2014), 43.

21. Ibid.

22. "The Hussein-McMahon Correspondence," Jewish Virtual Library, http://www.jewishvirtuallibrary.org/jsource/History/hussmac1.html (visited Jan. 18, 2017).

23. Sean McMeekin, *The Ottoman Endgame: War, Revolution, and the Making of the Modern Middle East, 1908–1923* (2015), 286.

24. Donald Quataert, *The Ottoman Empire, 1700–1922* (2005) 13, 61; Ian Black, "Middle East Still Rocking from First World War Pacts Made 100 Years Ago," *Guardian* (Dec. 30, 2015), http://www.theguardian.com/world/on-the-middle-east/2015/dec/30/middle-east-still-rocking-from-first-world-war-pacts-made-100-years-ago; "Sykes-Picot Agreement: 1916," Encyclopædia Britannica, http://www.britannica.com/event/Sykes-Picot-Agreement (visited May 2, 2016).

25. Dept. of State, International Boundary Study: Jordan-Syria Boundary (1969) (hereafter Jordan-Syria Boundary Study).

26. McMeekin, 284–88.

27. "Modern History Sourcebook: The Balfour Declaration," Fordham University, http://sourcebooks.fordham.edu/mod/balfour.asp (visited Jan. 10, 2017).

28. "Bolshevik," Encyclopædia Britannica, https://www.britannica.com/topic /Bolshevik (last updated July 14, 2009).

29. Isabel V. Hull, "Military Culture, Wilhelm II, and the End of the Monarchy in the First World War," in Annika Mombauer and Wilhelm Deist, eds., *The Kaiser* (2003), 235.

30. Adam Hochschild, *To End All Wars* (2011), 355.

31. Ibid.

32. Spencer C. Tucker, ed., *World War II: The Definitive Encyclopedia and Document Collection* (2016), 631.

33. Hochschild, 347–48.

34. Stefan Wolff, "Germany and German Minorities in Europe," in Tristan J. Mabry and John McGarry, eds., *Divided Nations and European Integration* (2013), 282.

35. "Treaty of Peace with Turkey, Aug. 10, 1920" (hereafter Treaty of Sèvres), http://treaties.fco.gov.uk/docs/pdf/1920/TS0011.pdf.

36. Erik Cornell, *Turkey in the 21st Century* (2001), 164.

37. "Treaty of Peace with Turkey and Other Instruments, July 24, 1923" (hereafter Treaty of Lausanne), article 16, http://treaties.fco.gov.uk/docs/pdf/1923 /ts0016-1.pdf (visited May 30, 2017).

38. Covenant of the League of Nations, article 22 (hereafter Covenant).

39. Abraham Bell and Eugene Kontorovich, "Palestine, *Uti Possidetis Juris*, and the Borders of Israel," *Arizona Law Review* 58 (2016), 633, 646 (internal citations omitted) (hereafter Bell and Kontorovich, "Borders of Israel").

40. The third paragraph of Article 22 described the foregoing principle as follows: "The character of the mandate must differ according to the stage of development of the people, the geographical situation of the territory, its economic condition and other similar circumstances." The fourth through the sixth paragraphs of Article 22 generally described differences among the mandates and what such differences meant for the respective Mandatory.

41. Covenant, paragraph 4 (emphasis added).

42. The fourth paragraph of Article 22 of the League of Nations Covenant reads, in pertinent part, as follows:

> *Certain communities* formerly belonging to the Turkish Empire have reached a stage of development where their existence as independent nations can be provisionally recognized subject to the rendering of administrative advice and assistance by a Mandatory until such time as they are able to stand alone. The wishes of these

communities must be a principal consideration in the selection of
the Mandatory.

43. "Convention Between the United States and Great Britain; Rights in Palestine. Signed at London, Dec. 3, 1924 . . ." (hereafter Anglo-American Treaty),
https://archive.org/stream/ldpd_11049065_000/ldpd_11049065_000_djvu
.txt.

44. The Principal Allied Powers were Great Britain, France, Italy, and Japan.
San Remo Resolution, Council on Foreign Relations (April 25, 1920), https://
world-media-watch.org/2013/03/10/65-jahre-moderner-staat-israel-oder
-die-volkerrechtlich-verbindliche-errichtung-einer-nationalen-heimstatte
-fur-die-juden-vor-91-jahren/delegation1920/.

45. Bell and Kontorovich, "Borders of Israel," 670.

46. "British Mandate for Palestine," *American Journal of International Law* 17,
no. 3 (Supp. 1923), 164 (hereafter Palestine Mandate), https://www.jstor.org
/stable/2212958?seq=1#page_scan_tab_contents.

47. Bell and Kontorovich, "Borders of Israel," 671.

48. Ibid., 673.

49. Ibid.

50. "The Weizmann-Feisal Agreement," Israel Ministry of Foreign Affairs,
http://www.mfa.gov.il/mfa/foreignpolicy/peace/mfadocuments/pages
/the%20weizmann-feisal%20agreement%203-jan-1919.aspx (visited Jan. 5,
2017).

51. Chaim Weizmann, *Trial and Error* (1949), 236. For more on the interactions
between Weizmann, Feisal, and T. E. Lawrence, see my book *Unholy Alliance*, 29–32.

52. Elie Podeh, *Chances for Peace* (2015), 22. Note that Feisal's handwritten remarks on the agreement were directed at the *British*, whom he mistrusted,
not at the Zionists.

53. "The Agreement Between Emir Feisal and Chaim Weizmann 1919," Peace
forourtime.org.uk, http://www.peaceforourtime.org.uk/page72.html (visited
Jan. 31, 2017) (emphasis added). Note, regarding the different spellings of
Emir Feisal's name, that there is no direct correspondence between the Arabic and Latin alphabets. Hence, Arabic names are transliterated, meaning
they are spelled as they sound to the hearer, which often leads to slight varia-
tions in spelling.

**Chapter 10: How the International Community Established the Modern
State of Israel**

1. "Winston Churchill on Palestine," IsraCast.com (March 2, 2017), http://
www.isracast.com/article.aspx?ID=764 (visited July 12, 2017).

2. Abraham Bell and Eugene Kontorovich, "Palestine, *Uti Possidetis Juris*, and
the Borders of Israel," *Arizona Law Review* 58 (2016), 633, 674 (hereafter Bell
and Kontorovich, "Borders of Israel") (internal citations omitted).

3. Ibid., 679.

4. Christian J. Tams, "League of Nations," Oxford Public International Law, paragraph 6, http://opil.ouplaw.com/view/10.1093/law:epil/9780199231690/law-9780199231690-e519 (last updated Sept. 2006).

5. See "International Status of South West Africa, Advisory Opinion," International Court of Justice (July 11, 1950), 128, 133, http://www.worldcourts.com/icj/eng/decisions/1950.07.11_status_of_SW_Africa.htm. This principle was reaffirmed by the ICJ in 1971. See "Legal Consequences for States of the Continued Presence of South Africa in Namibia (South West Africa) Notwithstanding Security Council Resolution 276, Advisory Opinion," International Court of Justice (June 21,1971), 16, 32–33, http://www.worldcourts.com/icj/eng/decisions/1971.06.21_namibia.htm.

6. G.A. Res. 181 (II) (Nov. 29, 1947). The results consisted of 33 members voting yes, 13 members voting no, and 10 members abstaining. Voting Record Search, A/Res/181(II)[A], United Nations Bibliographic Information System, http://unbisnet.un.org:8080/ipac20/ipac.jsp?session=F4859B448206F.5953&profile=voting&uri=full=3100023~!909562~!1&ri=1&aspect=power&menu=search&source=~!horizon (visited Feb. 1, 2017).

7. UN Charter, articles 9–22.

8. Ibid., article 80 ("Until such agreements [i.e., Trusteeship Agreements] have been concluded, nothing in this Chapter shall be construed in or of itself to alter in any manner the rights whatsoever of any states [e.g., Israel] or any peoples [e.g., Jews resident in "Palestine"] or the terms of existing international instruments [e.g., the Mandate for Palestine] to which Members of the United Nations may respectively be parties" (bracketed information added by author).

9. "Legal Consequences for States of the Continued Presence of South Africa in Namibia (South West Africa) Notwithstanding Security Council Resolution 276, Advisory Opinion," International Court of Justice (June 21,1971), paragraph 62 (emphasis added).

10. Howard Grief, "Article 80 and the UN Recognition of a 'Palestinian State,'" *Algemeiner* (Sept. 22, 2011, 10:58 a.m.), https://www.algemeiner.com/2011/09/22/article-80-and-the-un-recognition-of-a-%E2%80%9Cpalestinian-state%E2%80%9D/.

11. Eugene V. Rostow, "The Future of Palestine," ed. Kathleen A. Lynch, *Institute for National Strategic Studies* (1993), 15 n.1, https://www.files.ethz.ch/isn/23476/mcnair24.pdf (visited May 30, 2017).

12. Bell and Kontorovich, "Borders of Israel," 679.

13. Elon Gilad, "Israel—Day One: The Story of the Day of Independence," *Haaretz* (May 5, 2014, 1:07 p.m.), http://www.haaretz.com/israel-news/.premium-1.588927.

14. Bell and Kontorovich, "Borders of Israel," 679.

15. Youssef M. Ibrahim, "P.L.O. Proclaims Palestine to be an Independent State; Hints at Recognizing Israel," *New York Times* (Nov. 15, 1988), http://www

.nytimes.com/1988/11/15/world/plo-proclaims-palestine-to-be-an-inde
pendent-state-hints-at-recognizing-israel.html?pagewanted=all.

16. Bell and Kontorovich, "Borders of Israel," 679.

17. General Armistice Agreement, Isr.-Syria, art. 5, ¶ 1, Jul. 2, 1949, 42 U.N.T.S.
    327 (hereafter Armistice, Israel-Syria) (noting that the armistice line does
    not enshrine an "ultimate territorial [arrangement]"); General Armistice
    Agreement, Isr.-Jordan, art. 6, ¶ 9, Apr. 3, 1949, 42 U.N.T.S. 303 (hereafter
    Armistice, Israel-Jordan) (noting that the armistice line is "without preju-
    dice to future territorial settlements or boundary lines"); General Armistice
    Agreement, Isr.-Leb., art. 4, ¶ 2, Mar. 23, 1949, 42 U.N.T.S. 287 (hereafter
    Armistice, Israel-Lebanon) (noting that the "basic purpose" of the armistice
    line is to "delineate the line beyond which the armed forces of the respective
    Parties shall not move"); General Armistice Agreement, Isr.-Leb., art. 5, ¶
    2, Feb. 24, 1949, 42 U.N.T.S. 251 (hereafter Armistice, Israel-Egypt) (noting
    that the armistice line is "not to be construed . . . as a political or territorial
    boundary" and that the line is "delineated without prejudice" to the "ulti-
    mate settlement of the Palestine question").

18. "Armistice demarcation line," Free Dictionary, http://www.thefreediction
    ary.com/armistice+demarcation+line (visited Jan. 31, 2017).

19. *Ex Injuria Jus Non Oritur* Law and Legal Definition, USLegal, https://defini
    tions.uslegal.com/e/ex-injuria-jus-non-oritur/ (visited Jan. 26, 2017) (here-
    after *Ex Injuria*).

20. Marc Zell and Sonia Shnyder, "Palestinian Right of Return or Strategic
    Weapon?: A Historical, Legal and Moral Political Analysis," *Nexus* 8 (2003),
    77, n.15.

21. Restatement (Third) of Foreign Relations Law of the United States § 102(2)
    (Am. Law Inst. 1987).

22. Bell and Kontorovich, "Borders of Israel," 635.

23. Ibid. (emphasis added) (quoting Steven R. Ratner, "Drawing a Better Line:
    Uti Possidetis and the Borders of New States," *American Journal of Interna-
    tional Law* 90, no. 4 [Oct. 1996], 590).

24. In reference to Frontier Dispute (*Burk. Faso v. Mali*) (hereafter Frontier Dis-
    pute), Judgment, International Court of Justice (Dec. 22, 1986), 554, 565–67
    (emphasis added).

25. Ibid., 646 (emphasis added).

26. Bell and Kontorovich, "Borders of Israel," 635.

27. Frontier Dispute, 565–67.

28. Bell and Kontorovich, "Borders of Israel," 646–67 (giving numerous exam-
    ples regarding mandates).

29. See S.C. Res. 2334 (Dec. 23, 2016), "President Abbas Calls for World to Rec-
    ognise State of Palestine," Embassy of the State of Palestine, Dhaka, Bangla-
    desh (Jan. 2, 2017), http://palestineembassybd.com/?p=925. Note that many
    Palestinians regard the entire State of Israel as constituting "occupied Pales-

tinian territory." See, for example, Hamas Covenant, Art. 11 (Aug. 18, 1988), http://avalon.law.yale.edu/20th_century/hamas.asp.

30. Although Israel withdrew its military forces and all Jewish residents from the Gaza Strip in 2005, they never renounced their legal rights to the area.

31. *Ex Injuria*, at note 19.

32. Bell and Kontorovich, "Borders of Israel," 640 (emphasis added).

33. Ibid., 566 (emphasis added).

34. Ibid. (emphasis added).

35. Ibid., 642 (quoting Arbitration Commission of the International Conference for Former Yugoslavia, *Opinion No. 2* [Jan. 11, 1992], 31 I.L.M. 1497 [1992]) (emphasis added).

36. See, for example, S.C. Res. 2334 (Dec. 23, 2016) (calling Israel's settlement activity a "flagrant violation" of international law, demanding Israel's complete and total cessation of settlement activity, and showing no Palestinian compromises).

Chapter 11: Modern Israel vs. the Arab World

1. Muhammad Maqdsi, "Charter of the Islamic Resistance Movement (Hamas) of Palestine," *Journal of Palestine Studies* 22, no. 4 (1993), 122, 123, http://www.jstor.org/stable/2538093 (visited July 6, 2017).

2. Abraham Bell and Eugene Kontorovich, "Palestine, *Uti Possidetis Juris*, and the Borders of Israel," *Arizona Law Review* 58 (2016), 633, 679 (internal citations omitted) (hereafter Bell and Kontorovich, "Borders of Israel").

3. See Egyptian-Israeli General Armistice Agreement, Egypt-Isr., Art. I, ¶ 2, Feb. 24, 1949, http://peacemaker.un.org/sites/peacemaker.un.org/files/EG%20IL_490224_Egyptian-Israeli%20General%20Armistice%20Agreement.pdf (agreement stating that "no aggressive action by the armed forces— land, sea, or air—of either Party shall be undertaken, planned, or threatened against the people or the armed forces of the other").

4. See "The Sinai-Suez Campaign: Background & Overview (October– November 1956)," Jewish Virtual Library, http://www.jewishvirtuallibrary .org/background-and-overview-sinai-suez-campaign (visited July 5, 2017).

5. "The Suez Crisis, 1956," Office of the Historian, Bureau of Public Affairs, United States Department of State, https://history.state.gov/milestones/1953-1960/suez (visited July 5, 2017).

6. "Suez Crisis," Encyclopædia Britannica, https://www.britannica.com/event /Suez-Crisis (last updated Sept. 7, 2016); Ken Spiro, *Crash Course in Jewish History: From Abraham to Modern Israel* (rev. ed., 2011), 394.

7. See "Statement to the Knesset by Prime Minister Ben-Gurion, 23 January 1957," Israel Ministry of Foreign Affairs, http://mfa.gov.il/MFA/Foreign Policy/MFADocuments/Yearbook1/Pages/17%20Statement%20to%20 the%20Knesset%20by%20Prime%20Minister%20Ben-.aspx (visited July 6, 2017).

8. See Spiro, 393 (Egyptian President Gamal Nasser stating that "our basic objective will be the destruction of Israel").

9. Ibid.

10. Ibid., 394.

11. Ibid.

12. Martin Gilbert, *The Arab-Israeli Conflict: Its History in Maps* (2nd ed., 1976), 70.

13. S.C. Res. 242, ¶ 1 (Nov. 22, 1967) (hereafter Res. 242).

14. Yoram Meital, *Egypt's Struggle for Peace: Continuity and Change, 1967–1977* (1997), 49.

15. Peace Treaty Between Israel and Egypt, Egypt-Isr., Art. I, ¶ 2, Mar. 29, 1979, http://www.mfa.gov.il/mfa/foreignpolicy/peace/guide/pages/israel-egypt%20peace%20treaty.aspx.

16. Treaty of Peace Between the Hashemite Kingdom of Jordan and the State of Israel, Isr.-Jordan, annex I (Oct. 26, 1994), http://www.kinghussein.gov.jo/peacetreaty.html.

17. "Israel-Arab Peace Process: The Khartoum Resolutions (Sept. 1, 1967)," Jewish Virtual Library, http://www.jewishvirtuallibrary.org/the-khartoum-resolutions (visited July 6, 2017).

18. "Peace Treaty Between Israel and Egypt," Art. I, ¶ 2.

19. Res. 242. Note that Arab-Israeli wars have resulted in creating both Arab and Jewish refugees. Accordingly, the status of both groups of refugees needs to be considered in any final peace agreement.

20. U.N. SCOR, 22d Sess., 1382d mtg., U.N. Doc. S/PV.1382 (Nov. 22, 1967).

21. Avinoam Sharon, "Keeping Occupied: The Evolving Law of Occupation," *Regent Journal of Law & Public Policy* 1, no. 1 (Spring 2009), 145, 153–54 (citations omitted); see also Eugene V. Rostow, "Correspondence, to the Editor in Chief," *American Journal of International Law* 84 (1990), 717, 718 (responding to Professor Adam Roberts's article "Prolonged Military Occupation: The Israeli-Occupied Territories Since 1967," *American Journal of International Law* 84 [1990]) ("The right of the Jewish people to settle in Palestine has never been terminated for the West Bank").

22. Sharon, 155.

23. Ibid., 153–54.

24. Gilbert, 63 (stating that between 1968 and 1973 the Soviet Union provided approximately $2.6 billion worth of arms to the Arab states, including Egypt and Syria).

25. "Israel Military Intelligence: Intelligence During Yom Kippur War (1973)," Jewish Virtual Library, http://www.jewishvirtuallibrary.org/jsource/History/intel73.html (visited Jan. 18, 2017) ("In response to the Israeli Air Force's [IAF] attacks, Egyptian President Nasser asked the Soviets for help in defending Egyptian air space. 'The Soviets responded quickly, sending batteries of SAM's [Surface-to-Air], including the latest SAM-3s, with Soviet crews, and squadrons of MiG-21s, with Soviet pilots and ground crews'").

26. Spiro, 399.
27. Gilbert, 97 (showing the Egyptian forces trapped between Israeli forces approximately 101 kilometers from Cairo).
28. Ibid., 98 (using the distance key puts the Israeli frontlines within twenty to twenty-five miles of Damascus).
29. S.C. Res. 338 (Oct. 22, 1973).
30. G.A. Res. 3237 (XXIX), Observer Status for the Palestine Liberation Organization (Nov. 22, 1974).
31. G.A. Res. 3379, Elimination of All Forms of Racial Discrimination, (Nov. 10, 1975). The resolution was not rescinded until 1991. Paul Lewis, "U.N. Repeals Its '75 Resolution Equating Zionism with Racism," *New York Times* (Dec. 17, 1991), http://www.nytimes.com/1991/12/17/world/un-repeals-its -75-resolution-equating-zionism-with-racism.html.
32. "1976: Israelis Rescue Entebbe Hostages," BBC News: On This Day, http:// news.bbc.co.uk/onthisday/hi/dates/stories/july/4/newsid_2786000/2786967 .stm (visited Jan. 23, 2017).
33. Alan Taylor, "On This Day 36 Years Ago: The Signing of the Egypt-Israel Peace Treaty," *Atlantic* (March 26, 2015), http://www.theatlantic.com /photo/2015/03/on-this-day-36-years-ago-the-signing-of-the-egyptisrael -peace-treaty/388781/.
34. Spiro, 400. The IDF did not withdraw from Lebanon until May 2000. Ibid., 400–401.
35. "Intifada," Encyclopedea.com, http://www.encyclopedia.com/religion/ency clopedias-almanacs-transcripts-and-maps/intifada-0 (visited Jan. 23, 2017). An intifada is distinct from the normal Palestinian protests in that an intifada generally has "mass support from Palestinians across towns and villages as well as across social divisions." Damien McElroy, "Israel-Gaza Conflict: What Is an Intifada?," *Telegraph* (Nov. 6, 2014, 7:25 a.m. GMT), http://www .telegraph.co.uk/news/worldnews/middleeast/israel/10990699/Israel-Gaza -conflict-What-is-an-intifada.html.
36. Zachary Laub, "Hamas," Council on Foreign Relations, http://www.cfr.org /israel/hamas/p8968 (last updated Aug. 1, 2014). Hamas, originally an off-shoot of the Muslim Brotherhood, is a Palestinian group whose mission is to destroy Israel and establish an Islamic state in its place. Many nations, such as the United States and members of the European Union, have placed Hamas on their lists of known terrorist organizations. Ibid.
37. Youssef M. Ibrahim, "P.L.O. Proclaims Palestine to be an Independent State; Hints at Recognizing Israel, *New York Times* (Nov. 15, 1988), http://www .nytimes.com/1988/11/15/world/plo-proclaims-palestine-to-be-an-inde pendent-state-hints-at-recognizing-israel.html?pagewanted=all.
38. "1991: Bush Opens Historic Mid East Peace Conference," BBC News: On This Day, http://news.bbc.co.uk/onthisday/hi/dates/stories/october/30/news id_2465000/2465725.stm (visited July 6, 2017).
39. Spiro, 400.

40. Ibid.
41. Ibid.
42. Israeli-Palestinian Interim Agreement on the West Bank and the Gaza Strip, Isr.-P.L.O., Art. I, ¶¶ 1–2 (Sept. 28, 1995), http://www.unsco.org /Documents/Key/Israeli-Palestinian%20Interim%20Agreement%20on%20 the%20West%20Bank%20and%20the%20Gaza%20Strip.pdf.
43. "The Hebron Protocol," *Journal of Palestine Studies* 26 (1997), 131 (establishing the redeployment of Israeli troops to Hebron); "The Wye River Memorandum," U.S. Department of State (Oct. 23, 1998), https://2001-2009.state .gov/p/nea/rls/22694.htm (allowing for the transfer of certain areas of Israeli land into Palestinian control, the establishment of better security, and the ability to provide further redeployments).
44. See Spiro, 400–401 (showing Arafat walking out on talks with Israel and declaring the Second Intifada soon after).
45. "Al-Aqsa Intifada Timeline," BBC News, http://news.bbc.co.uk/2/hi/mid dle_east/3677206.stm (last updated Sept. 29, 2004, 07:50 GMT).
46. Ibid.
47. "A Performance-Based Roadmap to a Permanent Two-State Solution to the Israeli-Palestinian Conflict," U.S. Department of State (April 30, 2003), https://2001-2009.state.gov/r/pa/prs/ps/2003/20062.htm (laying out a three -year plan to create two states in Palestine).
48. Josef Federman, "Abbas Admits He Rejected 2008 Peace Offer from Olmert," *Times of Israel* (Nov. 19, 2015, 3:46 a.m.), http://www.timesofisrael .com/abbas-admits-he-rejected-2008-peace-offer-from-olmert/.
49. "Declaration Recognizing the Jurisdiction of the International Criminal Court," Palestinian National Authority Minister of Justice (Jan. 21, 2009), https://www.icc-cpi.int/nr/rdonlyres/74eee201-0fed-4481-95d4-c80710871 02c/279777/20090122palestiniandeclaration2.pdf.
50. "Situation in Palestine," Office of the Prosecutor, International Criminal Court (April 3, 2012), https://www.icc-cpi.int/NR/rdonlyres/C6162BBF -FEB9-4FAF-AFA9-836106D2694A/284387/SituationinPalestine0304 12ENG.pdf.
51. G.A. Res. 67/19, ¶ 2 (Dec. 4, 2012).
52. "Israel's Settlements Have No Legal Validity, Constitute Flagrant Violation of International Law, Security Council Reaffirms," Meetings Coverage and Press Releases, UN Security Council, U.N. Doc. SC/12657 (Dec. 23, 2016), https://www.un.org/press/en/2016/sc12657.doc.htm.
53. "Address by PM Netanyahu at Bar-Ilan University," Israel Ministry of Foreign Affairs (June 14, 2009), http://mfa.gov.il/MFA/PressRoom/2009/Pages/Ad dress_PM_Netanyahu_Bar-Ilan_University_14-Jun-2009.aspx. See also Jeffrey Goldberg, "The Tragic History of the Two-State Solution," Bloomberg (May 2, 2014), https://www.bloomberg.com/view/articles/2014-05-02/the -tragic-history-of-the-two-state-solution (explaining how Israel has sought to accommodate the Palestinians' desire for their own country for the last

eighty years, including attempts by Ariel Sharon and Ehud Olmert in the last two administrations).

54. Bell and Kontorovich, "Borders of Israel," 636–38.

55. Ibid., 679.

56. Rostow.

Section V: Jerusalem, the Eternal Capital of Israel

1. "Statements of the Prime Minister David Ben-Gurion Regarding Moving the Capital of Israel to Jerusalem," Knesset, https://knesset.gov.il/docs/eng /bengurion-jer.htm (visited July 13, 2017) (hereafter "Statements of the Prime Minister").

Chapter 12: Jerusalem's Spiritual and Historical Significance

2. Paul Goldman, "Church of the Holy Sepulchre in Jerusalem Gets Long-Awaited Refurbishment," NBC News (June 18, 2016, 4:49 p.m. ET), http://www.nbcnews.com/news/world/church-holy-sepulchre-jerusalem-gets-long-awaited-refurbishment-n591816.

3. Eoin Blackwell, "What's The Story Behind Jerusalem's Immovable Ladder?," *Huffington Post* (Feb. 12, 2016, 8:31 p.m. AEDT), http://www.huffingtonpost.com.au/2016/12/01/whats-the-story-behind-jerusalems-immovable-ladder_a_21617106/.

4. "Statements of the Prime Minister."

5. Basic Law: Jerusalem, Capital of Israel, 5740-2000, SH No. 980 p. 287 (Isr.).

6. Abigail Jacobson, *From Empire to Empire: Jerusalem Between Ottoman and British Rule* (2011), 2.

7. Basic Law: Jerusalem, Capital of Israel, 5740-2000, SH No. 980 p. 287 (Isr.).

8. Jacobson, 2.

9. Ibid. ("But, even those general problems of state and religion which appear to have counterparts in most modern countries—such as freedom of religion and religious establishment—cannot be understood properly without previous knowledge of the ideologies adhered to by the central groups confronting each other over the various issues.")

10. *Midrash Koheleth Rabbah* 1:1. Christian tradition likewise refers to Jerusalem as *Umbilicus Terra*. The Maharal of Prague explained this metaphorical analogy as signifying that just as "the umbilicus divides the body into its upper and lower halves, and is a sort of connecting link between the two, so, too, the land of Israel is a midway point. It links the physical world below with the spiritual worlds above. In this sense, it is the 'middle' of the world." Rabbi Yoel Schwartz, *Zion Today: Torah Perspective* (1986), 21.

11. "The Temple Mount," GoJerusalem.com, http://www.gojerusalem.com/article/186/The-Temple-Mount/ (visited July 13, 2017).

12. Jacobson, 9.

13. Professor Tom Meyer, "The Religious and Historical Claims to Jerusalem,"

Shasta Bible College and Graduate School (Dec. 3, 2013), http://www.shasta.edu/faculty-blogs/december-03rd-2013.

14. Yitzhak Reiter and Marwan Abu Khalaf, "Jerusalem's Religious Significance," *Palestine-Israel Journal of Politics, Economics and Culture* 8, no. 1 (2001).

15. Ibid.

16. Meyer.

17. Reiter and Khalaf.

18. Ibid.

19. Ibid.; see also Meyer.

20. See Amihai Mazar, "Archaeology and the Biblical Narrative: The Case of the United Monarchy," in Reinhard G. Kratz and Hermann Spieckermann, eds., *One God—One Cult—One Nation: Archaeological and Biblical Perspectives* (2010), 29–58.

21. Note that, while the 1006 B.C. date for King David's establishment of Jerusalem as the capital has been adopted by the Israeli government, dating of biblical era events remains both hotly contested by scholars and the subject of much ongoing archaeological exploration. See Israel Finkelstein and Neil Asher Silberman, *The Bible Unearthed: Archaeology's New Vision of Ancient Israel and the Origin of Its Sacred Texts* (reprint ed., 2002); and Israel Finkelstein and Amihai Mazar, *The Quest for the Historical Israel: Debating Archaeology and the History of Early Israel* (2007).

22. See Lee I. Levine, *Jerusalem: Portrait of the City in the Second Temple Period (538 B.C.E.–70 C.E.)* (2002).

23. See Geza G. Xeravits, *"Take Courage, O Jerusalem . . .": Studies in the Psalms of Baruch 4–5* (2015).

24. See Martin Goodman, *Rome and Jerusalem: The Clash of Ancient Civilizations* (reprint ed., 2007).

25. See Adrian J. Boas, *Jerusalem in the Time of the Crusades: Society, Landscape and Art in the Holy City Under Frankish Rule* (2001).

26. Roberto Mazza, *Jerusalem: From the Ottoman to the British* (reprint ed., 2009), 12–13.

27. Ibid., 12.

28. See Oded Peri, "Islamic Law and Christian Holy Sites: Jerusalem and Its Vicinity in Early Ottoman Times," *Islamic Law and Society* 6, no. 1 (1999), 97–111.

29. Mazza, 13.

30. Ibid., 12.

31. Jacobson, 2.

32. Ibid., 3.

33. Ashkenazi Jews include Jews from Northern and Eastern Europe (as well as their descendants from America). The term "Ashkenazi" comes from the old Hebrew word for Germany. Sephardic Jews include Jews of Mediterranean, Balkan, Aegean, and Middle Eastern heritage. The term comes from the old Hebrew word for Spain. Oriental Jews are those of African or Asian origin.

See "The Ashkenazi, Sephardi and Oriental," CountryStudies.us., http://
countrystudies.us/israel/49.htm (visited July 13, 2017).

34. Jacobson, 4.
35. Ibid., 4–5.
36. Ibid., 22–24, 27.
37. Ibid.,130.
38. Ibid., 1.
39. See Ibid., 118, 122, 129.
40. "The Palestine Mandate," Avalon Project, http://avalon.law.yale.edu/20th
_century/palmanda.asp (visited July 13, 2017).
41. Jacobson, 138.
42. Ibid., 139–42.
43. U.N. General Assembly, "Considerations Affecting Certain of the Provisions of the General Assembly Resolution on the 'Future Government of
Palestine': The City of Jerusalem," Working Paper Prepared by the Secre-
tariat, ¶ 1, U.N. Doc. A/AC.21/W.17 (Jan. 22, 1948), https://unispal.un.org
/DPA/DPR/unispal.nsf/5ba47a5c6cef541b802563e000493b8c/6362111f6897
24d705256601007063f2?OpenDocument.
44. "Statement to the Knesset by Prime Minister Ben-Gurion, 5 December 1949,"
Boston University, http://www.bu.edu/mzank/Jerusalem/tx/b-g-speech1949
.htm (visited July 17, 2017).
45. S.C. Res. 89, ¶ 6 (Nov. 17, 1950).
46. "Timeline of Jewish History: Modern Israel & the Diaspora (1950–1959),"
Jewish Virtual Library, http://www.jewishvirtuallibrary.org/timeline-of
-modern-israel-1950-1959-2#1953) (visited July 13, 2017).
47. "History of Jerusalem: Jordanian Annexation of the West Bank," Jewish Virtual Library, http://www.jewishvirtuallibrary.org/jordanian-annexation-of
-the-west-bank-april-1950 (visited July 13, 2017).
48. Ofra Friesel, "Israel's 1967 Governmental Debate About the Annexation of
East Jerusalem: The Nascent Alliance with the United States, Overshadowed
by 'United Jerusalem,' " *Law and History Review* 34, no. 2 (2016), 363 n.5.
49. Ibid., 365.
50. "Statement to the Knesset by Prime Minister Eshkol—12 June 1967," Israel Ministry of Foreign Affairs (June 12, 1967), http://mfa.gov.il/MFA/For
eignPolicy/MFADocuments/Yearbook1/Pages/23%20Statement%20to%20
the%20Knesset%20by%20Prime%20Minister%20Eshk.aspx.

Chapter 13: The Legal Basis for Jerusalem as Israel's Capital

1. "Statement to the Knesset by Prime Minister Ben-Gurion, 5 December 1949,"
Boston University, http://www.bu.edu/mzank/Jerusalem/tx/b-g-speech1949
.htm (visited July 13, 2017).
2. Basic Laws of the State of Israel, Israel Ministry of Foreign Affairs, http://
www.mfa.gov.il/mfa/aboutisrael/state/law/pages/basic%20laws%20of%20
the%20state%20of%20israel.aspx (visited July 13, 2017).

3. David B. Green, "1980: Israel Enacts the Symbolic 'Jerusalem, Capital of Israel' Law," *Haaretz* (visited July 30, 2015, 6:01 a.m.), http://www.haaretz .com/jewish/this-day-in-jewish-history/.premium-1.668420.

4. S.C. Res. 478, ¶ 3 (Aug. 20, 1980).

5. Basic Law: Jerusalem, Capital of Israel, 5740–1980, SH No. 980 p. 186 (Isr.); see also Ian S. Lustick, "Has Israel Annexed East Jerusalem?," *Middle East Policy* 5, no. 1 (Jan. 1997). 34–45.

6. Basic Law: Jerusalem, Capital of Israel, 5740–1980, SH No. 980 p. 186 (Isr.).

7. Ibid.

8. Tzippe Barrow, "Bill to Grant Jerusalem Priority Status," CBN News (Oct. 25, 2010), http://www.cbn.com/cbnnews/insideisrael/2010/october /bill-to-grant-jerusalem-priority-status/?mobile=false.

9. Tovah Lazaroff, "Netanyahu: 'Jerusalem is the Heart of the Nation. We'll Never Divide Our Heart,' " *Jerusalem Post* (visited May 28, 2014, 6:36 a.m.), http://www.jpost.com/National-News/Netanyahu-47-years-ago-Jerusalem -was-reunited-and-thats-how-it-will-stay-354589.

10. Tovah Lazaroff, "Poll: 72% of Jewish Israelis View J'lem as Divided," *Jerusalem Post* (visited June 5, 2016, 7:08 a.m.), http://www.jpost.com /Diplomacy-and-Politics/Post-poll-72-percent-of-Jewish-Israelis-view -Jlem-as-divided-315490.

11. Daniel Pomerantz, "Who Decides the Capital of Israel?," Honest Reporting (Sept. 15, 2016), http://honestreporting.com/capital-of-israel/.

12. "The Oslo Accords, 1993," U.S. Department of State, https://2001-2009 .state.gov/r/pa/ho/time/pcw/97181.htm (visited July 13, 2017).

13. Ibid.

14. See Kenneth W. Stein, ed., *History, Politics and Diplomacy of the Arab Israeli Conflict: A Source Document Reader High School, College, and Adult Education* (2nd ed., 2016), 23.

15. G.A. Res. 194 (III) (Dec. 11, 1948).

16. Ibid.

17. Ibid., paragraphs 7–10.

18. G.A. Res. 273 (III) (May 11, 1949).

19. Ibid.

20. Ibid.

21. S.C. Res. 242 (Nov. 22, 1967).

22. Ibid.

23. Ibid., paragraph 1.

24. See "Oslo Accords, 1993," University of Chicago, http://cis.uchicago.edu/old site/sites/cis.uchicago.edu/files/resources/CIS-090213-israelpalestine_38 -1993DeclarationofPrinciples_OsloAccords.pdf (visited July 13, 2017).

25. Harriet Dashiell Schwar and David S. Patterson, eds., *Foreign Relations of the United States, 1964–1968, Volume XVIII, The Arab-Israeli Dispute, 1964–1967*, Office of the Historian, Department of State (2000), 765–66, https://history .state.gov/historicaldocuments/frus1964-68v18.

26. Ibid., 996.

27. Ibid., 998.

28. William B. Quandt, *Peace Process: American Diplomacy and the Arab-Israeli Conflict Since 1967* (3rd ed., 2005), 443; Hugh Foot and Baron Caradon, *U.N. Security Council Resolution 242: A Case Study in Diplomatic Ambiguity* (1981).

29. Daniel S. Papp, ed., *As I Saw It: Dean Rusk as Told to Richard Rusk* (1990), 389.

30. President Ronald Reagan, "Address to the Nation on United States Policy for Peace in the Middle East," American Presidency Project (Sept. 1, 1982), http://www.presidency.ucsb.edu/ws/?pid=42911.

31. Foot and Caradon.

32. UN Security Council Minutes, 3351st Meeting, UN Doc. S/PV.3351 (March 18, 1994), https://unispal.un.org/DPA/DPR/unispal.nsf/0/1EB9794 F4BEEA0E8852560CB0070E091.

33. S.C. Res. 476 (Aug. 20, 1980).

34. "Israel Says UN Resolution Will Not Affect Jerusalem's Status as Capital," Jewish Telegraphic Agency (Aug. 22, 1980), http://www.jta.org/1980/08/22 /archive/israel-says-un-resolution-will-not-affect-jerusalems-status-as-cap ital.

35. UN Security Council Minutes, 2245th meeting, UN Doc. S/PV.2245 (Aug. 20, 1980), https://documents-dds-ny.un.org/doc/UNDOC/GEN/NL 8/000/25/PDF/NL800025.pdf?OpenElement.

36. Ibid.

37. Ibid.

38. See Shlomo Slonim, *Jerusalem in America's Foreign Policy, 1947–1997* (1998), 246.

39. Legal Consequences of the Construction of a Wall in the Occupied Palestinian Territory, Summary of the Advisory Opinion of 9 July 2004, International Court of Justice, The Hague, http://www.unrod.org/docs/ICJ -Advisory2004.pdf.

40. G.A. Res. 58/292 (May 17, 2004).

41. "Israel's Settlements Have No Legal Validity, Constitute Flagrant Violation of International Law, Security Council Reaffirms," United Nations Meetings Coverage and Press Releases. SC/12657 (Dec. 23, 2016), https://www .un.org/press/en/2016/sc12657.doc.htm.

42. See Tovah Lazaroff, Herb Keinon, Michael Wilner, and Adam Rasgon, "UNESCO Votes: No Connection Between Temple Mount and Judaism," *Jerusalem Post* (visited Oct. 13, 2016, 4:13 p.m.), http://www.jpost.com /Breaking-News/UNESCO-No-connection-between-Temple-Mount-and -Judaism-470050.

43. Uzi Baruch, "World Parliamentarians: Jerusalem Is Israel's Capital," Arutz Sheva: IsraelNationalNews.com (visited Oct. 21, 2016, 3:14), http://www.is raelnationalnews.com/News/News.aspx/219198.

44. See Harry S. Truman, "Statement by the President Announcing Recogni-

tion of the State of Israel," American Presidency Project (May 14, 1948), http://www.presidency.ucsb.edu/ws/?pid=12896.

45. Restatement (Third) of Foreign Relations Law of the United States § 203 cmt. a (Am. Law Inst. 1986).

46. See *Zivotofsky v. Kerry*, 135 S. Ct. 2076, 2085 (2015) (" '[S]tates may recognize or decline to recognize territory as belonging to, or under the sovereignty of, or having been acquired or lost by, other states'. . . . Recognition is often effected by an express 'written or oral declaration' "), https://www.law.cornell.edu/supremecourt/text/13-628.

47. Ibid.; Ian Brownlie, *Principles of Public International Law* (7th ed., 2008), 93.

48. See *Guaranty Trust Co. v. United States*, 304 U.S. 126, 137 (1938); *Nat'l City Bank of N.Y. v. Republic of China*, 348 U.S. 356, 358–59 (1955).

49. See *Oetjen v. Central Leather Co.*, 246 U.S. 297, 302–03 (1918).

50. John B. Moore, *A Digest of International Law* (1906), 72.

51. *Kerry*, 135 S. Ct. at 2084 (internal quotations omitted).

52. Ibid., 2094–95 (citing Art. II, § 3).

53. Ibid., 2085 (citing Emer de Vattel, *The Law of Nations* (1758), 461 ("[E]very state, truly possessed of sovereignty, has a right to send ambassadors" and "to contest their right in this instance" is equivalent to "contesting their sovereign dignity.") See also Cornelius van Bynkershoek, *On Questions of Public Law* (1737), 156–57 ("Among writers on public law it is usually agreed that only a sovereign power has a right to send ambassadors"); and Hugo Grotius, *On the Law of War and Peace* (1625), 440–41 (discussing the duty to admit ambassadors of sovereign powers).

54. *Kerry*, 135 S. Ct. at 2085 (citing Art. II, § 2, cl. 2).

55. Ibid.

56. See, e.g., *United States v. Pink*, 315 U.S. 203 (1942); *Banco Nacional de Cuba v. Sabbatino*, 376 U.S. 398, 410 (1964); *Kerry*, 135 S. Ct. at 2088.

57. Foreign Relations Authorization Act, Fiscal Year 2003, Pub. L. No. 107-228, 116 Stat. 1350 (2002).

58. Ibid., 1365.

59. Ibid., 1366.

60. George W. Bush, XLIII President of the United States: 2001–2009, Statement on Signing the Foreign Relations Authorization Act, Fiscal Year 2003 (Sept. 30, 2002), http://www.presidency.ucsb.edu/ws/?pid=63928.

61. *Kerry*, 135 S. Ct. at 2082.

62. Ibid. at 2094 (citations omitted).

63. *Zivotofsky ex rel. Zivotofsky v. Clinton*, 566 U.S. 189, 201 (2012).

64. *Kerry*, 135 S. Ct. at 2094 (citing Foreign Relations Authorization Act, Pub. L. No. 107-228, 116 Stat. 1365; see Sam F. Halabi, "Jerusalem in the Court and on the Ground," *Florida Journal of International Law* 26 [2014], 223).

65. H.R. Rep. No. 107–671, at 123 (2002), 2002 U.S.C.C.A.N. 869, 876 (Conf. Rep.).

66. *Kerry*, 135 S. Ct. at 2095–96 (citations omitted).

67. Ibid., 2090.
68. 141 *Congressional Record*, D1242-02 (daily ed. Oct. 24, 1995); 141 *Congressional Record*, H10680 (daily ed. Oct. 24, 1995).
69. Jerusalem Embassy Act of 1995, Pub. L. No. 104-45, 1995, U.S.C.C.A.N. (109 Stat) 398 (hereafter Jerusalem Embassy Act).
70. See Malvina Halberstam, "The Jerusalem Embassy Act," *Fordham International Law Journal* 19 (1996), 1379 n.6.
71. Jerusalem Embassy Act § 2.
72. Patrick Goodenough, "Will Trump Break with Predecessors and Move US Embassy to Jerusalem?," CNS News (last viewed Nov. 10, 2016, 4:13 a.m.), http://www.cnsnews.com/news/article/patrick-goodenough/will-trump -break-predecessors-and-move-us-embassy-jerusalem.
73. Jerusalem Embassy Act § 214.
74. *Kerry*, 135 S. Ct. at 2087 (emphasis added).
75. Michael Wilner, " 'Big Priority' Moving US Embassy to Jerusalem, Trump Aide Says," *Jerusalem Post* (Dec. 12, 2016), http://www.jpost.com/American -Politics/Big-priority-moving-US-embassy-to-Jerusalem-Trump-aide-says -475160.
76. See, e.g., Andrew Hanna and Yousef Saba, "Will Trump move the U.S. Embassy to Jerusalem?," *Politico* (last viewed Dec. 15, 2016, 9:00 p.m.), http:// www.politico.com/story/2016/12/trump-us-embassy-jerusalem-232724; Rebecca Shabad, "What Could Happen if Trump Moves the U.S. Embassy to Jerusalem?," CBS News (visited Dec. 20, 2016, 6:00 a.m.), http://www .cbsnews.com/news/what-could-happen-if-trump-moves-the-u-s-embassy -to-jerusalem/; Cecily Hilleary, "U.S. Embassy Move to Jerusalem Could Further Fuel Extremism," *Voice of America News* (visited Dec. 23, 2016, 2:31 p.m.), https://www.voanews.com/a/us-embassy-move-to-jerusalem-could -further-fuel-extremism/3648688.html.
77. See generally Alexander Smith, Paul Goldman, and Lawahez Jabari, "Trump Plan to Move Embassy from Tel Aviv to Jerusalem Poses Difficulties," NBC News (visited Dec. 18, 2016, 4:41 a.m.), http://www.nbcnews.com /news/world/trump-plan-move-embassy-tel-aviv-jerusalem-poses-challenges -n696396.
78. See Dave Clark, "Trump Plan for Jerusalem Embassy Blunts U.S. Peace Push," Yahoo News (Dec. 16, 2016), https://www.yahoo.com/news/trump -plan-jerusalem-embassy-blunts-us-peace-push-185635439.html; and "Erekat: 'Hope of Peace Will Vanish' if U.S. Moves Embassy to Jerusalem," Ma'an News Agency (visited Dec. 22, 2016, 8:30 p.m.), http://www.maannews.com /Content.aspx?ID=774517.
79. See Tessa Berenson, "Trump's Ambassador to Israel Recognizes Jerusalem as Capital," *Time* (Dec. 16, 2016), http://time.com/4604603/donald -trump-david-friedman-jerusalem/; and Andrew V. Pestano, "Trump Taps Hardliner David Friedman as U.S. Ambassador to Israel," UPI (visited Dec. 16, 2016, 9:24 a.m.), https://www.upi.com/Top_News

/US/2016/12/16/Trump-taps-hardliner-David-Friedman-as-US-ambassador
-to-Israel/1451481888257/.
80. *Kerry*, 135 S. Ct. at 241.

Section VI: Israel and the Law: Ancient Principles and Modern Lawfare

1. Ian Schwartz, "Kerry: Israel Can Either Be Jewish or Democratic, It Cannot Be Both," RealClearPolitics (Dec. 28, 2016), http://www.realclearpolitics
.com/video/2016/12/28/kerry_israel_can_either_be_jewish_or_democratic
_it_cannot_be_both.html.

Chapter 14: Loving Your Neighbor as a Model for Governance

2. David Ben-Gurion, *Rebirth and Destiny of Israel* (1954), 419.
3. See David Feldman, "The Structure of Jewish Law," in Menachem Marc Kellner, ed., *Contemporary Jewish Ethics* (1978), 21–38.
4. See Mark Goldfeder, "Defining and Defending Borders; Just and Legal Wars in Jewish Thought and Practice," *Touro Law Review* 30, no. 3 (2014); Mark Goldfeder, "Diritto e religione nel moderno d'Israele: l'antica uguaglianza come fondamento del diritto statale contemporaneo," *Quaderni costituzionali* (Fall 2015); and Mark Goldfeder, "Rights, Reservations, and Religion: International Human Rights Law and the Status of Women," *Crit: A Critical Legal Studies Journal* 6, no. 1 (Winter 2012).
5. Declaration of Establishment of State of Israel, Israel Ministry of Foreign Affairs (May 14, 1948), http://www.mfa.gov.il/mfa/foreignpolicy/peace
/guide/pages/declaration%20of%20establishment%20of%20state%20of
%20israel.aspx (hereafter Declaration).
6. Schwartz.
7. See Michael J. Perry, *The Idea of Human Rights* (1998), 11–41.
8. Jerusalem Talmud, *Nedarim* 9:4.
9. Babylonian Talmud, *Shabbat* 31a (Vilna Edition).
10. CA 3632/92 *Gabay v. State of Israel* 46(4) PD 487, 490 (1992) (Isr.).
11. Declaration (emphasis added).
12. Ben-Gurion, 419 (emphasis added).
13. *Mishneh Torah, Hilchos Daios* 6:3; see also *Sefer HaChinuch Mitzvah* 243 ("The elements included in this mitzvah follow the general principle that one should treat another person in the way he would treat himself, e.g. protecting his property, preventing him from being harmed, speaking only well of him, respecting him, and certainly not glorifying oneself at his expense.").
14. Basic Law: Human Dignity and Liberty, 5752–1992, SH No. 1391 p. 60 (Isr.) (emphasis added).
15. See Aharon Barak, "Israel Studies An Anthology: The Values of the State of Israel as a Jewish and Democratic State," Jewish Virtual Library (Aug. 2009), http://www.jewishvirtuallibrary.org/israel-studies-an-anthology-israel-as
-jewish-and-democratic-state.

16. Ibid.
17. See HCJ 6698/95 *Ka'adan v. Israel Lands Authority*, 54(1) PD 258 (2000) (Isr.); HCJ 2859/99 *Mkarina v. Minister of Interior* 59(6) PD 721 (2005) (Isr.).
18. Barak.
19. Commentary on the Torah, Leviticus 19:17–18; Babylonian Talmud, *Bava Metzia* 62a.
20. Babylonian Talmud, *Bava Metzia* 62a.
21. "Constitutionalism" here is used broadly to cover not only the Basic Laws but also the quasi-constitutional founding documents and semi-constitutional proclamations of the Israeli Supreme Court.
22. Arieh J. Kochavi, "Israel and the International Legal Arena," *Journal of Israeli History* 25, no. 1 (Aug. 18, 2006), 223.
23. UN GAOR, 30th Sess., 2400th plen. mtg. at 84, U.N. Doc. A/PV.2400 (Nov. 10, 1975).
24. Ibid. (Noting that on Dec. 16, 1991, the UN General Assembly revoked Resolution 3379 following a diplomatic battle that began when Israel conditioned its participation in the Madrid Peace Conference on the revocation of this resolution.)
25. Daphne Barak-Erez, "The International Law of Human Rights and Constitutional Law: A Case Study of an Expanding Dialogue," *International Journal of Constitutional Law* 2, no. 4 (Oct. 1, 2004), 611, 615 n.20 (quoting Aharon Barak; citations omitted).
26. See Ibid.; Convention Relating to the Status of Refugees art. 3, April 22, 1954, 189 U.N.T.S. 137; Barak-Erez, 623 (referring to HCJ 5100/94, *Public Committee Against Torture in Israel v. Government of Israel* 53[4] PD 817 [1999] [Isr.]); Ran Hirschl, "Constitutionalism, Judicial Review, and Progressive Change: A Rejoinder to McClain and Fleming," *Texas Law Review* 84, no. 2 (Dec. 2005), 471, 591, 507 n.109.
27. Ibid., 622–23. Compare HCJ 769/02, *Public Committee Against Torture in Israel v. Government of Israel* 56(5) PD 834 (2006) (Isr.), with *Hamdan v. Rumsfeld*, 548 U.S. 557 (2006). See Marko Milanovic, "Lessons for Human Rights and Humanitarian Law in the War on Terror: Comparing Hamdan and the Israeli Targeted Killings Case," *International Review of the Red Cross* 89, no. 866 (June 2007) 373, 393. ("The paradox that therefore emerges from comparing these two decisions is that *Hamdan*, the one which is on its face more favorable to the petitioners, might actually be less so in the long term. The Israeli Supreme Court is clearly superior to its US counterpart in applying humanitarian law to the phenomenon of terrorism, and it is even more so in its application of human rights law. This might actually prove to be the most enduring quality of the *Targeted Killings* judgment: that it shows so clearly how the relationship between human rights law and humanitarian law can be a two-way street, and how that relationship can be far more complex than is usually thought.")
28. J. Nicholas Kendall, "Israeli Counter-Terrorism: Targeted Killings Under International Law," *North Carolina Law Review* 80, no. 3 (2002), 1069, 1073.

29. See Jennie Rosenfeld, *Talmudic Re-Readings: Toward a Modern Orthodox Sexual Ethic* (2008), 278.
30. Babylonian Talmud, *Pesachim* 75a; Babylonian Talmud, *Ketubot* 37b; Babylonian Talmud, *Sotah* 8b; Babylonian Talmud, *Bava Kamma* 51a; Babylonian Talmud, *Sanhedrin* 45a, 52a–b.
31. Maimonides, *Hilchot De'ot* 1:5, 1:6.
32. Jerusalem Talmud, *Chagiga* 10a; Maimonides, *Hilchos Daios* 6:3.
33. The *Urim VeTumim* was a mystical and holy ornament that was worn with the high priest's breastplate and was used to seek prophetic answers. See Babylonian Talmud, *Sanhedrin* 16b, 20a, and 29b.
34. Laws of Kings 6:5. Maimonides understands the Jerusalem Talmud's discussion of this topic to require three distinct letters. Others, though, make the claim that one can fulfill the obligation by sending only one letter with all three texts. See Aruch HaShulchan, Laws of Kings 75:6–7.
35. Supplement of Nachmanides to *Maimonides's Book of Commandments*, Positive Commandment 4 (hereafter Supplement).
36. *Sefer HaKhinukh* 527 (published anonymously in thirteenth-century Spain).
37. Norman Solomon, "Judaism and the ethics of war," *International Review of the Red Cross* 87, no. 858 (June 2005), 295, 300.
38. Philo of Alexandria, "On the Special Laws," in Gregory M. Reichberg and Henrik Syse, eds., *Religion, War, and Ethics: A Sourcebook of Textual Traditions* (2014), 23.
39. See Flavius Josephus, "The Antiquities of the Jews," in *The Works of Josephus: Complete and Unabridged*, trans. by William Whiston (1980).
40. Supplement, Positive Commandment 6.
41. Laws of Kings 6:8; Supplement, Negative Commandment 57.
42. Laws of Kings 6:10.
43. *Sefer HaKhinukh, mitzvah* 529. See also Reuven Kimelman, *Warfare and Its Restrictions in Judaism*, Boston College, https://www.bc.edu/content/dam/files/research_sites/cjl/texts/current/forums/Isr-Hez/kimleman_war.htm (visited July 14, 2017).
44. Available online at http://www.billydreskin.net/wp-content/uploads/2016/07/JudaismWar.RabbiBillyDreskin.zip (visited July 16, 2017).
45. IDF Code of Ethics, Israel Defense Forces, https://www.idfblog.com/about-the-idf/idf-code-of-ethics/ (visited July 14, 2017).
46. Ibid.
47. Ibid.
48. Israeli Military Advocate General Headquarters manual, *Laws of War in the Battlefield* (1998), 35, 52.
49. On tolerance of non-Jews: Joel H. Golovensky, "The Discriminatory Laws That Do Not Discriminate," *Jerusalem Post* (Aug. 9, 2016), http://www.jpost.com/Opinion/The-discriminatory-laws-that-do-not-discriminate-463677. On LGBT tolerance: "State-Sponsored Homophobia: A World Survey of Laws Criminalising Same-Sex Sexual Acts Between Consenting Adults,"

International Lesbian, Gay, Bisexual, Trans and Intersex Association (May 2012), http://ilga.org/downloads/ILGA_State_Sponsored_Homopho bia_2012.pdf; *2011* "Human Rights Report: Israel and the Occupied Territories," U.S. Department of State (May 24, 2012), https://www.state.gov /documents/organization/187889.pdf. On honor killings: "Freedom in the World 2012," Freedom House, https://freedomhouse.org/report/freedom -world/freedom-world-2012 (visited July 14, 2017); "2010 Human Rights Report: Iran," U.S. Department of State (April 8, 2011), https://www.state .gov/documents/organization/160461.pdf; Sherifa Zuhur, "Considerations of Honor Crimes, FGM, Kidnapping/Rape, and Early Marriage in Selected Arab Nations," UN Division for the Advancement of Women (May 11, 2009), http://www.un.org/womenwatch/daw/egm/vaw_legislation_2009 /Expert%20Paper%20EGMGPLHP%20_Sherifa%20Zuhur%20-%20II _.pdf; On religious tolerance: "Mission Statement," Justice for Jews from Arab Countries, http://www.justiceforjews.com/mission.html (visited July 14, 2017); Ethan Bronner, "Mideast's Christians Losing Numbers and Sway," *New York Times* (May 12, 2009), www.nytimes.com/2009/05/13 /world/middleeast/13christians.html?pagewanted=1&_r=1; "Guide: Christians in the Middle East," BBC News (Oct. 11, 2011), http://www.bbc.com /news/world-middle-east-15239529; "Israel in Figures 2010," Central Bureau of Statistics, Jerusalem, http://www.cbs.gov.il/publications/isr_in_n10e.pdf (visited July 14, 2017). On elections: "Freedom in the World 2014," Freedom House, www.freedomhouse.org/report/freedom-world/freedom-world-2014 (visited July 14, 2017). On women's rights: "Social Institutions & Gender Index," OECD Development Centre, Israel, http://www.genderindex.org /country/israel (visited July 14, 2017); "2011 Human Rights Report: Israel and the Occupied Territories," U.S. Department of State (May 24, 2012), https://www.state.gov/documents/organization/187889.pdf; "The World Factbook: Israel," Central Intelligence Agency, https://www.cia.gov/library /publications/the-world-factbook/geos/is.html (visited July 14, 2017); "Israel," World Bank, http://data.worldbank.org/country/israel?view=chart (visited July 14, 2017). On free media: "Freedom of the Press 2012," Freedom House, www.freedomhouse.org/report/freedom-press/freedom-press -2012 (visited July 14, 2017); "Freedom of the Press 2011," Freedom House, www.freedomhouse.org/report/freedom-press/freedom-press-2011 (visited July 14, 2017); "2011 Report on International Religious Freedom: Israel," U.S. Department of State (July 30, 2012), https://www.state.gov/docu ments/organization/193099.pdf; "West Bank 2012," Freedom House, www .freedomhouse.org/report/freedom-world/2012/west-bank (visited July 14, 2017); "2011 Human Rights Report: Israel and the Occupied Territories," U.S. Department of State (May 24, 2012), https://www.state.gov/documents /organization/187889.pdf; "2010 Human Rights Report: Iran," U.S. Department of State (April 8, 2011), https://www.state.gov/documents/organiza tion/160461.pdf.

Chapter 15: How We Are Defeating the BDS Movement

1. "Netanyahu Lands Unexpected Endorsement: The Boycott Israel Movement," *Haaretz* (Aug. 12, 2014), http://www.haaretz.com/misc/haaretzcomsmartphoneapp/.premium-1.630645 (last visited July 17, 2017).

2. "Inside Bush's Supreme Team," *BusinessWeek* (April 25, 2005); "The 25 Most Influential Evangelicals in America," *Time* (Feb. 7, 2005), http://content.time.com/time/specials/packages/article/0,28804,1993235_1993243_1993317,00.html.

3. *McConnell v. FEC*, 540 U.S. 93 (2003); *Operation Rescue v. National Organization for Women, Inc.*, 537 U.S. 808 (2002); *Santa Fe Independent School District v. Doe*, 530 U.S. 290 (2000); *Lamb's Chapel v. Center Moriches Union Free School District*, 508 U.S. 384 (1993); *Board of Airport Commissioners v. Jews for Jesus, Inc.*, 482 U.S. 569 (1987).

4. See Jay Sekulow, "Standing Against Anti-Israel BDS Movement at the U.N.," American Center for Law and Justice (May 31, 2016), https://aclj.org/israel/standing-against-the-anti-israel-bds-movement-at-the-un; see also Ian F. Fergusson, "The Export Administration Act: Evolution, Provisions, and Debate," Congressional Research Service (July 15, 2009), https://fas.org/sgp/crs/secrecy/RL31832.pdf.

5. Export Administration Act of 1979, Pub . L. No. 93-72, 93 Stat. 503 (1979).

6. 42 U.S.C. 2000d (2012).

7. "Dear Colleague" Letter, U.S. Department of Education (Oct. 26, 2010), https://www2.ed.gov/about/offices/list/ocr/letters/colleague-201010.pdf.

8. David Epstein, "Much Ado About No Change," Inside Higher Ed (April 4, 2006), https://www.insidehighered.com/news/2006/04/04/ocr.

9. As'ad AbuKhalil, "A Critique of Norman Finkelstein on BDS," Al-Akhbar English (visited Feb. 17, 2012, 2:59 p.m.), http://english.al-akhbar.com/node/4289.

10. Jennifer Lipman, "Activist: BDS Does Mean End of the Jewish State," *Jewish Chronicle* (Oct. 19, 2010), https://www.thejc.com/news/world/activist-israel-boycott-does-mean-end-of-jewish-state-1.19059.

11. In *Davis v. Monroe County Board of Education*, 526 U.S. 629, 652 (1999), the Supreme Court defined peer-on-peer harassment in the educational context as conduct that is so severe, pervasive, and objectively offensive, and that so undermines and detracts from the victims' educational experience, that the victim-students are effectively denied equal access to an institution's resources and opportunities. See Samantha Harris, "Misunderstanding 'Harassment,' " *FIRE* (Oct. 16, 2012), https://www.thefire.org/misunderstanding-harassment (visited July 17, 2017).

12. " 'Working Definition' of Anti-Semitism," U.S. Department of State (Feb. 8, 2007), https://2001-2009.state.gov/g/drl/rls/56589.htm.

13. Ibid.

14. "EUMC Working Definition of Antisemitism," European Parliament

Working Group on Antisemitism, http://www.antisem.eu/projects/eumc
-working-definition-of-antisemitism/ (visited July 13, 2017).

15. Ibid.

16. Ibid.; "Defining Anti-Semitism," U.S. Department of State (Jan. 20, 2017),
https://www.state.gov/s/rga/resources/267538.htm.

17. Lea Speyer, "Campus Watchdog: Jewish Students Single Largest Target
of Systematic Suppression of Civil Rights at American Universities (In-
terview)," *Algemeiner* (July 26, 2016, 2:38 p.m.), https://www.algemeiner
.com/2016/07/26/campus-watchdog-jewish-students-single-largest-target
-of-systematic-suppression-of-civil-rights-at-american-universities-inter
view/.

18. See "Report on Antisemitic Activity in 2015 at U.S. Colleges and Universities
with the Largest Jewish Undergraduate Populations," AMCHA Initiative,
http://www.amchainitiative.org/wp-content/uploads/2016/03/Antisemitic
-Activity-at-U.S.-Colleges-and-Universities-with-Jewish-Populations
-2015-Full-Report.pdf.

19. "Boycott of Israeli Academic Institutions," American Studies Association
(Dec. 4, 2013), https://www.theasa.net/about/advocacy/resolutions-actions
/resolutions/boycott-israeli-academic-institutions.

20. *What Does the Boycott Mean?*, American Studies Association, https://www
.theasa.net/about/advocacy/resolutions-actions/resolutions/boycott-israeli
-academic-institutions/what-does (last visited July 13, 2017).

21. Letter from CeCe Heil, Senior Counsel, ACLJ, to Michael Czarcinski, General Manager, Westin Bonaventure Hotel & Suites (Oct. 13, 2014), http://
media.aclj.org/pdf/westin-bonaventure-letter.pdf.

22. "Historic: UAW 2865, UC Student-Worker Union, Becomes First Major U.S. Labor Union to Support Divestment from Israel by Membership
Vote," U.S. Student-Workers Union, http://www.uaw2865.org/historic-uaw
-2865-uc-student-worker-union-becomes-first-major-u-s-labor-union-to
-support-divestment-from-israel-by-membership-vote/ (visited July 13, 2017).

23. Letter from CeCe Heil, Senior Counsel, ACLJ, to Janet Napolitano, University of California (Nov. 24, 2014), http://media.aclj.org/pdf/UAW-boycott
-israel.pdf.

24. "UAW Strikes Down BDS Resolution Approved by Local Branch," Jewish Telegraphic Agency (visited Dec. 17, 2015, 2:01 p.m.) http://www.jta
.org/2015/12/17/news-opinion/united-states/uaw-strikes-down-bds-resolu
tion-approved-by-local-branch.

25. Letter from Zionist Organization of America to Mark S. Schlissel, President, University of Michigan (Dec. 4, 2015), http://www.amchainitiative.org
/wp-content/uploads/2015/12/letter-to-President-Schlissel-re-Jesse-Arm
-12-4-15.pdf.

26. Ibid.

27. Jackie Charniga, "SAFE Representatives Call for Dismissal of CSG Mem-

ber," *Michigan Daily* (visited Nov. 24, 2015, 10:00 p.m.), https://www.michi gandaily.com/section/news/csg-meeting-2.

28. "#BDSFail: Jewish Student Unanimously Beats Ethics Probe After Standing Up To Anti-Israel Protesters," Judean People's Front (Dec. 8, 2015), http://judeanpf.com/2015/12/08/BDSFail-UMichigan (visited July 17, 2017).

29. Sam Kestenbaum, "CUNY Graduate Students Vote for Academic Boycott of Israel," *Forward* (Apr. 15, 2016), http://forward.com/news/breaking -news/338760/cuny-graduate-students-vote-for-academic-boycott-of-is rael/.

30. "Academic Boycott of Israel at CUNY," Doctoral Students' Council, https:// cunyboycott.wordpress.com/resolution-2/ (visited July 13, 2017).

31. Sean Kennedy, "The Adjunct Project Endorses the Boycott of Israeli Academic Institutions," Adjunct Project: A Resource for Graduate Center Student-Workers and CUNY Adjuncts (April 12, 2016), http://cunyad junctproject.org/2016/04/12/the-adjunct-project-endorses-the-boycott-of -israeli-academic-institutions/.

32. Carly F. Gammill, "CUNY Responds to ACLJ's Anti-BDS Letter," American Center for Law and Justice (May 24, 2016), https://aclj.org/israel/cuny-presi dent-responds-to-acljs-anti-bds-letter-commits-to-take-appropriate-action.

33. Ibid.

34. Ibid.

35. *United States v. Rumely*, 345 U.S. 41, 56 (1953) (Douglas, J., concurring).

Chapter 16: Closing Arguments

1. Antonin Scalia and Bryan A. Garner, *Making Your Case: The Art of Persuading Judges*, (2008), 37.

2. Abraham Bell and Eugene Kontorovich, "Palestine, *Uti Possidetis Juris*, and the Borders of Israel," *Arizona Law Review* 58 (2016), 633, 635.

3. Ibid.

4. Rick Gladstone, "Tempest at U.N. over Report Saying Israel Practices Apartheid," *New York Times* (March 15, 2017), https://www.nytimes .com/2017/03/15/world/middleeast/un-israel-palestine-apartheid.html.

5. Economic and Social Commission for Western Asia (ESCWA), "Israeli Practices Towards the Palestinian People and the Question of Apartheid," E/ESCWA/ECRI/2017/1 (2017), https://archive.is/08Q5b.

6. Kerry Picket, "Haley Slams UN Report As 'Anti-Israel Propaganda,'" *Daily Caller* (visited March 15, 2017, 7:57 p.m.), http://dailycaller.com/2017/03/15 /haley-slams-un-report-as-anti-israel-propaganda/.

READ MORE FROM
JAY SEKULOW

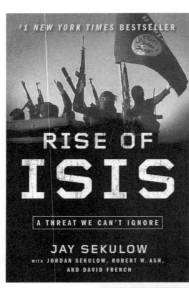

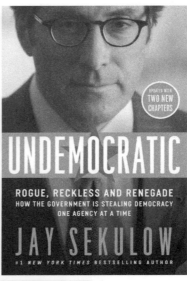

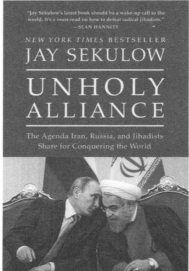